TYPOGRAPHY NOW TWO

TYPOGRAPHY NOW TWO

implosion

EDITED BY RICK POYNOR

First published in 1996
First published in paperback in 1998
Reprint paperback 2000
by Booth-Clibborn Editions
12 Percy Street, London W1P 9FB

ISBN 1 86154 023 X

Published and distributed in the United Kingdom

Worldwide direct mail rights:
Internos Books
12 Percy Street
London W1P 9FB
England

Printed and bound in Hong Kong by Dai Nippon Printing Co.

EDITOR, COMPILER AND WRITER — RICK POYNOR

ASSISTANT EDITOR — EMILY KING

ART DIRECTORS — JONATHAN BARNBROOK, STEPHEN COATES

COVER, INTRODUCTION AND DIVIDER PAGE DESIGN — JONATHAN BARNBROOK

PAGE DESIGN — JASON BEARD

The captions and artwork in this book are based on material supplied by those whose work is included. While every effort has been made to ensure their accuracy, Booth-Clibborn Editions does not under any circumstances accept any responsibility for any errors or omissions.

Sources for divider page quotations

PAGES 16/17

John Plunkett
"Plugged in"
Metropolis, October 1994

Joshua Berger
"Regarding the design, typography and legibility of this publication"
Plazm no. 6, 1994

Tobias Frere-Jones
"Towards the cause of grunge"
Zed no. 1, 1994

Rudy VanderLans
"Radical commodities"
Emigre no. 34, Spring 1995

Jan van Toorn
Thinking design: issues in culture and values
Western Carolina University, 1993

PAGES 78/79

P. Scott Makela
quoted in Michael Rock
"P. Scott Makela is wired"
Eye no. 12 vol. 3, 1994

Katherine McCoy
interviewed by Rick Poynor
Eye no. 16 vol. 4, 1995

Jonathan Barnbrook
interviewed by Rick Poynor
Eye no. 15 vol. 4, 1994

PAGES 106/107

Edward Fella
letter to Rick Poynor, 1995

Lorraine Wild
quoted in Anne Burdick
"A sense of rupture"
Eye no. 14 vol. 4, 1994

Louise Sandhaus
"An introduction from the designer of this journal"
Errant Bodies, Winter 1994

J. Abbott Miller,
"Must books be ugly, too?"
AIGA Journal of Graphic Design
vol. 11 no. 2, 1993

PAGES 182/183

Brian Schorn
letter to Rick Poynor, 1995

Michael Worthington
Hypertype, featured on California Institute of the Arts' 25th Anniversary CD-ROM, 1995

Jeffery Keedy
Fast Forward
California Institute of the Arts, 1993

FR

The five years that have passed since first publication of this book's predecessor, *Typography Now: The Next Wave,*

have seen the mainstreaming of experimental approaches to typography

that were until quite recently much more likely to be identified with "hothouse" design schools, or obscure arts journals with tiny circulations, than with the contents of the commercial break or the newsstand magazine. In 1991, when *Typography Now* was in preparation, such work, even within the design community, seemed to be a minority taste. Interesting as it was to observers like myself, it still came as a genuine surprise that a publisher was prepared to put out a book that concentrated – to the exclusion of all other forms of typography – on what many regarded as a wholly ignorable lunatic fringe.

BY RICK POYNOR

EEZING

¶*Typography Now Two*'s purpose is therefore both different from the first book's, and the same. It is different in the sense that, while I hope the book contains many unfamiliar examples, work of this kind is by now sufficiently familiar as a genre, even to those who still don't like it, not to require any special introduction (explanation is another matter). Whether it is seen as a regrettable fad that will eventually pass when the deluded finally see sense, or as an established and legitimate design method with plenty of remaining potential, ***the "new typography" can no longer be said to be especially shocking – within the design profession, at least – or even particularly new. And, like any cultural form that sets out to kick over the traces, only to find itself applauded for the effort, its less thoughtful manifestations are subject to the law of diminishing returns.***

¶What *Typography Now Two* does share with its predecessor is a documentary intention. Enough time has elapsed for significant developments to have occurred and this book attempts to chart them. One of the most immediate differences in putting it together was the sheer volume of material to choose from five years on. The first wave of experimentally inclined typographers, whose careers began in the 1980s or earlier, have been joined in the 1990s by countless others inspired by their example. Designers who were undergraduates in 1991 now have work experience or second degrees behind them. The effect of earlier influences is noticeable at an institution such as London's Royal College of Art. It wasn't until the college's 1995 degree show that a marked sense of engagement with typographic concerns dating back anything from five to ten years in the United States surfaced across the body of student work. To give a sense of where typography may be heading in the next few years, this book looks at postgraduate work from the Royal College of Art, Cranbrook Academy of Art and, perhaps the most significant centre of new typography in the 1990s, California Institute of the Arts.

Press advertisement
Designer: Geof McFetridge
Client: California Institute of the Arts
USA, 1994–95

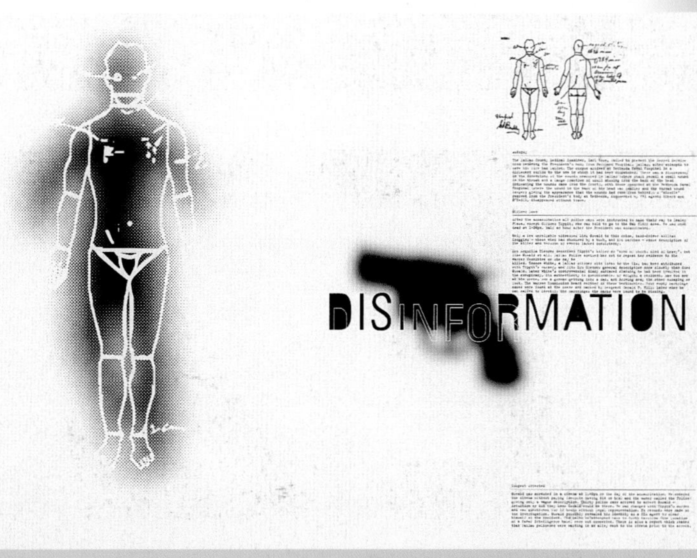

Student project on the Kennedy assassination
Designer: Carlo Tartaglia
Royal College of Art
Great Britain, 1995

Cover of *Climax* no. 1
Designers: Alessandro Manfredi, Fabrizio Schiavi
Client: Happy Books
Italy, 1995

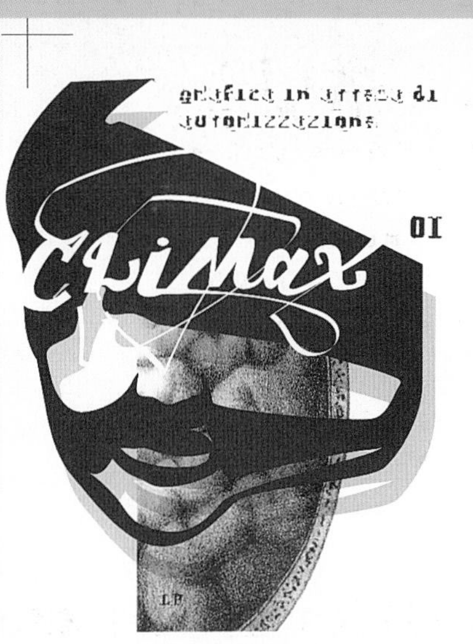

¶Given the international dimension and scale of these developments (which are still under way) no claims to definitiveness can be made for a collection of this size. *Typography Now Two* aims instead to give a selective but representative account of the experimental typography that characterised the period and a picture of some of the key ideas that accompanied it. The book shows significant minor projects that have a particular story to tell, or simply deserve to be better known, alongside more familiar examples, such as *Emigre* or *Raygun*, which must, by any reckoning, be regarded as central to typographic change in the 1990s.

¶These changes have not been accomplished without loud cries of pain from some sections of the design community. Even as the first *Typography Now* was going to press, Massimo Vignelli was publicly blasting *Emigre* as a "factory of garbage". "That is a national calamity. It's not a freedom of culture, it's an aberration of culture . . . They show no responsibility. It's just like freaking out, in a sense. The kind of expansion of the mind that they're doing is totally uncultural."[1] Two years later, Paul Rand pitched in against "indecipherable, zany typography; tiny type with miles of leading; text in all caps (despite indisputable proof that lowercase letters are more readable, less formal, and friendlier); ubiquitous letterspacing; visually annotated typography; revivalist caps and small caps; pseudo Dada and Futurist collages; and whatever 'special effects' a computer makes possible."[2]

Poster for "New Typography" exhibition
Designer: Zsolt Czakó
Hungary, 1994

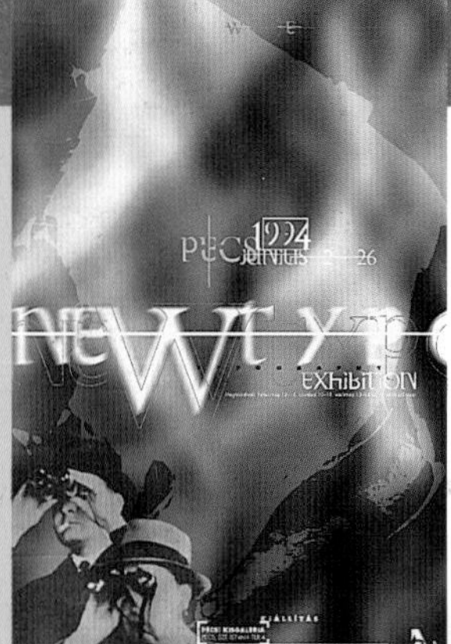

¶If that didn't seem to leave many options open to the would-be typographic rebel, New York art director Henry Wolf was even more specific. He singled out a particular offender for detailed stylistic rebuttal, P. Scott Makela's *Living Surfaces* poster (reproduced on page 97), doubting "that history will repeat itself here".[3] But the most sustained and incisive attack on the perceived excesses of the new typography came from Steven Heller in his now notorious essay "Cult of the ugly". Heller's polemic triggered a fusillade of angry letters from supporters of typographic experimentation on both sides of the Atlantic and inspired an issue of *Emigre* (taken to task in the essay) devoted to probing Heller, eliciting the responses of some of those he had criticised, and clearing up what the magazine believed to be a misunderstanding of the purpose and context of the new design.[4]

Advertisement in *Blur* magazine
Designer: Scott Clum
Client: FontShop Canada
USA, 1993

¶The irony of these attacks was that it was already too late. While conservative critics focused on work produced within the insulated sanctum of the academy, or aimed at other designers, hotly contesting its relevance to the "real world", the genie of typographic inspiration (or vandalism, depending on your point of view) was already at large in the culture. The first issue of *Raygun*, art directed by David Carson, appeared in November 1992 and the magazine's immediate North American impact and rapport with its young readership helped to confirm and consolidate advertising and communication trends that had been gathering momentum since the 1980s. *Raygun*'s pyrotechnic type treatments, much like those of *The Face* ten years earlier, appeared to offer a fail-safe set of graphic codes for reaching a generation – "Generation X", as the novelist Douglas Coupland dubbed it – increasingly unmotivated by conventional means of address.

¶The difference, this time round, was that the advertising agencies did not dilute the message by making their own pale copies, as they had with Neville Brody's work in the mid-1980s. They bought the product straight from source. Nike's US agency, Wieden & Kennedy, was one of the first to set a premium on fashionable type by calling in Brody himself to help sell training shoes in 1988. In Europe, in the 1990s, Nike has commissioned type-led campaigns by Why Not Associates, David Carson and the London-based multidisciplinary team Tomato. Robert Nakata, a Cranbrook Academy of Art-educated typographer known for boldly experimental projects at Studio Dumbar, left the Hague-based company to join Wieden & Kennedy's Amsterdam office, where he has created print campaigns for Nike and Microsoft. ***At the same time, designers of high-impact type effects have forged an emotive new genre of ambient typography in their contributions to television commercials, pop promos and other moving-image projects, initially as typographers, but increasingly as directors, too.***

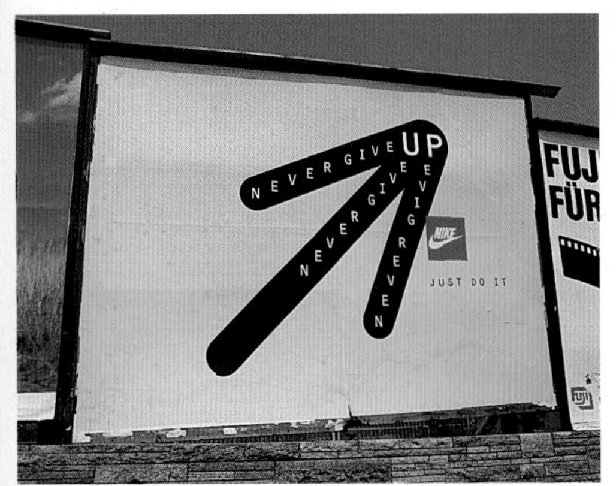

Outdoor brand campaign
Designer: Robert Nakata
Agency: Wieden & Kennedy
Client: Nike Europe
The Netherlands, 1992

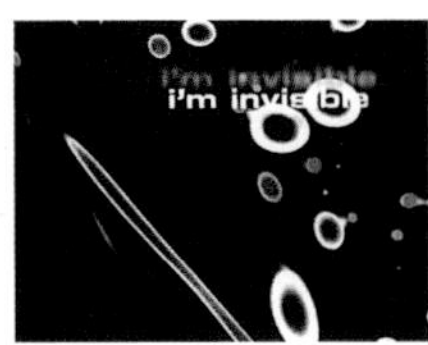

Video for the song "Cowgirl"
Directors: Graham Wood, Robert Shackleton
Design company: Tomato
Client: Underworld
Great Britain, 1993

In Britain, Tomato, Why Not Associates and Jonathan Barnbrook probably have the highest profile; David Carson, Barry Deck and P. Scott Makela are perhaps the most strongly identified with the movement in the United States.

¶Type and typography are receiving more public attention in 1996 than at any previous time. The worldwide explosion, in the wake of Emigre Fonts, of small independent type foundries firing off little catalogues offering faces made with Fontographer that run the gamut from sublime to ridiculous has helped to put typographic design on the media map. David Carson is probably the only graphic designer at this point whose celebrity can command television coverage or a profile in *Newsweek*, but it is still not uncommon in the 1990s for *Esquire* to run an article on the grunge font phenomenon, for *Wired* to profile type designers Barry Deck and Jonathan Hoefler, or for a newspaper such as the *Chicago Tribune* to take a long, hard look at local goings-on in the typographic undergrowth – which led it to conclude, with laudable balance, that "New fonts have something to say, even if you can't always read them."[5]

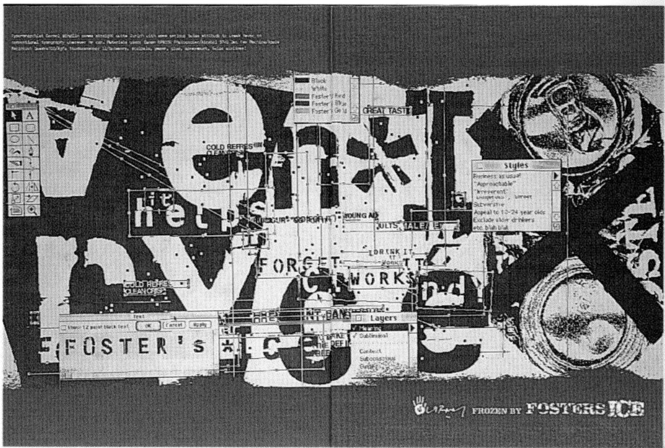

Press advertisement for Foster's Ice beer
Designer: Cornel Windlin
Creative director: Ian Swift
Client: Scottish Courage
Great Britain, 1996

¶A telling instance of the emerging media belief that typography and the people who produce it are interesting to non-designers (or ought to be) came in a recent advertisement designed by Cornel Windlin for Foster's Ice beer. The double-page ad, a fractured collage of broken type and Macintosh screen commands, appears to mock its own claim to offer – in its own words – a "subversive appeal to 18-24 year olds". The ironic foregrounding of the usually hidden marketing and design thinking that underpins the ad is reinforced by the panel of copy at the top: "Typo-anarchist Cornel Windlin comes straight outta Zurich with some serious Swiss attitude to wreak havoc on conventional typography wherever he can." This is followed by a list of the materials and technology used by Windlin to create the image.

¶There is something quite poignant about an ad which employs the typographic signifiers of "subversion" to acknowledge its own complicity in the commercial process. But the ad's very knowingness poses larger questions about the purpose, within the commercial arena, of "experimental" or "radical" design. If the aim of the new typographers working within advertising (apart from making some money) is to enlarge the available repertoire of visual languages and shake off the design profession's last few remaining rules and constraints, then the battle appears to have been won.

Aesthetically, almost anything is possible now.

Soft drink can
Design company: Reed Design
Client: Woolworths
Great Britain, 1995

But the question remains: **what exactly, in broader communication terms, is the new typography for?**

Advertisers might reply that the new advertising is open-ended, that viewers are free to pursue their own private associations and make of it what they like. But this apparent openness is merely a means to an end, and this end, not unreasonably, is the same as it ever was: *buy our product.* The Foster's ad tries to achieve it with a double bluff: "Look, we're being 'subversive' and we know you know it's a pose – we're OK." But the only small option for subversion, however original the design, is also the same as it ever was:

savour the aesthetics by all means, but don't buy the product.

¶If radical typography's purpose amounts to nothing more challenging than a new way to shift the goods – and amuse the designer in the process – it is destined to last only as long as it continues to intrigue the consumer. Within the cultural arena, too, experimental typography faces similar pressing questions of purpose. In hard communication terms, leaving aside the deconstructionist theory, which few typographers can be said truly to understand, what is it for? Exciting as it may be to look at, does it represent a functional improvement on more conventional ways of delivering the same essential message? It is easy to justify extreme manipulations of small quantities of text in a poster or a television commercial when the emotion of the message is as important as what the words have to say and, historically, designers have always sought to achieve a balance between typographic legibility and the need for expression.

Spread from *Raygun* no. 14
Designer: Rodney Shelden Fehsenfeld
Art director: David Carson
Client: Ray Gun Publishing
USA, 1994

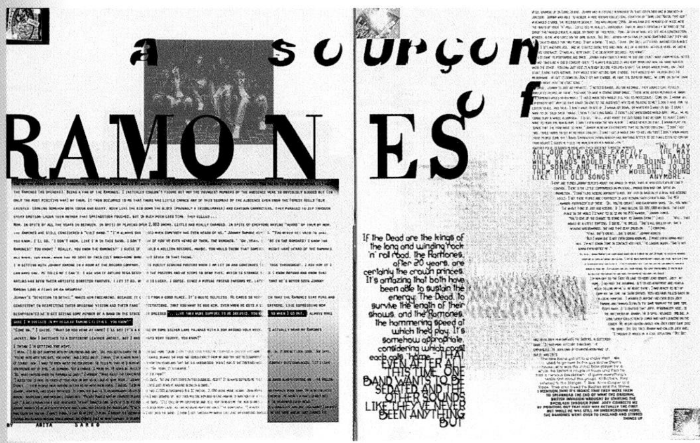

¶But longer texts for continuous reading pose more demanding problems of interpretation for the typographer. In 30 issues of *Raygun*, David Carson and his design assistants pulled text typography as far from convention as it has ever been taken in a mass-market publication. Carson argued that his intention was to encourage reluctant MTV-generation readers to read, and they wrote to the magazine in droves to say that they liked the approach. Other American designers advanced similar arguments. "Television has conditioned everyone at being very good at discerning what an image is and 'getting' it within a few frames," explained Rick Valicenti. "If you don't like it, you hit the remote control. So print, quite often, does the same thing: it freezes a moment where a lot of things are happening to provide an impression. People can either stay there and engage the interesting aspects, or turn the page."[6]

¶While such claims rapidly became almost axiomatic in some sections of the design world, they remain entirely untested in any rigorous sense of the word. What impact do such typographic strategies have on reading speed and comprehension?

Is it really the case that a text that is typographically demanding to read is more memorable once deciphered? And how much previous commitment to the subject matter do you need to even want to begin to decipher it?

¶There are certainly many who question the need for designers to intervene so deterministically in the reading process. ***Reading, argues British information designer Paul Stiff, is a highly complex, far from passive set of activities, operating on many levels. "When people read," he notes, "they make strategic choices, constantly generating inferences and hypotheses – about intention, relevance, tone of voice, and so on."[7]***

American critic Marc Treib points out that an over-activated text is "like getting a book that is already underlined, and if you have some idiot who is marking phrases that are unimportant in terms of your reading of the book, it's something you have to overcome to get back to the original message."[8] In an issue of the *American Center for Design Journal*, published in 1994, the designers' typographic interpretation of an article, based on footprint shapes, became a source of public bad feeling expressed in a special note tacked on to the article itself by the writers: "As authors, we feel compelled to state our objections to the layout . . . First, we believe that setting the text in the shape of footprints compromises legibility and discourages people from reading . . . Second, while our article compares dancing to interdisciplinary collaboration, dance is a metaphor and not the true subject of the article."[9]

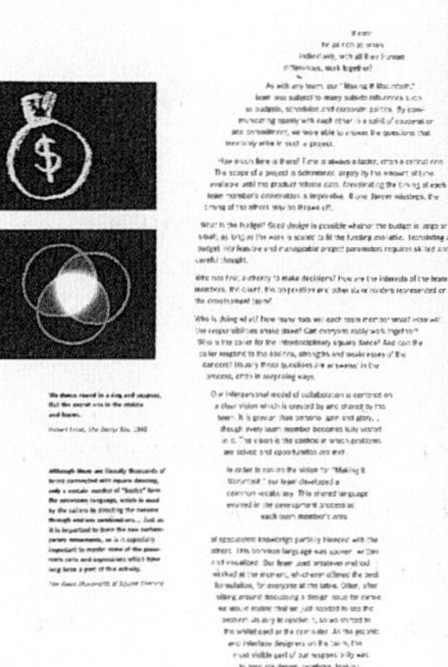

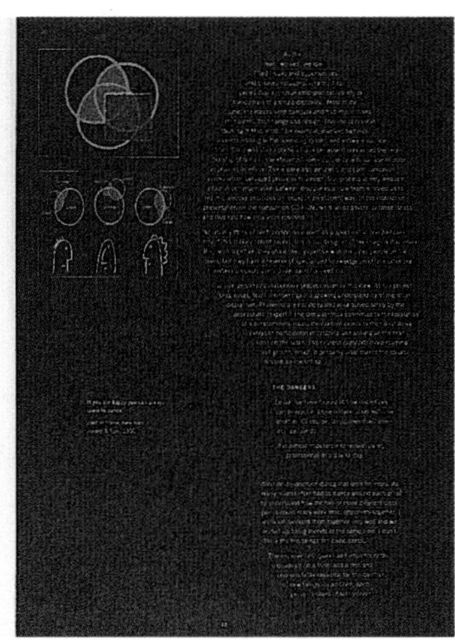

Spread from *American Center for Design Journal* vol. 8 no. 1
Design company: Tanagram
Client: American Center for Design
USA, 1994

¶If a clash such as this, within a journal publicly committed to design as a "form of authorship", suggests there is some way to go before designers and writers routinely coexist in a state of happy interaction, *Typography Now Two* shows that such collaboration can sometimes be achieved. *Emigre*, though it has the self-referential advantage of being a publication about design, continues to offer a model for a typographic articulation of text achieved in a way that is engagingly expressive, genuinely functional and a lasting contribution to practical research. The design journals *Form + Zweck* and *Zed*, publications very much in the *Emigre* tradition, also exhibit a high degree of thoughtfulness in their exploration of the experimental interface of writing and design.

Project from *Zed* no. 2
"Selected notes to ZeitGuys"
Designer: Bob Aufuldish
Writer: Mark Bartlett
Client: Virginia Commonwealth University
USA, 1995

¶In publishing's mainstream, such approaches are still not as common as their academic and advertising impact might lead one to expect, perhaps because the traditional hierarchies and divisions of responsibility are much slower to shift than in small independent publications. *Raygun* aside, *Wired* is perhaps the most striking example of a newsstand publication which attempts to meld typography and image in the service of an editorial vision. *Wired*'s pre-contents introductory pages are "advertisements", inspired by the books of Marshall McLuhan and Quentin Fiore, for key techno-cultural ideas from the heart of the magazine, conceived and realised at journalistic speed in scintillating verbal and visual metaphors for the fluid information transfers of the digital realm.

Spread from *Wired* no. 2.08
Creative director: John Plunkett
Designers: John Plunkett, Eric Adigard
Design company: Plunkett + Kuhr
Client: Wired Ventures
USA, 1994

¶It is too early to say whether the liquid condition of the emerging screen-based typography – see Michael Worthington's *Hypertype* project on page 218 – will have a lasting reciprocal influence on the typography of the paper realm. Print will continue to exist for the foreseeable future, though, and it seems likely that many of the experimental approaches gathered here will become permanent features of typographic practice. More than anything, the picture that emerges from *Typography Now Two* is one of flux and transition. ***The implosion of traditional typography may, like a sloughed skin, be a sign of renewal, or it may prove to have been a marker of millennial anxiety, profound uncertainty in an accelerating culture, perhaps even long-term decline.*** That is for future historians to decide. What can be said with some certainty is that the mutations of typography in the 1990s reflect a deep scepticism about received wisdom and a questioning of established authorities, traditional practices and fixed cultural identities, which has parallels throughout society. They tell us a great deal about the increasing value we place, as a culture, in the mediating power of typography as an interpreter of the reality we inhabit. They encapsulate the moment while also, in the largest sense, being wholly of their time.

Subscription card for *Now Time* magazine
Designer: Edward Fella
Client: A.R.T. Press
USA, 1993

1 "Massimo Vignelli vs. Ed Benguiat (sort of)", *Print* XLV:V, September/October 1991.
2 Paul Rand, "From Cassandre to chaos" in *Design, Form and Chaos*, Yale University Press, New Haven and London, 1993.
3 Henry Wolf, "The view of a curmudgeon, junior grade", *AIGA Journal of Graphic Design*, vol. 11 no. 4, 1993.
4 Steven Heller, "Cult of the ugly", *Eye* no. 9 vol. 3, 1993. *Emigre* no. 30, "Fallout", Spring 1994. The "fallout" continued up to the time of writing. In 1996, a digital type foundry, Beaufonts, based in Manchester, England, published a brochure, *Beaufonts 1, Excess Baggage*, containing a text that wittily mangles the words of Heller's original essay to make a perverse kind of (non)sense.
5 Hugh Hart, "It takes all types", *Chicago Tribune*, 2 June 1995.
6 Quoted in Hugh Hart, *Chicago Tribune*.
7 Paul Stiff, "Stop sitting around and start reading", *Eye* no. 11 vol. 3, 1993.
8 Quoted in Michael Dooley, "Kicking up a little dust" in Michael Bierut, William Drenttel, Steven Heller & D. K. Holland (eds.), *Looking Closer: Critical Writings on Graphic Design*, Allworth Press, New York, 1994.
9 Lauralee Alben and Jim Faris, "The interdisciplinary dance (shall we?)", *American Center for Design Journal*, "Interact", vol. 8 no. 1, 1994.

We’re trying to create visual metaphors on a static, printed page to represent its opposite: the electronic, nonlinear, infinitely malleable nature of the Net. We’re equally interested in the eerie “perfection” of computer-generated images and low-tech, hand-made imagery . . . ‘high tech/high touch”.

John Plunkett

SOME READERS MAY CHOOSE TO INTERPRET A LAYOUT AS BEING UNREADABLE; AS HAVING CROSSED THAT LINE BETWEEN FORM AND FUNCTION. THE QUESTION IS: IF WE DIDN'T EXPERIMENT, IF WE SET ALL OUR TYPE IN A THREE COLUMN GRID, WOULD YOU EVEN BE INTERESTED? PROBABLY NOT. THE CLEAN GRID OF MODERNITY HAS BEEN FORMALLY REJECTED BY THE NIHILISM OF INDUSTRIAL YOUTH CULTURE. *Joshua Berger*

The new ability has become the new aesthetic … Like the arabesques of the 1880s and the swashes of the 1970s, the contortions of the 1990s will fall out of favour, but not before showing us what the new tools can do.

Tobias Frere-Jones

SALES

Massimo Vignelli

commercial

Instead of always looking at it from the point of view that mass consumption is a bad thing, and anything assisting it is guilty by association, perhaps a bit of credit is due to the mainstream for taking some risks, and to the avant-garde for infiltrating mainstream culture … I'm not saying that the avant-garde exists simply to supply the commercial world with the means to sell more products, but I do think it can be beneficial for both to occasionally share ideologies.

Rudy VanderLans

THE POWER OF CAPITALIST CULTURE TO COMMODIFY AND CONTROL HAS DISPERSED THE DESIGNER'S FORMS AND INSTRUMENTS OF CRITICISM AND MADE THEM HARMLESS IN THE DAZZLING SPECTACLE …

JAN VAN TOORN

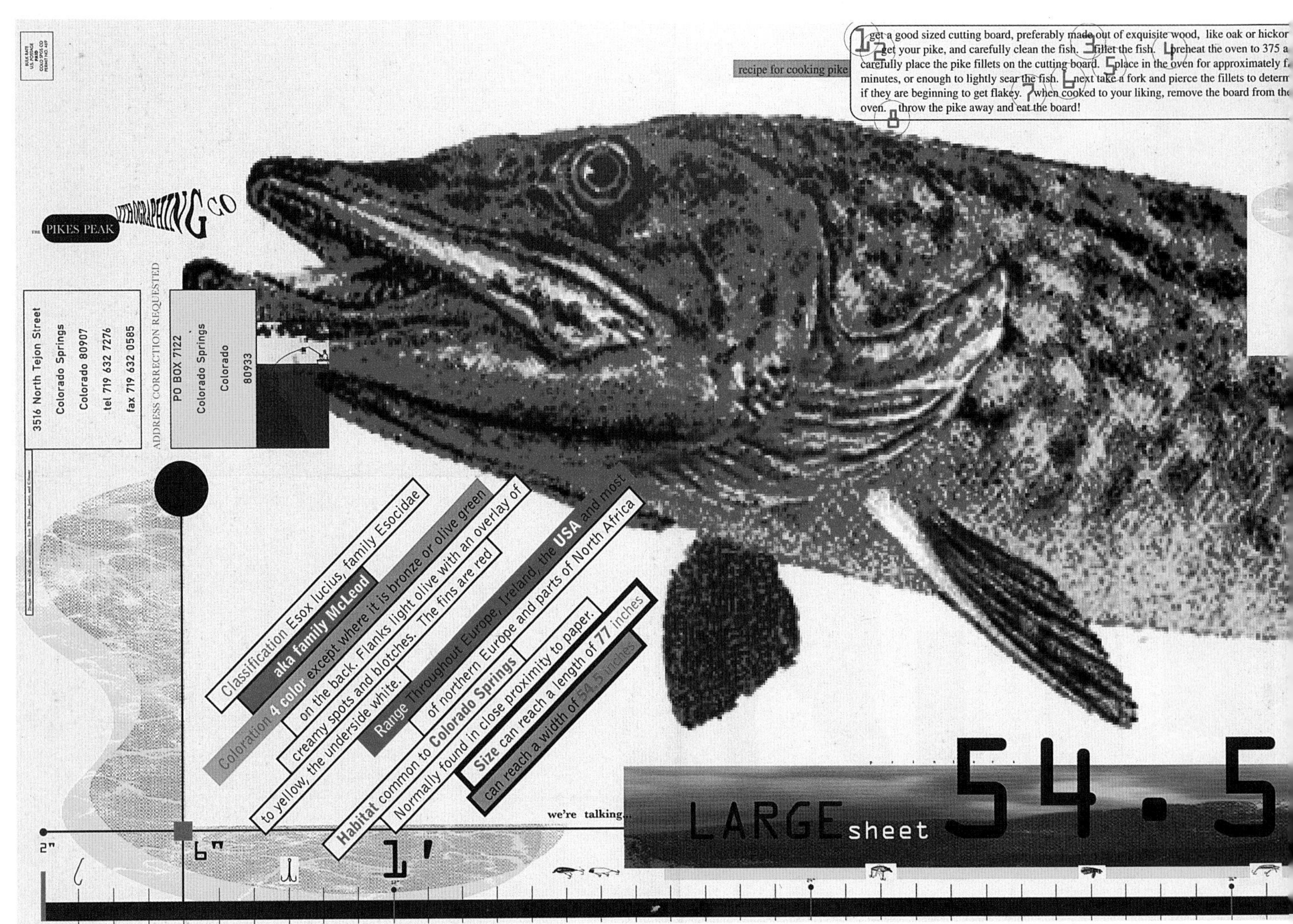

Promotional poster for a large-sheet printer

DESIGNER/ILLUSTRATOR April Greiman

PRINCIPAL TYPEFACES Baskerville, DIN Mittelschrift, OCRA, Bell Gothic

CLIENT Pikes Peak Lithographing

USA, 1994

Better call Scott. I think we got a big one!
since 1949 PIKES PEAK LITHOGRAPHING CO
77"
inches
54.5"
5' 5" or 65"
76"
65"
77"
Perfectly adapted for a life of murder and mayhem, the pike blends in with beds of water weed. The fins and tail are large, giving the fish rapid acceleration as and when required. The head of the pike is flattened and the large eyes are set high up in the skull. It's jaws are large, strong and bony. The teeth are long and pointed and there is a ridge of sharp but small teeth on the roof of the fish's mouth. Lazy by inclination, pike are often happy to scavenge on dead food. They are also active and effective hunters, more than capable of catching fish of up to half their own body weight.

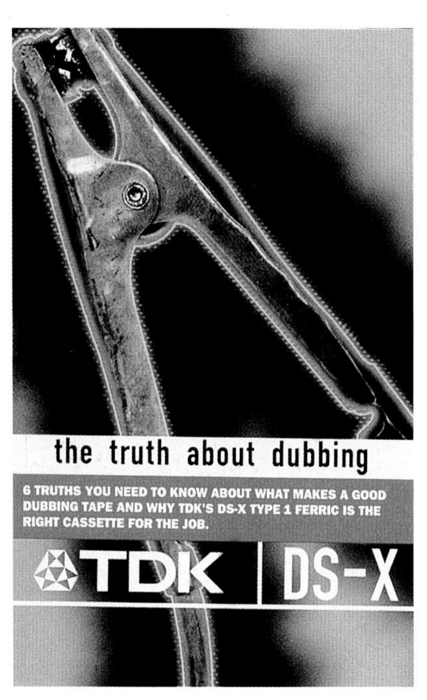

The Truth Series

Promotional mailers

ART DIRECTOR Steve Farrar
DESIGNERS Kirk James, Andrew Szurley, Richard Curren
DESIGN COMPANY Jager Di Paola Kemp Design
PRINCIPAL TYPEFACES Franklin Gothic, DIN
CLIENT TDK

USA, 1993-94

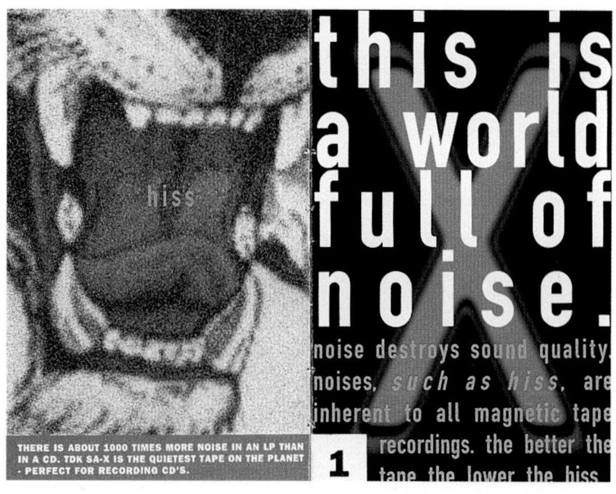

Team TDK is a progamme developed to deliver product information, services and merchandising tools to the sales forces of music and audio stores. Each of the three mailers contained a blank cassette and a cassette-sized educational booklet aimed at design-aware retail managers and sales people. By keeping copy short and direct and reinforcing it with dynamic conceptual imagery, the designers hoped to make information easier to absorb and recall.

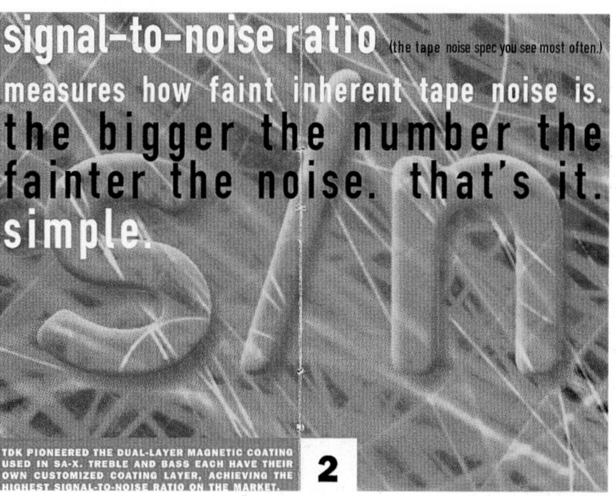

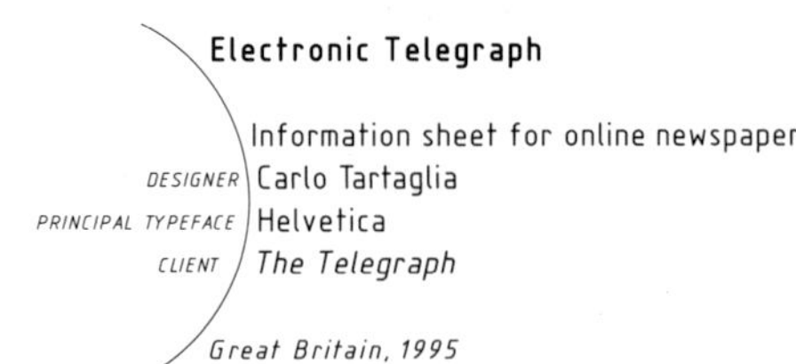

Electronic Telegraph

Information sheet for online newspaper
DESIGNER Carlo Tartaglia
PRINCIPAL TYPEFACE Helvetica
CLIENT *The Telegraph*

Great Britain, 1995

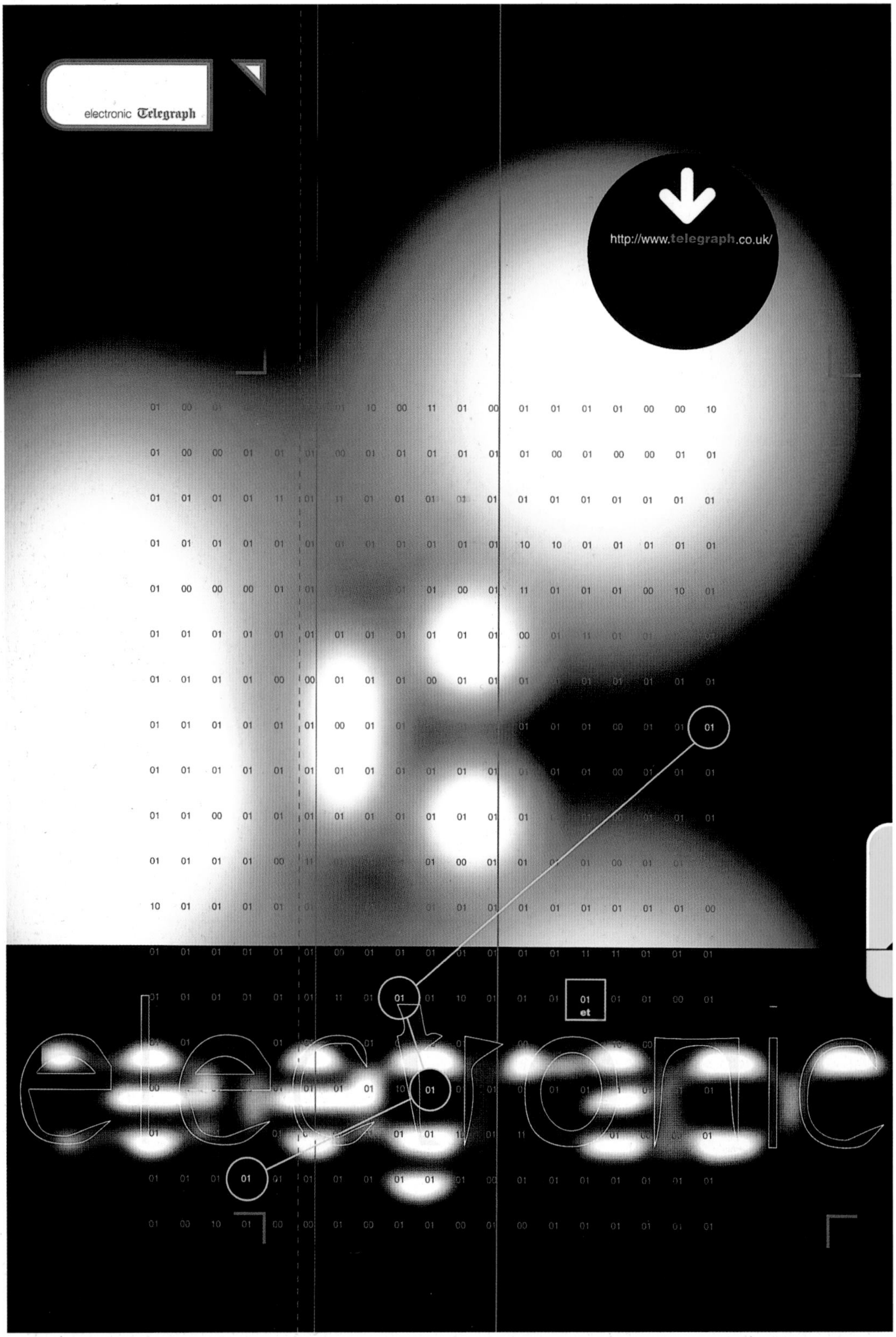

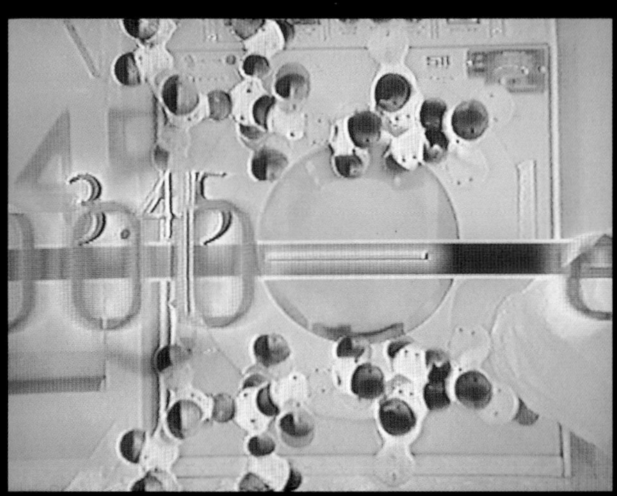

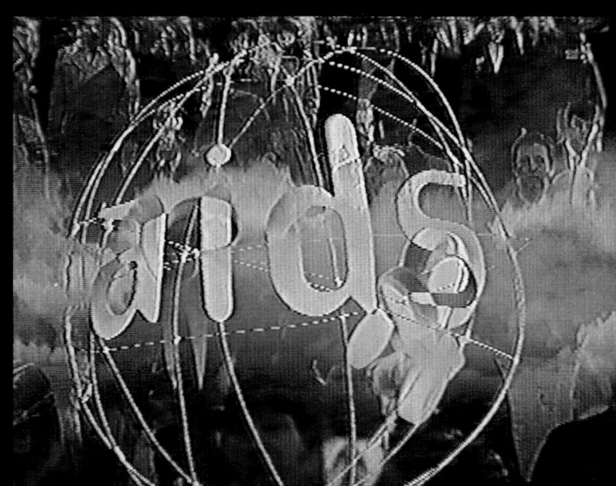

Punctvox

Graphic stings for a German news channel

DESIGNERS Andy Altmann, David Ellis
DESIGN COMPANY Why Not Associates
PHOTOGRAPHER Rocco Redondo
PRINCIPAL TYPEFACE Template Gothic
CLIENT Vox TV

Great Britain, 1994

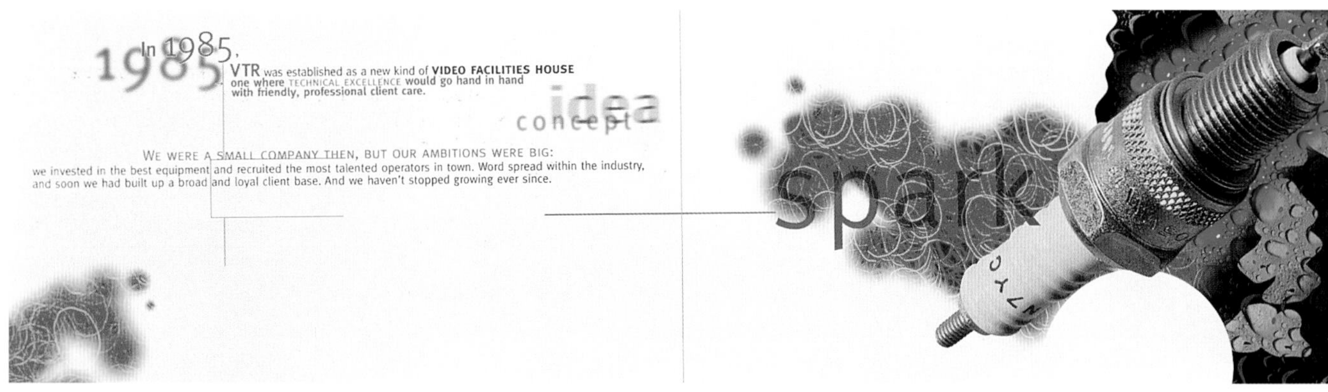
1985
In 1985,
VTR was established as a new kind of VIDEO FACILITIES HOUSE
one where TECHNICAL EXCELLENCE would go hand in hand
with friendly, professional client care.
idea
concept
WE WERE A SMALL COMPANY THEN, BUT OUR AMBITIONS WERE BIG:
we invested in the best equipment and recruited the most talented operators in town. Word spread within the industry,
and soon we had built up a broad and loyal client base. And we haven't stopped growing ever since.
spark

growth
We are now one of London's TOP
post-production houses, employing more than 80 staff.
We also have two sister companies whose resources complement our own:
THE MACHINE ROOM TAPE-TO-TAPE CONVERSION AND DUPLICATION
BLUE BROADCAST POST-PRODUCTION
Although we've expanded, the VTR philosophy remains the same:
we believe that technical wizardry is only part of the picture –
teamwork is what makes us succeed.

Promotional brochure for a TV and video facilities house

DESIGNERS Andy Altmann, David Ellis, Patrick Morrissey
DESIGN COMPANY Why Not Associates
PHOTOGRAPHERS Photonica, PhotoDisc
PRINCIPAL TYPEFACE Meta
CLIENT VTR

Great Britain, 1995

We want every job to be as
worry-free
AS POSSIBLE, FROM concept meeting right through to completion.

THAT'S WHERE THE
VTR PRODUCTION TEAM
COMES IN:
they are there to provide clients with PROFESSIONAL ADVICE and friendly support from start to finish, and to keep a close eye on bookings and costs.

WE ALSO HAVE A TRAINED ENGINEERING DEPARTMENT ON HAND AT ALL TIMES TO ENSURE THE SMOOTH RUNNING OF OUR EQUIPMENT.

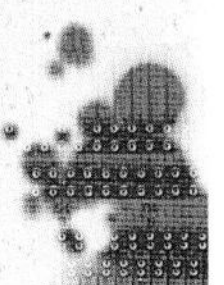

AXIAL
D.C.P.
MATADOR
SGI EXTREMES
ALIAS
HENRY
URSA GOLD
PARALLAX ADVANCE
SOFTIMAGE 3D

With a broad range of the best equipment there is – including Henrys, Ursa Gold telecines, Axial edit suites, Parallax Advance, Alias and Softimage 3D–we can find the solution for even the most demanding project, whether it's multi-layering, morphing or any other special effect. But although we're at the forefront of technological innovation, we put the emphasis firmly on user-friendliness:
we want to dazzle you with the results, not blind you with science.

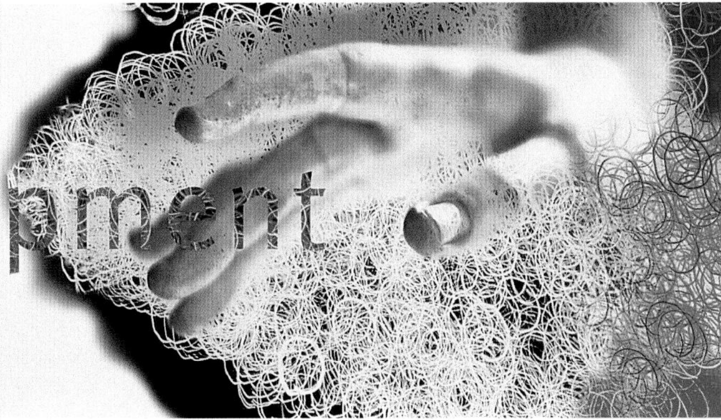

Utne Reader no. 67

Magazine cover

DESIGNER DIRECTORS Jan Jancourt, Andrew Henderson
ASSOCIATE ART DIRECTOR Andrew Henderson
DESIGN COMPANY Jancourt & Associates
PRINCIPAL TYPEFACE Officina
CLIENT LENS Publishing

USA, 1995

Utne Reader no. 68

Magazine cover and spreads

DESIGN DIRECTORS Jan Jancourt, Andrew Henderson
ASSOCIATE ART DIRECTOR Andrew Henderson
DESIGN COMPANY Jancourt & Associates
PRINCIPAL TYPEFACE Officina
CLIENT LENS Publishing

USA, 1995

Utne Reader is an independently published digest of new writing and articles of interest selected from other publications, both marginal and mainstream. In 1994, eleven years after it was founded by Eric Utne, the magazine's editorial philosophy was rethought and a redesign was commissioned to embody its new vision. The *Reader*'s new format is both livelier than before and more rigorous in mood, while transmitting the urgency of its socially and culturally attuned content.

> "There is no there there."
GERTRUDE STEIN (SPEAKING OF OAKLAND)

> "It ain't no Amish barn-raising in there . . ."
BRUCE STERLING (SPEAKING OF CYBERSPACE)

CYBERHOOD VS NEIGHBORHOOD

Is There a There in Cyberspace?

SPECIAL TO *UTNE READER* | John Perry Barlow

I am often asked how I went from pushing cows around a remote Wyoming ranch to my present occupation (which *Wall Street Journal* recently described as "cyberspace cadet"). I haven't got a short answer, but I suppose I came to the virtual world looking for community.

Unlike most modern Americans, I grew up in an actual place, an entirely nonintentional community called Pinedale, Wyoming. As I struggled for nearly a generation to keep my ranch in the family, I was motivated by the belief that such places were the spiritual home of humanity. But I knew their future was not promising.

At the dawn of the 20th century, over 40 percent of the American workforce lived off the land. The majority of us lived in towns like Pinedale. Now fewer than 1 percent of us extract a living from the soil. We just became too productive for our own good.

Of course, the population followed the jobs. Farming and ranching communities are now home to a demographically insignificant percentage of Americans, the vast majority of whom live not in ranch houses but in more or less identical split-level "ranch homes" in more or less identical suburban "communities." Generica.

In my view, these are neither communities nor homes. I believe the combination of television and suburban population patterns is simply toxic to the soul. I see much evidence in contemporary America to support this view.

Meanwhile, back at the ranch, doom impended. And, as I watched community in Pinedale growing ill from the same economic forces that were killing my family's ranch, the Bar Cross, satellite dishes brought the cultural infection of television. I started looking around for evidence that community in America would not perish altogether.

I took some heart in the mysterious nomadic City of the Deadheads, the virtually physical town that follows the Grateful Dead around the country. The Deadheads lacked place, touching down briefly wherever the band happened to be playing, and they lacked continuity in time, since they had to suffer a new diaspora every time the band moved on or went home. But they had many of the other necessary elements of community, including a culture, a religion of sorts (which, though it lacked dogma, had most of the other, more nurturing aspects of spiritual practice), a sense of necessity, and, most importantly, shared adversity.

I wanted to know more about the flavor of their interaction, what they thought and felt, but since I wrote Dead songs (including "Estimated Prophet" and "Cassidy"), I was a minor icon to the Deadheads, and was thus inhibited, in some socially Heisenbergian way, from getting a clear view of what really went on among them.

Then, in 1987, I heard about a "place" where Deadheads gathered where I could move among them without distorting too much the field of observation. Better, this was a place I could visit without leaving Wyoming. It was a shared computer in Sausalito, California, called the Whole Earth 'Lectronic Link, or WELL. After a lot of struggling with modems, serial cables, init strings, and other computer arcana that seemed utterly out of phase with such notions as Deadheads and small towns, I found myself looking at the glowing yellow word "Login:" beyond which lay my future.

"Inside" the WELL were Deadheads in community. There were thousands of them there, gossiping, complaining (mostly about the Grateful Dead), comforting and harassing each other, bartering, engaging in religion (or at least exchanging their totemic set lists), beginning and ending love affairs, praying for one another's sick kids. There was, it seemed, everything one might find going on in a small town, save dragging Main Street and making out on the back roads.

I was delighted. I felt I had found the new locale of

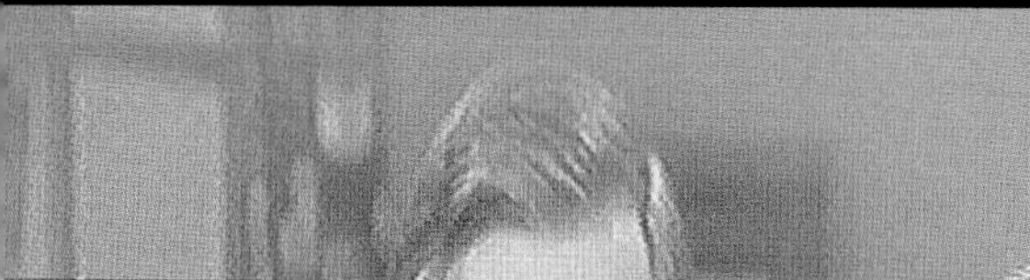

> Computer networking can help bring community back to the center of modern life

CYBERHOOD VS NEIGHBORHOOD

The Virtual Community

Howard Rheingold

In the summer of 1986, my then-2-year-old daughter picked up a tick. There was this blood-bloated *thing* sucking on our baby's scalp, and we weren't quite sure how to go about getting it off. My wife, Judy, called the pediatrician. It was 11 o'clock in the evening. I logged onto the WELL, the big Bay Area infonet, and contacted the Parenting conference (a conference is an on-line conversation about a specific subject). I got my answer on-line within minutes from a fellow with the improbable but genuine name of Flash Gordon, M.D. I had removed the tick by the time Judy got the callback from the pediatrician's office.

What amazed me wasn't just the speed with which we obtained precisely the information we needed to know, right when we needed to know it. It was also the immense inner sense of security that comes with discovering that real people—most of them parents, some of them nurses, doctors, and midwives—are available, around the clock, if you need them. There is a magic protective circle around the atmosphere of the Parenting conference. We're talking about our sons and daughters in this forum, not about our computers or our opinions about philosophy, and many of us feel that this tacit understanding sanctifies the virtual space.

The atmosphere of this particular conference—the attitudes people exhibit to each other in the tone of what they say in public—is part of what continues to attract me. People who never have much to contribute in political debate, technical argument, or intellectual gamesmanship turn out to have a lot to say about raising children. People you knew as fierce, even nasty, intellectual opponents in other contexts give you emotional support on a deeper level, parent to parent, within the boundaries of this small but warmly human corner of cyberspace.

In most cases, people who talk about a shared interest don't disclose enough about themselves as whole individuals on-line to inspire real trust in others. But in the case of the subcommunity called the Parenting conference, a few dozen of us, scattered across the country, few of whom rarely if ever saw the others face to face, have a few years of minor crises to knit us together and prepare us for serious business when it comes our way. Another several dozen read the conference regularly but contribute only when they have something important to add. Hundreds more read the conference every week without comment, except when something extraordinary happens.

Jay Allison and his family live in Massachusetts. He and his wife are public-radio producers. I've never met them face to face, although I feel I know something powerful and intimate about the Allisons and have strong emotional ties to them. What follows are some of Jay's postings on the WELL:

"Woods Hole. Midnight. I am sitting in the dark of my daughter's room. Her monitor lights blink at me. The lights used to blink too brightly so I covered them with bits of bandage adhesive and now they flash faintly underneath, a persistent red and green, Lillie's heart and lungs.

"Above the monitor is her portable suction unit. In the glow of the flashlight I'm writing by, it looks like the plastic guts of a science-class human model, the tubes coiled around the power supply, the reservoir, the pump.

"Tina is upstairs trying to get some sleep. A baby monitor links our bedroom to Lillie's. It links our sleep to Lillie's too, and because our souls are linked to hers, we do not sleep well.

"I am naked. My stomach is full of beer. The flashlight rests on it, and the beam rises and falls with my breath. My daughter breathes through a white plastic tube inserted into a hole in her throat. She's 14 months old."

Sitting in front of our computers with our hearts racing and tears in our eyes, in Tokyo and Sacramento and Austin, we read about Lillie's croup, her tracheostomy, the

autumn winter
cakewalk
95
cakewalk

Double-sided point-of-sale promotion
for a children's clothing manufacturer

DESIGNERS Andy Altmann, David Ellis, Patrick Morrissey
DESIGN COMPANY Why Not Associates
PRINCIPAL TYPEFACE Template Gothic
CLIENT Cakewalk

Great Britain, 1995

this isn't the
Next big
Idea

works

this how
FUTURE
will look

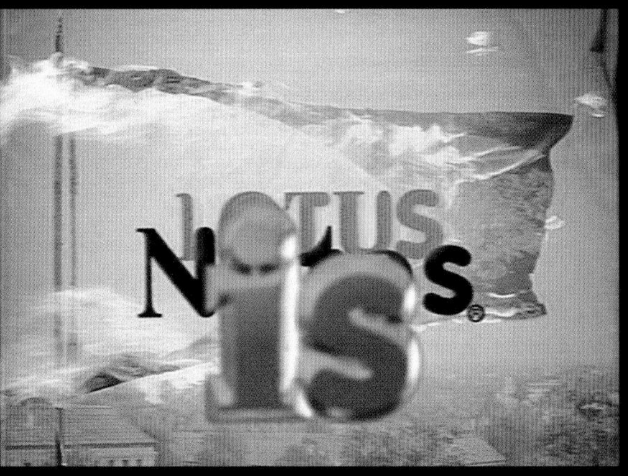
LOTUS
is

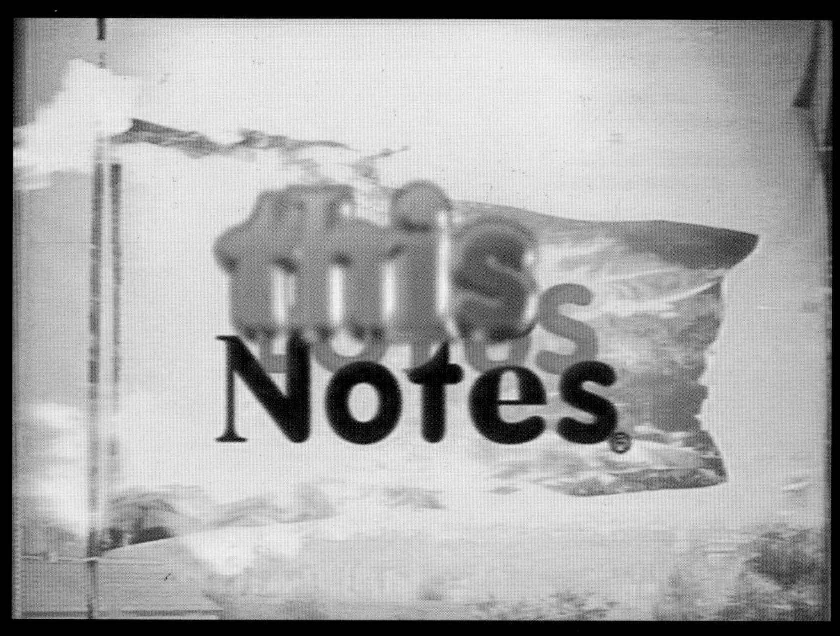

Lotus: This is Notes

Television commercial

DIRECTOR	Jeffrey Plansker
ART DIRECTOR	Steve Sumne
DESIGN DIRECTOR	P. Scott Makela
DESIGN COMPANY	Words and Pictures for Business and Culture
SPECIAL PHOTOGRAPHY	Laura Plansker
PRINCIPAL TYPEFACES	Dead History, Barmeno
CLIENT	Lotus Software Corporation

USA, 1994

Everything + Nothing

Audio CD cover for David Sylvian

DESIGNER	P. Scott Makela
DESIGN COMPANY	Words and Pictures for Business and Culture
PHOTOGRAPHER	Billy Phelps
PRINCIPAL TYPEFACE	WAC Mittelschrift
CLIENT	Virgin Records

USA, 1994

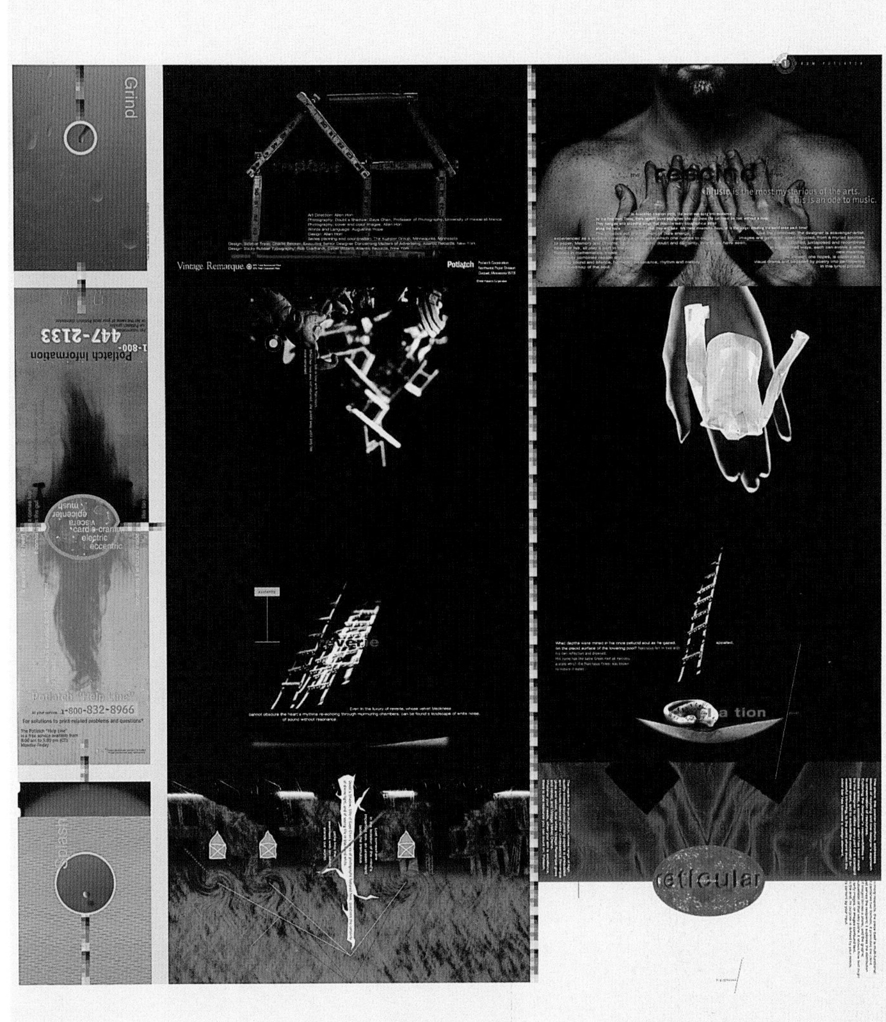

The Rescinded Muse

Poster/brochure for a paper company

DESIGNERS	Allen Hori, Charlie Becker, Rob Eberhardt
DESIGN COMPANY	Bates Hori
WRITER	Augustine Hope
PHOTOGRAPHERS	Gaye Chan, Allen Hori
PRINCIPAL TYPEFACES	Helvetica, News Gothic, Bell Gothic
CLIENT	Potlatch Corporation

USA, 1994

Allen Hori's paper promotion is a complex "ode to music" which equates the poetic discoveries of the design process with the intuitive explorations of music-making. The recycled paper's character is reflected in the way the press sheet is structured to eliminate trimming and unnecessary wastage. The viewer can treat the piece as a double-sided poster, or use its perforations to take it apart and reassemble it as a brochure.

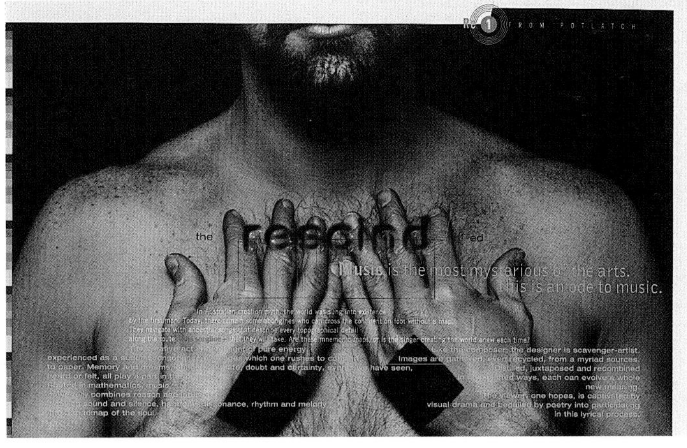

Wired's pre-contents introductory pages are a rare example of structural innovation within a commercial newsstand magazine. Each issue, a quotation from a main editorial feature embodying a key cultural or technological idea becomes the designers' starting point for a McLuhanesque four-page visual essay. Often the typography is woven into the image so tightly that the two become almost indivisible – a new style of journalistic communication that is simultaneously both highly suggestive and editorially specific.

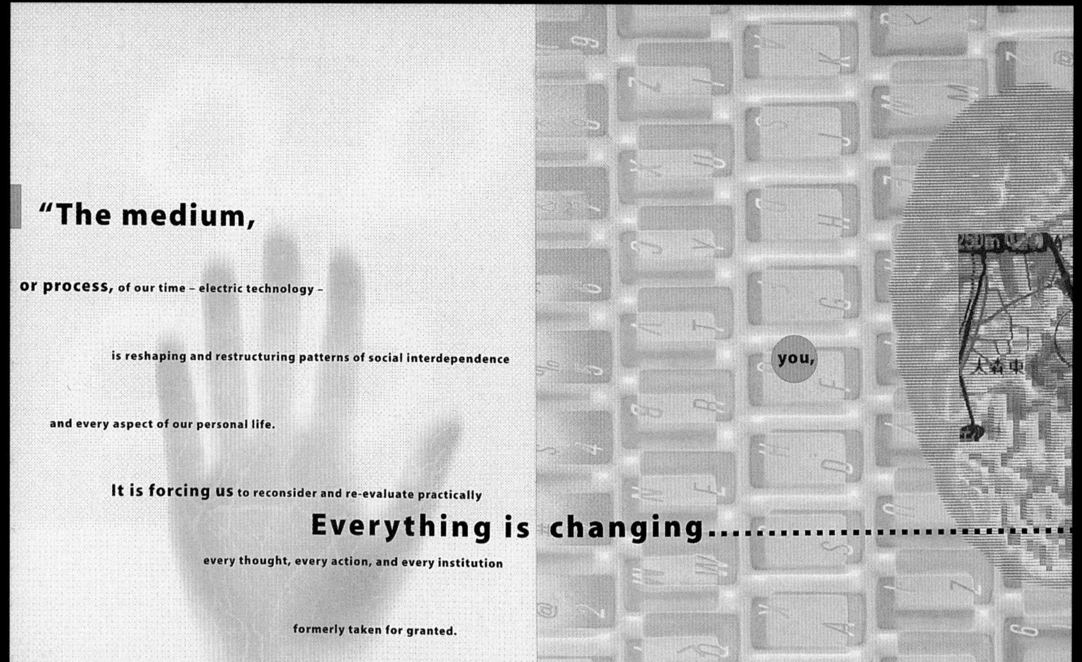

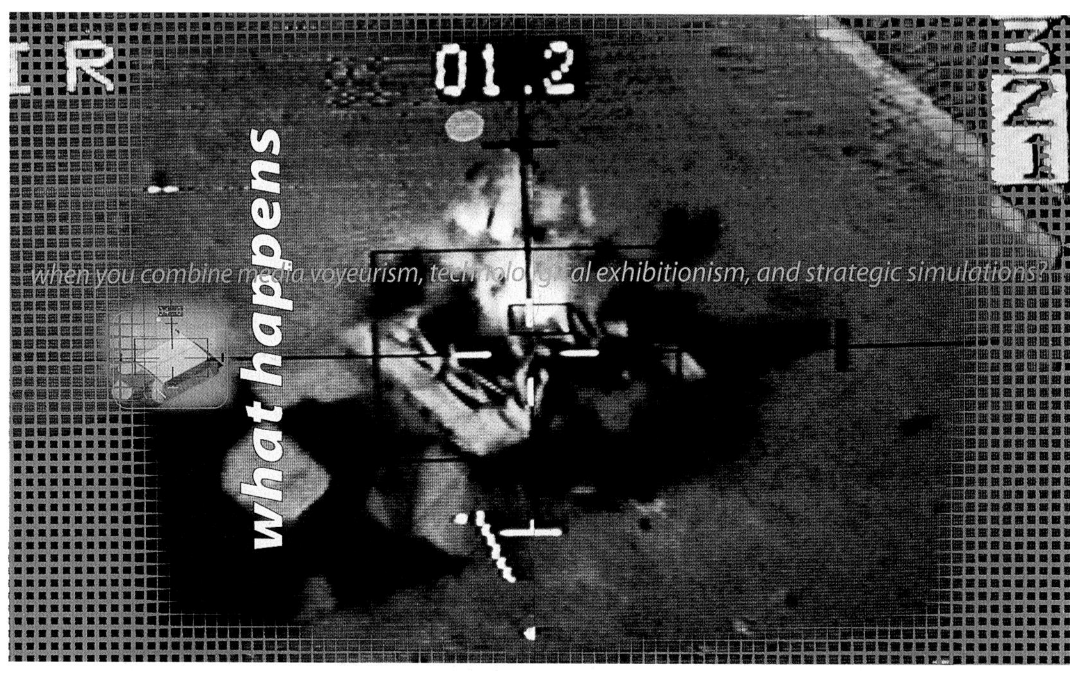

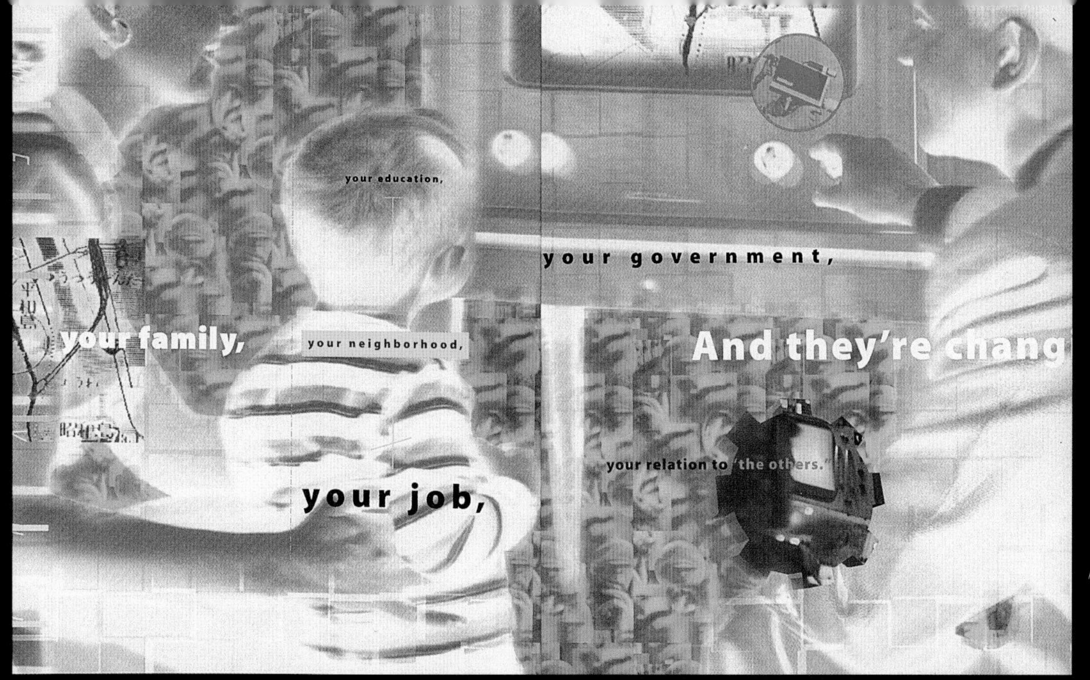

Wired no. 1.1

Magazine spreads
CREATIVE DIRECTOR John Plunkett
DESIGNERS John Plunkett, Eric Adigard
DESIGN COMPANY Plunkett + Kuhr
ILLUSTRATOR Eric Adigard
PRINCIPAL TYPEFACE Myriad
CLIENT Wired USA

USA, 1993

Wired no. 2.09

Magazine spreads
CREATIVE DIRECTOR John Plunkett
DESIGNERS John Plunkett, Thomas Schneider
DESIGN COMPANY Plunkett + Kuhr
ILLUSTRATOR Eric Adigard
PRINCIPAL TYPEFACE Myriad
CLIENT Wired Ventures

USA, 1994

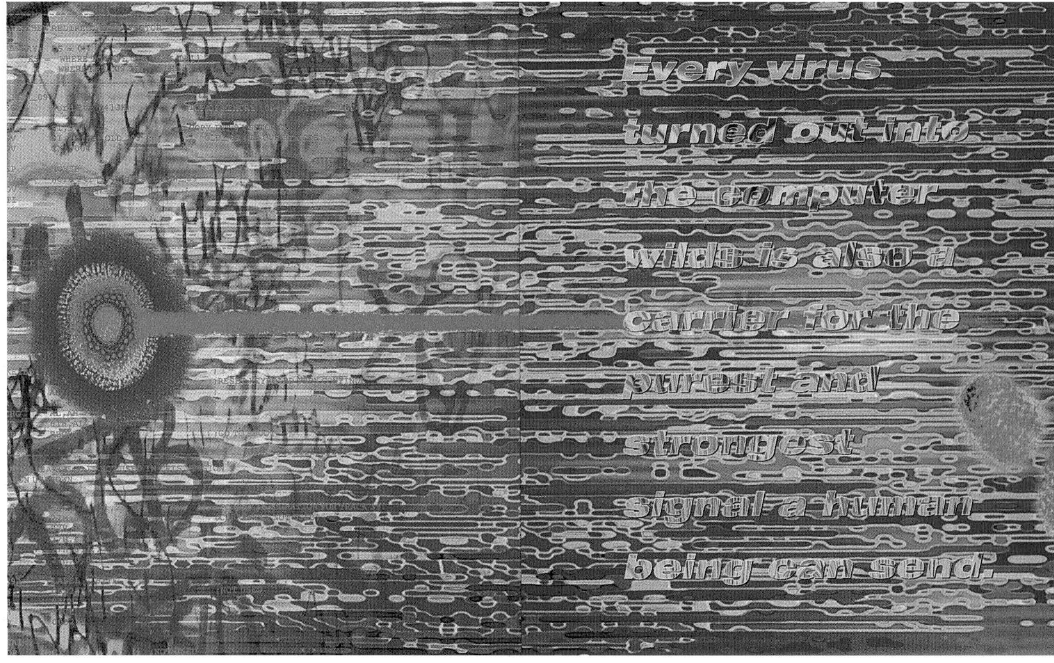

Wired no. 3.02

Magazine spreads

CREATIVE DIRECTORS John Plunkett, Barbara Kuhr

DESIGNERS Thomas Schneider, Johan Vipper

PRINCIPAL TYPEFACE Helvetica

CLIENT Wired Ventures

USA, 1995

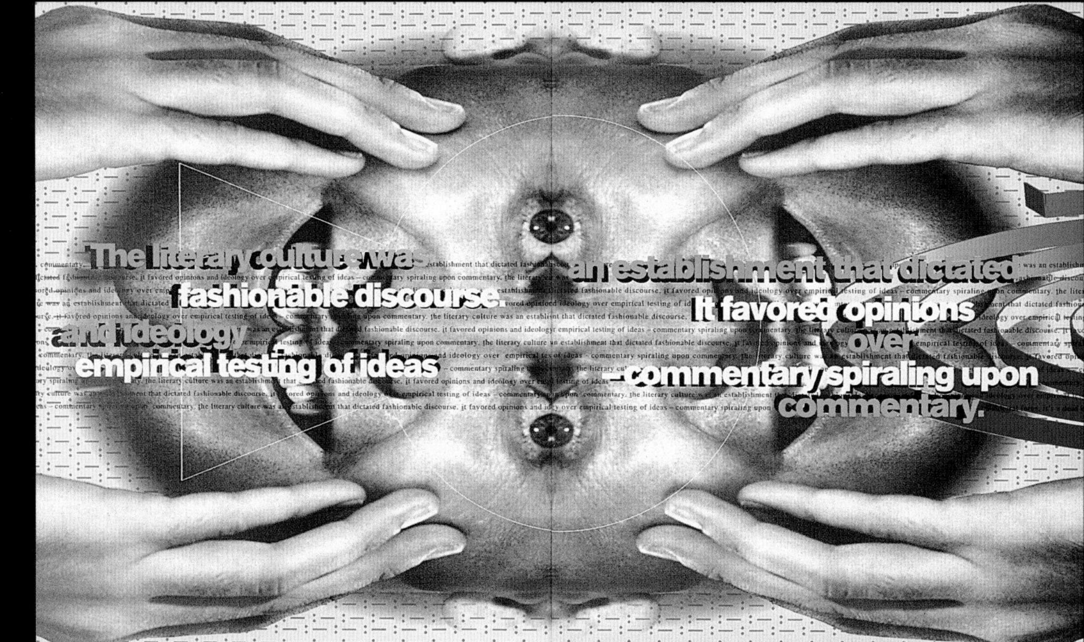

Wired no. 3.08

Magazine spreads

CREATIVE DIRECTORS John Plunkett, Barbara Kuhr

DESIGNERS John Plunkett, Thomas Schneider, Eric Adigard

ILLUSTRATOR Eric Adigard

PRINCIPAL TYPEFACE Akzidenz Grotesk

CLIENT Wired Ventures

USA, 1995

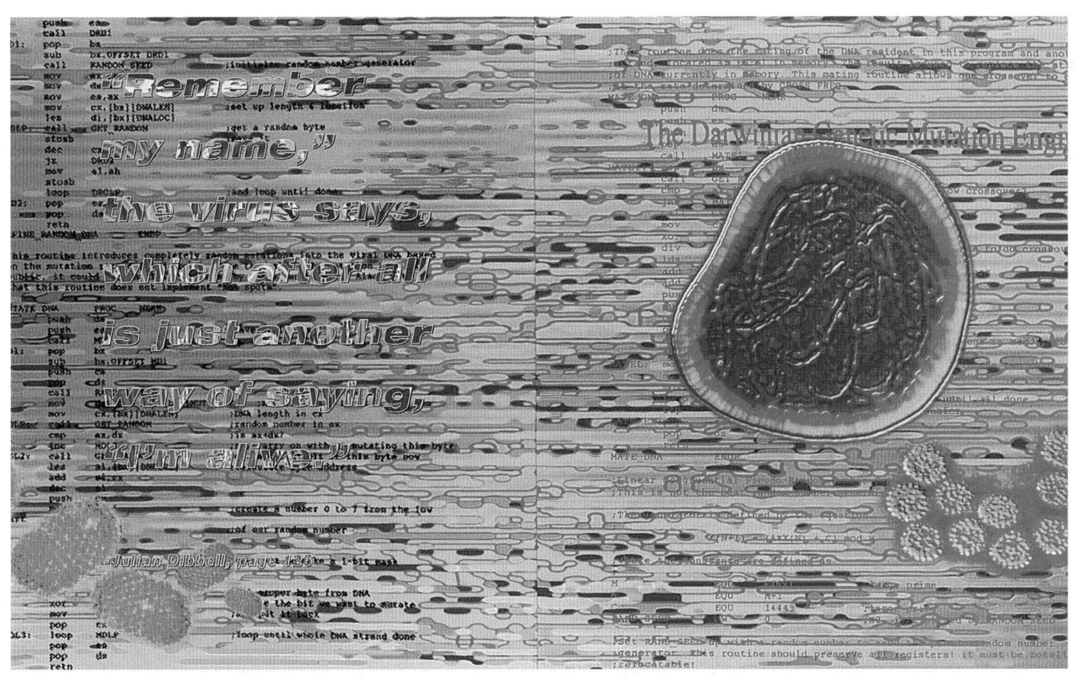
"Remember
my name,"
the virus says,
which after all
is just another
way of saying,
'I'm alive.'"
Julian Dibbell, page 126
The Darwinian Genetic Mutation Engine

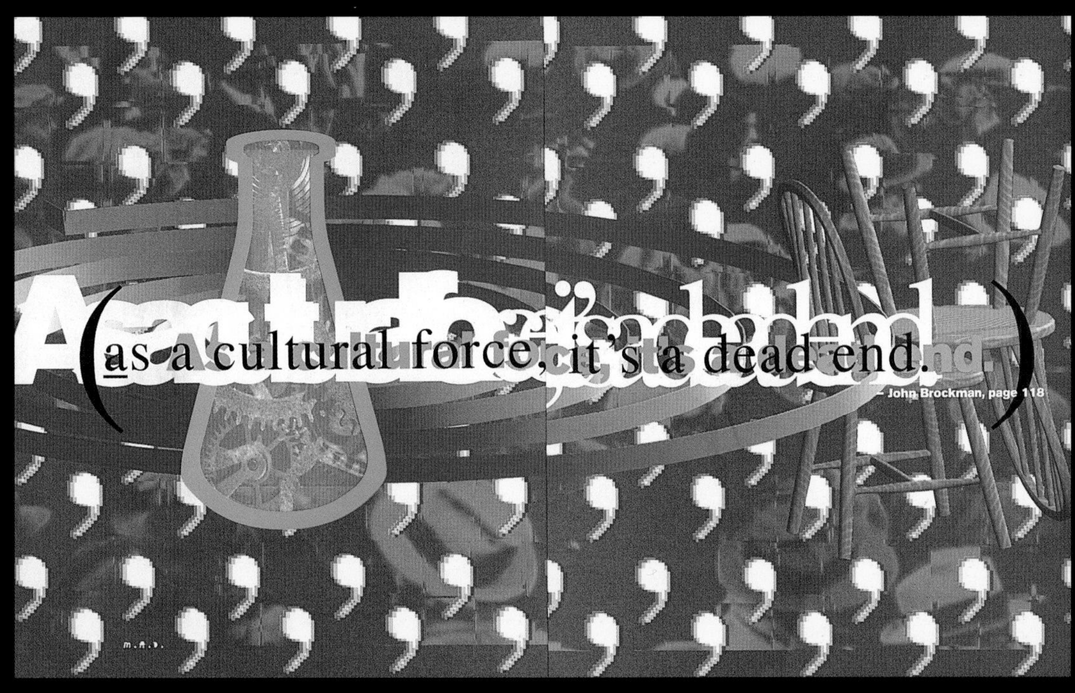
as a cultural force, it's a dead end.
– John Brockman, page 118

The Future's Paper

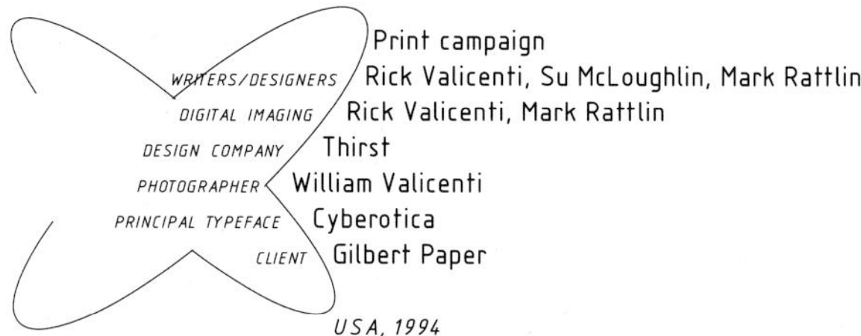

Print campaign

WRITERS/DESIGNERS Rick Valicenti, Su McLoughlin, Mark Rattlin

DIGITAL IMAGING Rick Valicenti, Mark Rattlin

DESIGN COMPANY Thirst

PHOTOGRAPHER William Valicenti

PRINCIPAL TYPEFACE Cyberotica

CLIENT Gilbert Paper

USA, 1994

"The Future's Paper" print campaign authored by Thirst consisted of two trilogies and each of the double-page ads ran just once in *Wired*.

For the more "human" second series, "Realize Change", familiar iconography – Clark Kent, Betty Crocker, Elvis – was futuristically recast. In a non-typographic extension of the project, Rick Valicenti's photographer brother took life-sized enlargements of the figures to a Midwestern shopping mall, where he invited shoppers to pose with their preferred character – a "twisted look", Valicenti claims, at contemporary confusions between fantasy and reality.

THIRST chicago
realize
change
the future's paper
For the technology driven work that lies ahead.
Samples...call GILBERT paper at USA 800 445 7329 e mail usmedsdx@ibmmail.com
NEUTECH®: high performance laser paper
Jet-Tech™: high resolution ink jet paper

change
realize
the future's paper
Samples...call GILBERT paper at USA 800 445 7329 e mail usmedsdx@ibmmail.com
NEUTECH®: high performance laser paper
Jet-Tech™: high resolution ink jet paper

Nike: The Shoe

Print campaign
DESIGNERS Chris Priest, Andy Altmann, David Ellis
DESIGN COMPANY Why Not Associates
AGENCY Wieden Kennedy
PHOTOGRAPHER Hans Pieterse
PRINCIPAL TYPEFACE Franklin Gothic
CLIENT Nike

Great Britain, 1992

Tant qu'il y aura des dunks

Poster/brochure to promote a five-on-five basketball tournament
DESIGNER Robert Nakata
AGENCY Wieden & Kennedy
WRITER Ernest Lupinacci
PHOTOGRAPHER Hans Pieterse
PRINCIPAL TYPEFACE Monaco
CLIENT Nike France

The Netherlands, 1994

NIKE
Coca-Cola
Le
Nike
5 x 5
5 x 5 Tant qu'il y aura des dunks
Tant qu'il y aura des dunks
Le tournoi de basket
24-25 sept.,
Parc Départemental
de Bron-Parilly,
15 rue du Clos Verger,
Vennissieux;
5
Le tournoi de basket 5x5 de Nike débarque à Lyon, samedi 24 septembre.
4
Amène tes baskets et tes 36 cm de détente sèche au parc départemental de Bron-Parilly - 15 rue du Clos Verger à Vénnissieux - à 13 heures tapantes et Nike te mettra dans une équipe avec 4 autres joueurs.
3
Reste dans le coin et reviens dimanche à 11 heures. Ce sera la dernière phase de qualification, avant la finale à Paris, du Raid Outdoor 3x3 de Nike.
2
2 supers tournois de basket pour le dernier week-end de l'été...t'es gâté!
1
Au coucher du soleil, quand les derniers sifflets se seront tus et que le panier aura fini de trembler, nous saurons qui est vraiment le numéro 1.
Le tournoi est gratuit et ouvert à tous.
Alors fonce chez INTERSPORT ou MAG SPORT pour t'inscrire avant le 22 septembre.
Pour te rendre au tournoi:
En voiture: prends le périphérique, sors à Saint-Priest Centre et au 1er feu, à gauche. En métro: prends la ligne D et descends à la station Parilly.
Rhône

1 The new Air Trainer Max²™ shoe's dual air pressure technology matches the movement and impact of the foot.
2 Ken Griffey, Jr., baseball player, wears the Air Trainer Max² cross-training shoe from Nike.
3 In running, the heel strikes first, so 5 psi (at inflation), lower density air is located in the center of the heel Air-Sole® unit. This "softer" air provides maximum cushioning after jumps. Higher density, 25 psi (at inflation), air wraps around the heel for firmness and stability.
4 The "air" used is actually a gas that won't deflate over the lifetime of the shoe.
5 A forefoot Air-Sole® unit gives extra cushioning.
25 PSI
5 PSI
What is
technology
but mind
pushing the limits
of
muscle
NIKE

Nike Running

Print campaign
DESIGNER Robert Nakata
AGENCY Wieden & Kennedy
WRITER Evelyn Monroe
PRINCIPAL TYPEFACE DIN Mittelschrift
CLIENT Nike Europe

The Netherlands, 1994

Nike Running

Print campaign
DESIGNER Robert Nakata
AGENCY Wieden & Kennedy
WRITERS Ernest Lupinacci, Giles Montgomery, Bob Moore
PHOTOGRAPHER John Huet
PRINCIPAL TYPEFACES Argos, DIN Mittelschrift
CLIENT Nike Europe

The Netherlands, 1995

Microsoft Office

Print campaign
DESIGNER Robert Nakata
AGENCY Wieden & Kennedy
WRITER Bob Moore
PHOTOGRAPHER Dieter Eikelpoth
PRINCIPAL TYPEFACE Corporate S
CLIENT Microsoft

The Netherlands, 1994-95

Each of the three portraits – rock star, businessman, young boy – is followed by an "image" spread and, through the copy's emphasis and lack of visible computer, it is hoped the viewer will understand that Microsoft makes software and not hardware. The typography suggests the ease and fluidity with which information can be manipulated in the digital realm, as well as its personal dimension, without resorting to an obviously "computer" look in the choice of typeface.

Altmann's Tongue

Book jacket

DESIGNER Barbara De Wilde

DESIGN COMPANY De Wilde Design

PRINCIPAL TYPEFACE Brodovitch Albro

CLIENT Knopf

USA, 1994

The Unusual Life of Tristan Smith

Book jacket
DESIGNER Chip Kidd
DESIGN COMPANY Chip Kidd Design
PRINCIPAL TYPEFACE Univers
CLIENT Knopf

USA, 1994

The Information

Book jacket
DESIGNER Chip Kidd
DESIGN COMPANY Chip Kidd Design
PRINCIPAL TYPEFACE Bulmer
CLIENT Harmony Books

USA, 1995

Cowgirl

Promotional poster for a single by Underworld

DESIGNER John Warwicker

DESIGN COMPANY Tomato

PRINCIPAL TYPEFACES Custom-made for the project

CLIENT Junior Boys Own

Great Britain, 1994

underw orld: born slippy. ,

underw orld: born slippy .TEL EMATIC ; cowg irl; (W INJER MIX .)

a side, born slippy; TELEMATIC. b side, cowgirl (WINJER MIX). written/produced/mixed by UNDERWORLD (smith/hyde/emerson). ⓟ + ⓒ junior boys own, 1995. junior recordings ltd, the saga centre, 326 kensal road, london w10 5bz, tel 0181 960 4495, fax 0181 960 3256. published by underworld/sherlock holmes music. management: jukes productions, tel 0171 286 9532. manufactured and distributed by rtm/pinnacle. made in england.

jbo29R JUNIOR BOY'S OWN 5 026734 002900 >

Born Slippy

Record sleeve for a 12-inch single by Underworld

DESIGNERS Jason Kedgley, Graham Wood

Revolution Radio

Television commercial
DIRECTOR Walter Pitt
ANIMATOR/EDITOR/PHOTOGRAPHER Alexei Tylevich
PRINCIPAL TYPEFACES Custom-made for the project
CLIENT Rev 105

USA, 1994

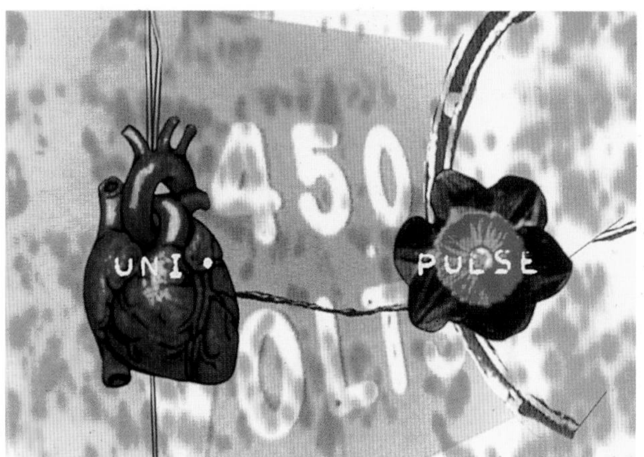

Revolution Radio, an alternative music station based in Minneapolis, gave Alexei Tylevich complete freedom in his choice of imagery and use of editing for a TV commercial. Tylevich's animation was one of a number of segments assigned to different designers. The segments were then spliced together in a televisual version of Exquisite Corpse, the Surrealist game in which each player contributes a section of a drawing without seeing what the other players have drawn.

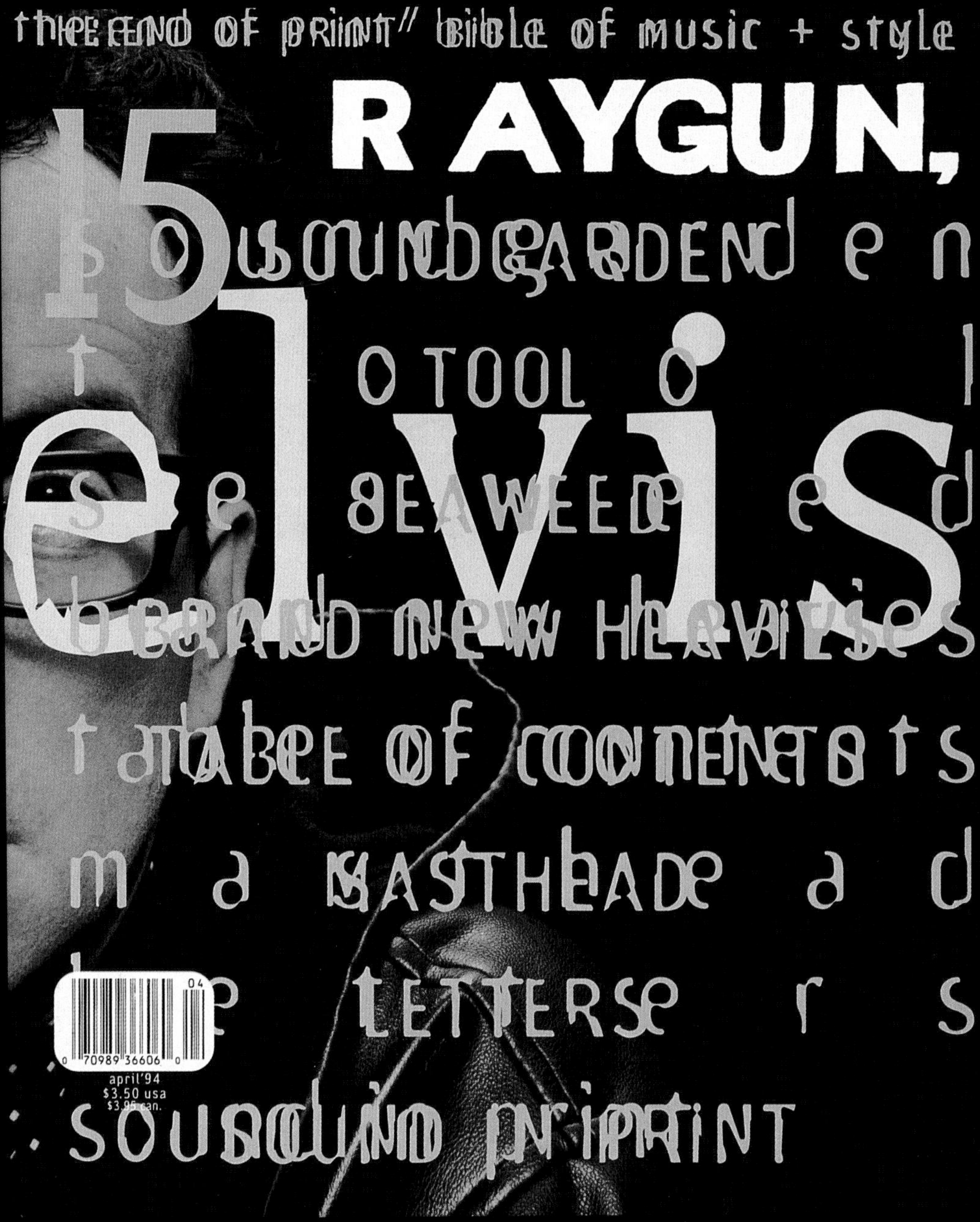

Raygun no. 15

Magazine cover

ART DIRECTOR/DESIGNER David Carson
PHOTOGRAPHERS Davies and Starr
CLIENT Ray Gun Publishing

USA, 1994

Raygun no. 5

Magazine cover
ART DIRECTOR/DESIGNER David Carson
ILLUSTRATOR Jim Sherraden
PHOTOGRAPHER Merlyn Rosenberg
CLIENT Ray Gun Publishing

USA, 1993

Raygun no. 19

Magazine cover
ART DIRECTOR/DESIGNER David Carson
PHOTOGRAPHER Colin Bell
PRINCIPAL TYPEFACE Teenager
CLIENT Ray Gun Publishing

USA, 1994

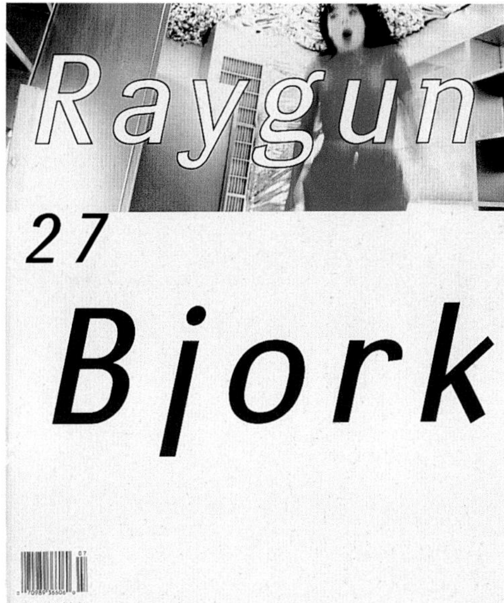

Raygun no. 27

Magazine cover
ART DIRECTION/DESIGNER David Carson
PHOTOGRAPHER David Stewart
PRINCIPAL TYPEFACE Neulin Sans
CLIENT Ray Gun Publishing

USA, 1995

Raygun no. 31

Magazine cover
ART DIRECTORS/DESIGNERS Hal Wolverton, Alicia Johnson
DESIGN COMPANY Johnson & Wolverton
PHOTOGRAPHER Doug Aitken
PRINCIPAL TYPEFACE Interstate
CLIENT Ray Gun Publishing

USA, 1995

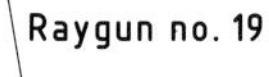

Raygun no. 19

Magazine spread
ART DIRECTOR/DESIGNER David Carson
ILLUSTRATOR Christian Northeast
PRINCIPAL TYPEFACE Teenager
CLIENT Ray Gun Publishing

USA, 1994

Raygun no. 14

Magazine spread
ART DIRECTOR/DESIGNER David Carson
PHOTOGRAPHER Chris Cuffaro
CLIENT Ray Gun Publishing

USA, 1994

Raygun no. 15

Magazine spread

ART DIRECTOR/DESIGNER David Carson

ILLUSTRATOR Malcolm Tarlofsky

CLIENT Ray Gun Publishing

USA, 1994

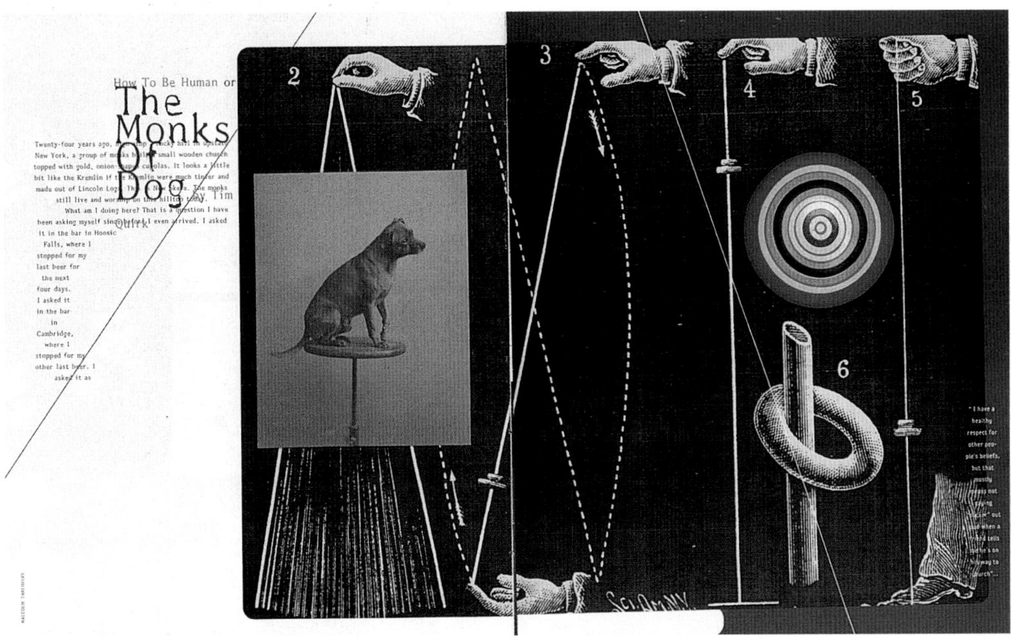

How To Be Human or

The Monks Of Dog

By Tim Quirk

Twenty-four years ago, high atop a rocky hill in upstate New York, a group of monks built a small wooden church topped with gold, onion-shaped cupolas. It looks a little bit like the Kremlin if the Kremlin were much tinier and made out of Lincoln Logs. This is New Skete. The monks still live and worship on this hilltop today.

What am I doing here? That is a question I have been asking myself since before I even arrived. I asked it in the bar in Hoosic Falls, where I stopped for my last beer for the next four days. I asked it in the bar in Cambridge, where I stopped for my other last beer. I asked it as

Songs in the Key of Life

It might have been a chord, a voice, a chorus. Maybe a lyric, a look, an attitude, a concept. . .

Let's say you're a teen, settled into a compromising position in the backseat of Dad's wagon — a song comes on the radio you've heard a thousand times before, yet somehow, amid the passionate mauling and slobbering and groping and uncertainty, it sounds so astounding, so enlightening, you swear you've never heard it quite that way before.

Unless you're a troglodyte living in a peat bog somewhere, music of some sort has provided your life with a lengthy soundtrack, a musical accompaniment, marking the different phases you've been through. Most likely, at some point along your journey, music assumed such an essential role it actually overwhelmed you, took over your thoughts, influenced your decisions, helped you see, gave you direction when you thought none existed.

We wanted to find out what songs some of today's rock 'n' rollers would single out as revelatory, the sounds they heard that changed their lives wholly and irrevocably. Here's what a few of them said.

BY BOB GULLA

PHOTO: ALLEN MESSER / HATCH SHOW PRINT

Raygun no. 18

Magazine spread

ART DIRECTOR/DESIGNER David Carson

PHOTOGRAPHER Allen Messer

CLIENT Ray Gun Publishing

USA, 1994

Raygun no. 19

Magazine Spreads

ART DIRECTOR David Carson

DESIGNER Martin Venezky

CLIENT Ray Gun Publishing

USA, 1994

Raygun no. 29

Magazine spread
ART DIRECTOR/DESIGNER David Carson
ILLUSTRATORS Vera Daucher, Sarah Cromwell, Nick Whiting
PRINCIPAL TYPEFACE Neulin Sans
CLIENT Ray Gun Publishing

USA, 1995

RootDOWN
the essence
of DUB

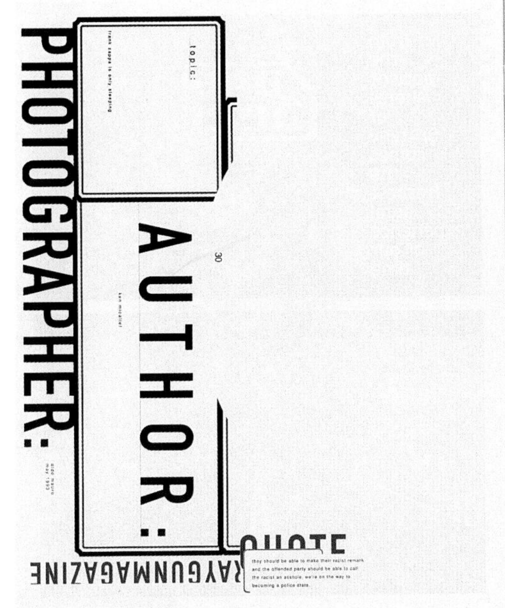

Raygun no. 30

Magazine spread
ART DIRECTOR/DESIGNER David Carson
PHOTOGRAPHER Aldo Mauro
CLIENT Ray Gun Publishing

USA, 1995

In the issues leading up to David Carson's departure from *Raygun*, there was already evidence of a move towards a much quieter typography described by the magazine's publisher, Marvin Scott Jarrett, as "a new simplicity". This was most starkly apparent in issue 30, Carson's swansong, where in place of his customary fractured headline treatments he devised a label-like credit box that emphasised the contributors' functions rather than their bylines.

Bikini no. 3

Magazine spread

DESIGN DIRECTOR	Scott Clum
DESIGN COMPANY	Ride Design
PHOTOGRAPHER	Cynthia Levine
ILLUSTRATOR	Scott Clum
PRINCIPAL TYPEFACES	Matrix, Osprey
CLIENT	Ray Gun Publishing

USA, 1994

52

Dylan McDermott grew up in the New York saloon culture. That's what makes him literary.

By Anita Sarko

Photographed by Cynthia Levine for KeswickHamilton-Sygma
Grooming: Katrina Borgstrom/Celestine
Stylist: Ariana Lambert/Cloutier

I Was a Teenage BAR • FRY

Don't hate Dylan McDermott because he's beautiful ... or a very hot young actor ... What was that? You know you've heard of him, but you're not *quite* sure why or how? Okay, I know what the problem is ... it's that name. Just remember: He's not Dermot Mulroney; nor D.W. Moffet; nor D.B. Sweeney; nor, if you're *really* confused, Delbert McClinton (*he's* a singer, you moron).

McDermott broke out of the aforementioned Blarney Bunch (though he's actually half Italian), after many false starts, last summer, by being the soft, sensitive, utterly tortured center between Eastwood, Malkovich and Russo in the mega-macho(a) movie blockbuster, *In the Line of Fire*. He's, also the most classically hunky of his contemporaries with similar monikers, which, at one point, before she changed her tastes, might have contributed to his inclusion in another crowded collective: Julia's boys. Yes, *that* Julia. Dylan seemed to have started her trend towards coupling with her co-stars. This was before either of them was who they are now, since they were both enjoying their first brush with a degree of substantial success as husband and wife in *Steel Magnolias*. Life imitated art through a subsequent engagement. Not that he's ever had major babe problems, from what I've heard. I know one gorgeous actress, a close friend of mine, who nixed accompanying me to see *In the Line of Fire* because she has a rule: "I never see movies starring old boyfriends". (She doesn't catch too many films these days.) They dated many years ago and she seems to recall that the affair began after he won a pool game over another interested suitor. "Is he still a drunk?" she asked me.

I am happy to say, the answer is NO! The road to this momentous decision is far more interesting than most of the stories he's had to act his way through. Some enterprising member of even younger Hollywood (Leonardo? Macaulay?) should start saving his money to grab the option since he's already 60 pages into a book that's "... autobiographical, in a way, but it's still fiction." But, we'll get to that later. For now, let's just say that McDermott saw the light, when , 10 years ago, at the age of 22, after years of being a waiter and tending bar (What? An actor working as a waiter and bartender? An Irish guy with a drinking problem?), Dylan cleaned up his act and then learned how to. Not so easy, when your father owns the bar. It just so happens that this major Greenwich Village hangout is located right on the end of my very own block. How convenient ! I suggest we meet there, so he'll feel at home and I won't have to stray far from mine. And, would you believe, it's location is:

POSITIVELY WEST FOURTH STREET

Shades of Mr. Zimmerman and Mr. Thomas ... who, incidentally, dropped dead from drink at another Village tavern a few blocks to the west. Can't get away from this guy's name.

Our Dylan ambles in, flashes a friendly grin and greeting, leading me to a quiet table in the back room.. He informs me that he's seen me in the neighborhood over the years and, when he was an impressionable Punk/New Wave loving 16-year-old, used to be a regular at the Mudd Club, when I was the DJ. "I've been going more jazzy now," he explains, "Miles and Coltrane. You don't want to leave your house. I guess it doesn't lift you up. It doesn't get your energy going, but it's more where my energy's going somehow." It's amazing that he's even got energy after the life he's led. But, we'll get to that.

For now we talk about how funny his press kit is, since it's basically a wad of contradictory shit padded with an inordinate amount of fashion spreads. "For a while I couldn't get any press ... they're always willing to put me into clothes, but they're not willing to give me the article," he explains with a laugh." Years ago, I had to do whatever it takes. You learn." I point out that he's almost had to fight the same sort of "I want to be taken seriously" bit that sexy female starlets are always whining about. He takes solace in the fact that Paul Newman once had the same problem. Maybe that's why Dylan is such an inspired pool player ... but, I keep my mouth shut concerning that particular coincidence.

"You're a serious actor who's studied for years, done multiple movies and stage work and you're still considered, by most, to be just another pretty boy with an Irish name who was one of the cast of thousands claiming Julia Roberts as a former fiancée. Finally, *In the Line of Fire* breaks you out and now you're following it with *The Cowboy Way*, whose current release date is April, which, besides co-starring Woody Harrelson, co-stars *Keifer Sutherland* . You know what the hook is going to be in the

53

THE VERY EXCITING WORLD OF DRAGSTERS

ie, a large explosion between the legs.

by Cole Coonce photos by Cole too.

34

35

YEAH, YEAH, YEAH. I know, I know: You are young, beautiful, and you live in Babylon Hills, California, 90210. You are trying to get a handle on this Grand Guignol play a/k/a "life." You are frustrated, misunderstood, beat up by the pain of being alive, and at the same time you are seeking out the proper mode of expression, the milieu that trims your foliage. You are seeking your muse, but at this point will settle for a job.

The truth is thus: the denizens of White Flight, California comprise a society of complainers, bellyachers, cable teevee fuckoffs, and pampered bourgeoisie boneheads, indifferent and/or oblivious to the fact that there is fuckall to give their dreary lives meaning. Kids today are bored, jaded, and unlike, say, our youth-gone-mad predecessors of the 1960's.

Now, the kids of the 60's were some busy buckaroos. That's right: hippies were more ambitious than you! What with campus demonstrations, love-ins, extended holidays in Southeast Asia, multi-media slide shows projected on the likes of Nico and Edie Sedgewick, riots on Sunset Strip and a whole lot of consciousness expansion—who had time to complain about the futility of existence?

Back in the day, the kids was also shakin' some action at the local drag strip. This was where the young gearheads displayed their gumption, bravado, and intellect. They showcased these attributes in machinery they crafted themselves (generally speaking)—contraptions that resembled a spaceship as much as anything else. These were formally known as "rails" or "dragsters."

"Drag strips," "rails," "dragsters." What the hell is drag racing, you may wonder? It is a socio-technological phenomena that is louder, faster, and more primal than either grindcore or the Big Bang itself, that's what.

Drag racing was born at the dry lake beds and the abandoned military airstrips of post World War II Southern California, and these locations remain a staple of hot rodding. The mood and vibrations at these exhibitions of unbridled horsepower are very primal, chaotic, and apocalyptic. Despite the clouds of smoke and fire that might obscure the action, a message cuts through the haze and fumes—a message the gearheads and hepcats and kittens intuitively understand: speed is a metaphor for freedom.

Bikini no. 11

Magazine spread

DESIGN DIRECTOR	Scott Clum
DESIGN COMPANY	Ride Design
PHOTOGRAPHER	Cole Coonce
PRINCIPAL TYPEFACE	Blur
CLIENT	Ray Gun Publishing

USA, 1995

Bikini no. 2

Magazine spread

DESIGN DIRECTOR Scott Clum

DESIGNERS Rey International

THE YOUNG AMERICANS

photoGraphy by
MELODIE MCDANIEL

StYLing by
RACHEL SAGE

welcome to the

CHELSEA HOTEL

Legend precedes the Chelsea Hotel.

by N. Hollis Brown

The gold-colored, imprinted plaques marking either side of the building's entrance boast the fact that both Dylan Thomas and Arthur Miller once made the hotel their homes—Thomas lapsed into a fatal coma in Room 205. Warhol filmed many of his early avant-garde films there, including The Chelsea Girls. Leonard Cohen exalted Janis Joplin in his song, "Chelsea Hotel #2." The 1978 stabbing of Nancy Spungen by Sex Pistol Sid Vicious was immortalized in the film Sid and Nancy. And the list goes on.

The Chelsea Hotel, 222 West 23rd Street, is literally a historic landmark, officially designated to the National Register of Historic Places by the United States Department of the Interior. As the Chelsea's owner Stanley Bard, a youthful 60-year-old, sits behind his cluttered desk, he speaks proudly of his ongoing friendship with his clientele, whom he describes as "the intelligentsia: the poet, writer, playwright, dancer, artist, painter, sculptor." Bard revels in the building's history.

The Chelsea Hotel was built in 1884 as an apartment building—it was the first building in New York to have 12 stories and penthouses. After going bankrupt in 1903, reopening as a hotel in 1905 and going bankrupt again in 1939, it was purchased by Bard's father, David. Stanley took over operation of the hotel in 1957, and has been joined by his son, David, and his daughter Michelle. In the lobby, dust has settled on the dried eucalyptus, long-since arranged in a green jar on one of two silver-and-glass deco coffee tables in the lobby. Blue leather benches are arranged around the fireplace, which is flanked by matching griffin statuettes. The walls, a single window, and the ceiling are crowded with an array of art, much of which has been donated by residents, or even bartered for rent—which, at $1,400 a month for a tiny loft, is expensive, even by New York standards.

But legend and cost don't make the hotel an exclusive haven for the elite. From among the 70% of its 250 rooms occupied by long-term residents, there are a number of fairly

Speak, preview issue

Magazine spreads

ART DIRECTOR/DESIGNER Martin Venezky
CONTRIBUTING DESIGNERS Bob Aufuldish, Fred Bower, Bill Bowers, Elliott Peter Earls, Geoff Kaplan
PHOTOGRAPHERS Melodie McDaniel, Michael Darter, Paige Stuart
PRINCIPAL TYPEFACES Univers, Bodoni, Franklin Gothic, Spartan Classified, Century Expanded, custom-made for the project
PUBLISHER Dan Rolleri

USA, 1995

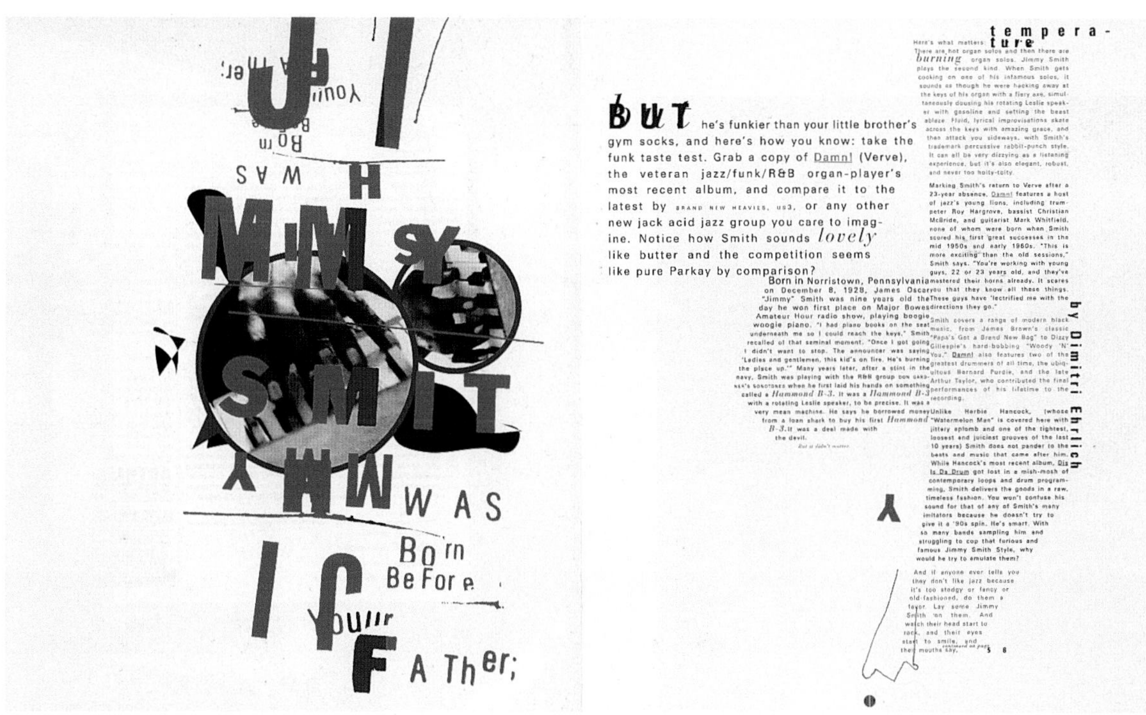

BUT he's funkier than your little brother's gym socks, and here's how you know: take the funk taste test. Grab a copy of Damn! (Verve), the veteran jazz/funk/R&B organ-player's most recent album, and compare it to the latest by BRAND NEW HEAVIES, US3, or any other new jack acid jazz group you care to imagine. Notice how Smith sounds *lovely* like butter and the competition seems like pure Parkay by comparison?

Born in Norristown, Pennsylvania on December 8, 1928, James Oscar "Jimmy" Smith was nine years old the day he won first place on Major Bowes Amateur Hour radio show, playing boogie woogie piano. "I had piano books on the seat underneath me so I could reach the keys," Smith recalled of that seminal moment. "Once I got going I didn't want to stop. The announcer was saying 'Ladies and gentlemen, this kid's on fire. He's burning the place up.'" Many years later, after a stint in the navy, Smith was playing with the R&B group DON GARDNER'S SONOTONES when he first laid his hands on something called a *Hammond B-3*. It was a *Hammond B-3* with a rotating Leslie speaker, to be precise. It was a very mean machine. He says he borrowed money from a loan shark to buy his first *Hammond B-3*. It was a deal made with the devil.

But it didn't matter.

temperature

Here's what matters: There are hot organ solos and then there are *burning* organ solos. Jimmy Smith plays the second kind. When Smith gets cooking on one of his infamous solos, it sounds as though he were hacking away at the keys of his organ with a fiery axe, simultaneously dousing his rotating Leslie speaker with gasoline and setting the beast ablaze. Fluid, lyrical improvisations skate across the keys with amazing grace, and then attack you sideways, with Smith's trademark percussive rabbit-punch style. It can all be very dizzying as a listening experience, but it's also elegant, robust, and never too hoity-toity.

Marking Smith's return to Verve after a 23-year absence, Damn! features a host of jazz's young lions, including trumpeter Roy Hargrove, bassist Christian McBride, and guitarist Mark Whitfield, none of whom were born when Smith scored his first great successes in the mid 1950s and early 1960s. "This is more exciting than the old sessions," Smith says. "You're working with young guys, 22 or 23 years old, and they've mastered their horns already. It scares you that they know all these things. These guys have 'lectrified me with the directions they go."

Smith covers a range of modern black music, from James Brown's classic "Papa's Got a Brand New Bag" to Dizzy Gillespie's hard-bobbing "Woody 'N' You." Damn! also features two of the greatest drummers of all time, the ubiquitous Bernard Purdie, and the late Arthur Taylor, who contributed the final performances of his lifetime to the recording.

Unlike Herbie Hancock, (whose "Watermelon Man" is covered here with jittery aplomb and one of the tightest, loosest and juiciest grooves of the last 10 years) Smith does not pander to the beats and music that came after him. While Hancock's most recent album, Dis Is Da Drum got lost in a mish-mosh of contemporary loops and drum programming, Smith delivers the goods in a raw, timeless fashion. You won't confuse his sound for that of any of Smith's many imitators because he doesn't try to give it a '90s spin. He's smart. With so many bands sampling him and struggling to cop that furious and famous Jimmy Smith Style, why would he try to emulate them?

And if anyone ever tells you they don't like jazz because it's too stodgy or fancy or old-fashioned, do them a favor. Lay some Jimmy Smith on them. And watch their head start to rock, and their eyes start to smile, and their mouths say,

continued on page 58

by Dimitri Ehrlich

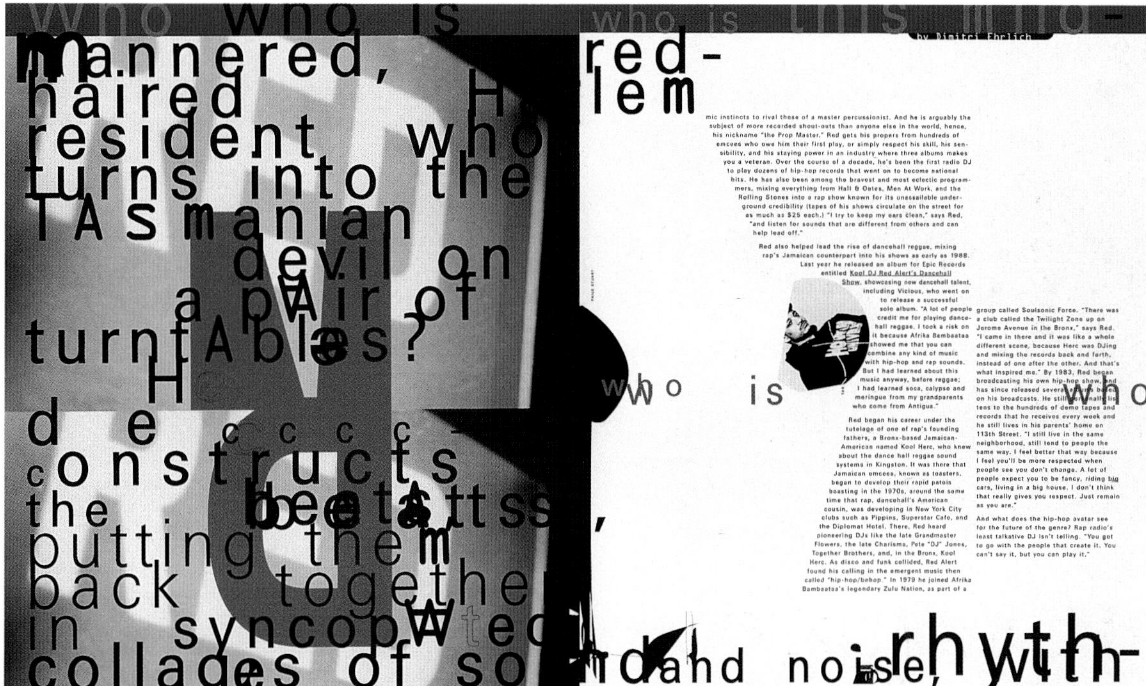

mic instincts to rival those of a master percussionist. And he is arguably the subject of more recorded shout-outs than anyone else in the world, hence, his nickname "the Prop Master." Red gets his propers from hundreds of emcees who owe him their first play, or simply respect his skill, his sensibility, and his staying power in an industry where three albums makes you a veteran. Over the course of a decade, he's been the first radio DJ to play dozens of hip-hop records that went on to become national hits. He has also been among the bravest and most eclectic programmers, mixing everything from Hall & Oates, Men At Work, and the Rolling Stones into a rap show known for its unassailable underground credibility (tapes of his shows circulate on the street for as much as $25 each.) "I try to keep my ears clean," says Red, "and listen for sounds that are different from others and can help lead off."

Red also helped lead the rise of dancehall reggae, mixing rap's Jamaican counterpart into his shows as early as 1988. Last year he released an album for Epic Records entitled Kool DJ Red Alert's Dancehall Show, showcasing new dancehall talent, including Vicious, who went on to release a successful solo album. "A lot of people credit me for playing dancehall reggae. I took a risk on it because Afrika Bambaataa showed me that you can combine any kind of music with hip-hop and rap sounds. But I had learned about this music anyway, before reggae; I had learned soca, calypso and meringue from my grandparents who come from Antigua."

Red began his career under the tutelage of one of rap's founding fathers, a Bronx-based Jamaican-American named Kool Herc, who knew about the dance hall reggae sound systems in Kingston. It was there that Jamaican emcees, known as toasters, began to develop their rapid patois boasting in the 1970s, around the same time that rap, dancehall's American cousin, was developing in New York City clubs such as Pippins, Superstar Cafe, and the Diplomat Hotel. There, Red heard pioneering DJs like the late Grandmaster Flowers, the late Charisma, Pete "DJ" Jones, Together Brothers, and, in the Bronx, Kool Herc. As disco and funk collided, Red Alert found his calling in the emergent music then called "hip-hop/bebop." In 1979 he joined Afrika Bambaataa's legendary Zulu Nation, as part of a group called Soulsonic Force. "There was a club called the Twilight Zone up on Jerome Avenue in the Bronx," says Red. "I came in there and it was like a whole different scene, because Herc was DJing and mixing the records back and forth, instead of one after the other. And that's what inspired me." By 1983, Red began broadcasting his own hip-hop show, and has since released several albums based on his broadcasts. He still personally listens to the hundreds of demo tapes and records that he receives every week and he still lives in his parents' home on 113th Street. "I still live in the same neighborhood, still tend to people the same way. I feel better that way because I feel you'll be more respected when people see you don't change. A lot of people expect you to be fancy, riding big cars, living in a big house. I don't think that really gives you respect. Just remain as you are."

And what does the hip-hop avatar see for the future of the genre? Rap radio's least talkative DJ isn't telling. "You got to go with the people that create it. You can't say it, but you can play it."

Raygun's impact with readers, advertisers and the design community made it inevitable that others would attempt to apply its lessons. *Speak* magazine, published in San Francisco, is a quarterly review of fashion, lifestyle and the arts. Martin Venezky, art director for the preview issue, had created a number of pages for *Raygun* and his design for *Speak* achieves a balance between readability in the main copy and expression in its display typography and other visual devices. David Carson was appointed art director from the second issue.

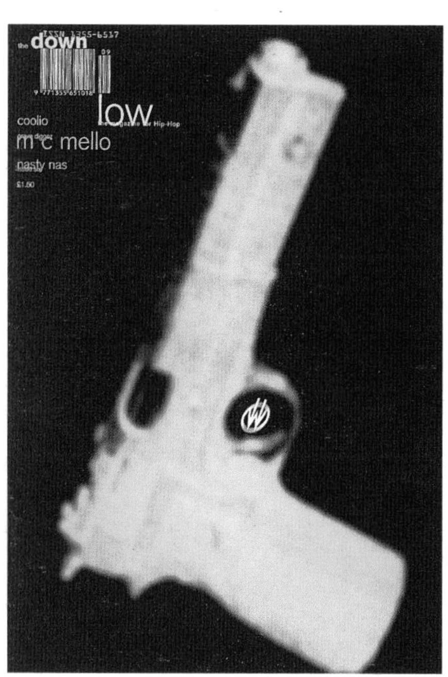

The Downlow no. 6 — Hip-hop magazine cover and spread

DESIGNERS Dominic Lippa, Mark Diaper, Rachel Dinnis, Michael Davies

DESIGN COMPANY Lippa Pearce Design

PRINCIPAL TYPEFACE Template Gothic

CLIENT *The Downlow*

Great Britain, 1995

The Downlow no. 9

Hip-hop magazine cover and spread
DESIGNERS Michael Davies, Mark Diaper, Birgit Eggers
PRINCIPAL TYPEFACES Triplex, Citizen, OCRB, News Gothic
CLIENT *The Downlow*

Great Britain, 1995

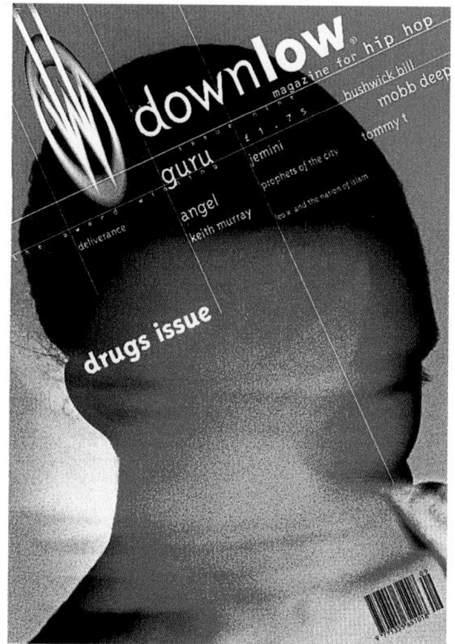

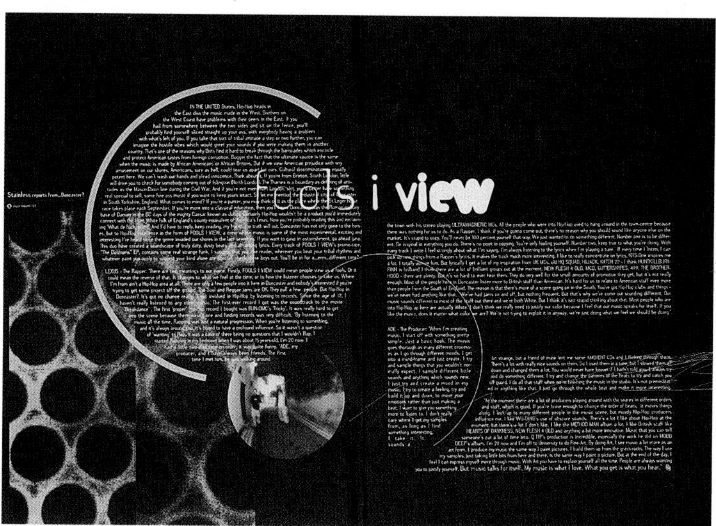

The Downlow no. 10

Hip-hop magazine spread
DESIGNERS Michael Davies, Mark Diaper, Birgit Eggers, MC Colosseum, Shaun O'Mara, Glen Thornley, Alan King
PRINCIPAL TYPEFACE Template Gothic
CLIENT *The Downlow*

Great Britain, 1996

Blah Blah Blah no. 1

Magazine cover and spread

ART DIRECTORS/DESIGNERS	Chris Ashworth, Neil Fletcher, Amanda Sissons
DESIGN COMPANY	Substance
PHOTOGRAPHER	Alison Dyer
PRINCIPAL TYPEFACE	DIN
CLIENT	Ray Gun Publishing

Great Britain, 1996

Blah Blah Blah no. 2

Magazine spread

ART DIRECTORS/DESIGNERS	Chris Ashworth, Neil Fletcher, Amanda Sissons
DESIGN COMPANY	Substance
PHOTOGRAPHER	Joseph Cultice
PRINCIPAL TYPEFACE	Compacta
CLIENT	Ray Gun Publishing

Great Britain, 1996

Blah Blah Blah no. 3

Magazine spread

ART DIRECTORS/DESIGNERS	Chris Ashworth, Neil Fletcher, Amanda Sissons
DESIGN COMPANY	Substance
PHOTOGRAPHER	Kevin Westenberg
PRINCIPAL TYPEFACE	Univers
CLIENT	Ray Gun Publishing

Great Britain, 1996

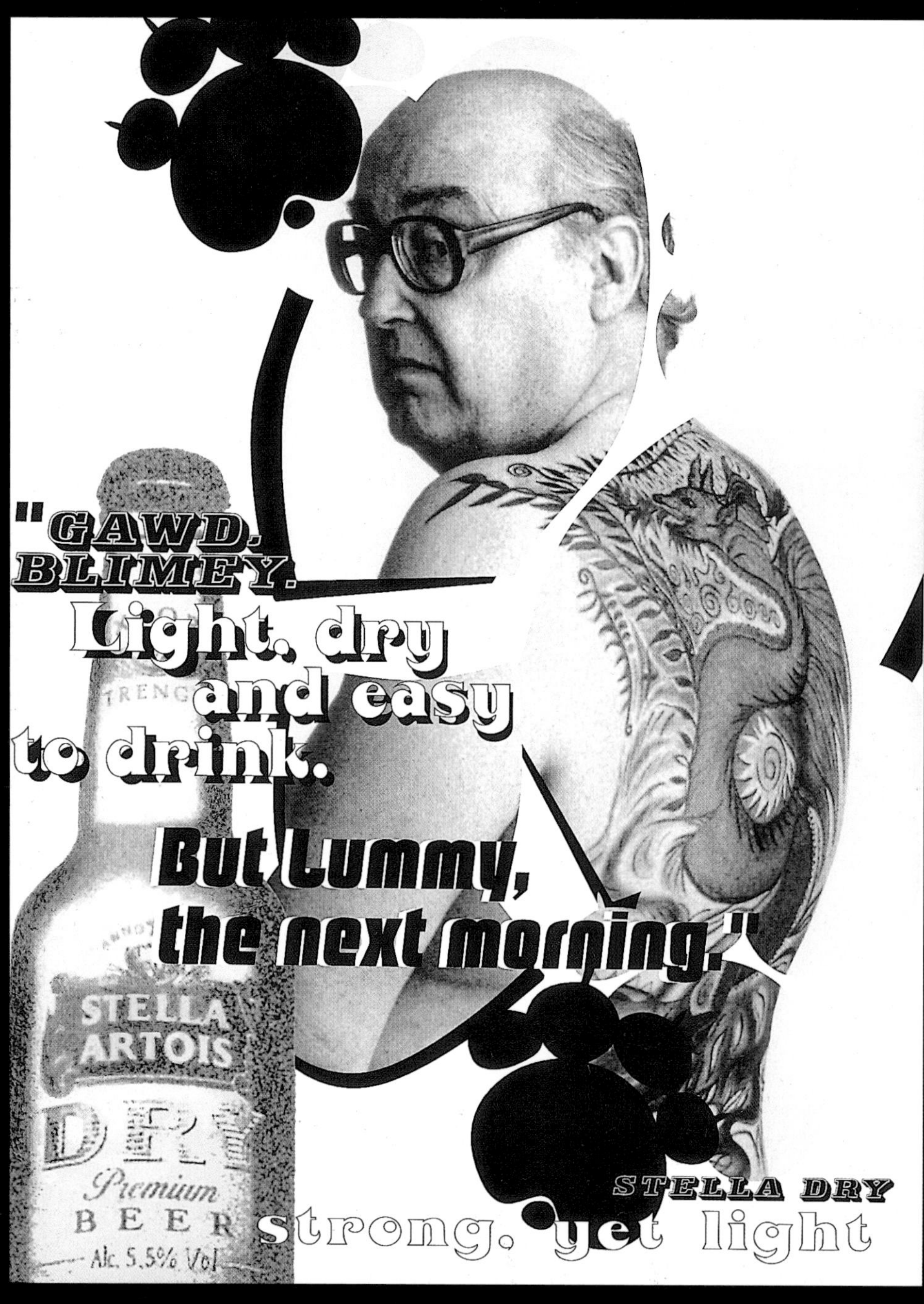

Stella Artois Dry

Print campaign
ART DIRECTOR Simon Butler
DESIGNERS/ILLUSTRATORS Whitney Lowe, Somi Kim, Lisa Nugent, James Moore
DESIGN COMPANY ReVerb
PHOTOGRAPHER Tim O. Sullivan (tattoo)
PRINCIPAL TYPEFACES Abbess, Altoona, Acropilis, Dolmen Decorated, Egbert, Enlivan, Falstaff, Siena, Garage Gothic, Helvetica, Melody, Monster, Narly, Pinwheel, Phrastic,
AGENCY Lowe Howard-Spink
CLIENT Whitbread

Great Britain, 1995

"would you credit it? my tastebuds were being tickled by this delicate, light sensation.
THEN D.R.Y."
STELLA ARTOIS
Premium
BEER
Alc. 5.5% Vol
stella dry
strong yet light
Strong yet Light
275ml
"IT SAT ON MY TONGUE, SWIRLED AROUND AND DISAPPEARED IN A BEAUTIFUL LIGHT CRISP MANNER,
AFTER THAT..."
STELLA DRY
STRONG yet light

The Bearded Lady

Television commercial

DIRECTOR Kinka Usher
ART DIRECTOR Todd Grant
CREATIVE DIRECTOR Bo Coyner
DESIGNER/ANIMATOR Alexei Tylevich
AGENCY Goodby, Silverstein & Partners
PRINCIPAL TYPEFACES Custom-made for the project
CLIENT Sega

USA, 1994

The bizarre narrative of Sega's commercial for a 32-bit game system was set in an amusement park freak show. Alexei Tylevich's animated typographic segments for both 30 and 60 second versions reflect the hallucinatory theme of the commercial's live action.

Print campaign

DESIGNER Simon Taylor
DESIGN COMPANY Tomato
AGENCY Bates Dorland
PHOTOGRAPHER Simon Taylor
PRINCIPAL TYPEFACES DIN Engschrift, Aachen
CLIENT Grolsch

Great Britain, 1995

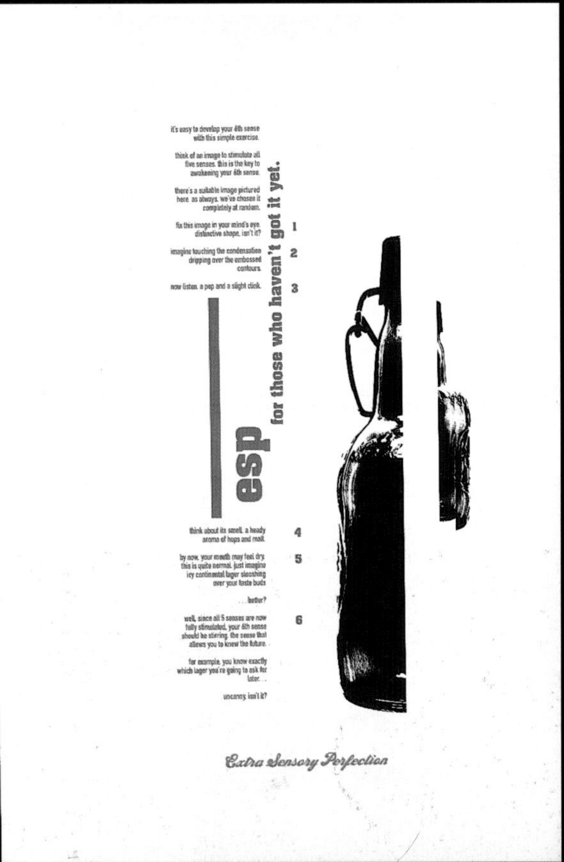

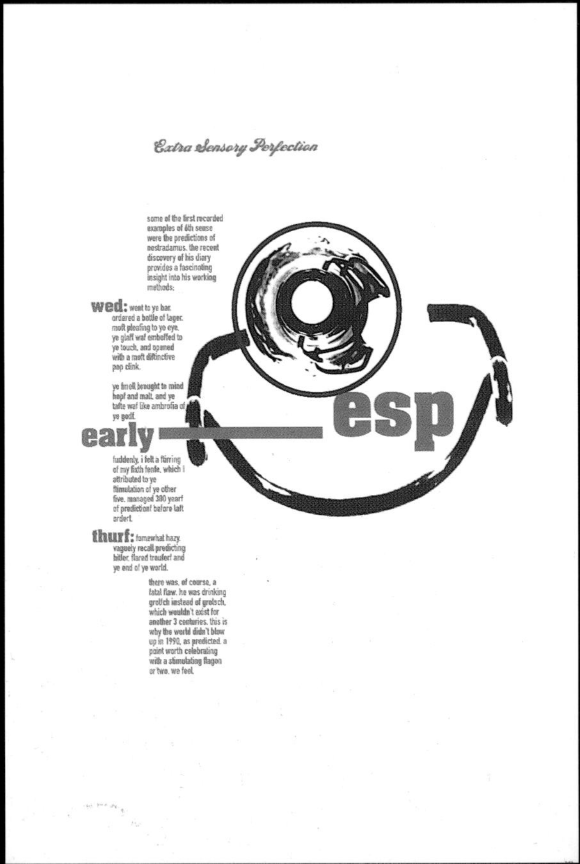

it's easy to develop your 6th sense with this simple exercise.

think of an image to stimulate all five senses. this is the key to awakening your 6th sense.

there's a suitable image pictured here. as always, we've chosen it completely at random.

1 fix this image in your mind's eye. distinctive shape, isn't it?

2 imagine touching the condensation dripping over the embossed contours.

3 now listen. a pop and a slight clink.

esp **for those who haven't got it yet.**

4 think about its smell. a heady aroma of hops and malt.

5 by now, your mouth may feel dry. this is quite normal. just imagine icy continental lager sloshing over your taste buds

. . . better?

6 well, since all 5 senses are now fully stimulated, your 6th sense should be stirring. the sense that allows you to know the future.

for example, you know exactly which lager you're going to ask for later. . .

uncanny, isn't it?

Extra Sensory Perfection

Extra Sensory Perfection

some of the first recorded examples of 6th sense were the predictions of nostradamus. the recent discovery of his diary provides a fascinating insight into his working methods:

wed: went to ye bar. ordered a bottle of lager. moft pleafing to ye eye. ye glaff waf emboffed to ye touch, and opened with a moft diftinctive pop clink.

ye fmell brought to mind hopf and malt, and ye tafte waf like ambrofia of ye godf.

early esp

fuddenly, i felt a ftirring of my fixth fenfe, which i attributed to ye ftimulation of ye other five. managed 300 yearf of predictionf before laft ordert.

thurf: fomewhat hazy. vaguely recall predicting hitler, flared troufert and ye end of ye world.

there was, of course, a fatal flaw. he was drinking grolfch instead of grolsch, which wouldn't exist for another 3 centuries. this is why the world didn't blow up in 1990, as predicted. a point worth celebrating with a stimulating flagon or two, we feel.

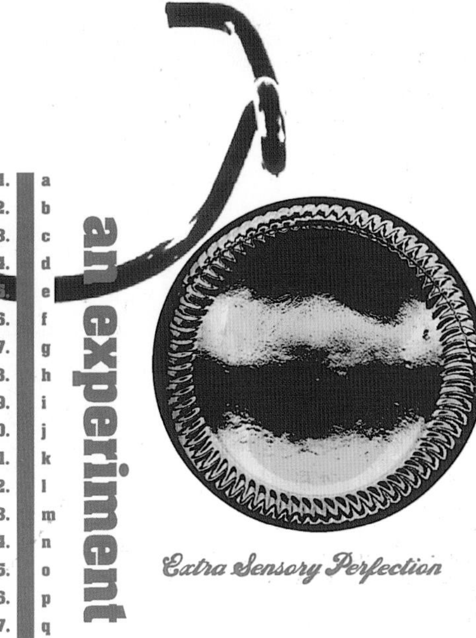

an experiment into esp

1.	a
2.	b
3.	c
4.	d
5.	e
6.	f
7.	g
8.	h
9.	i
10.	j
11.	k
12.	l
13.	m
14.	n
15.	o
16.	p
17.	q
18.	r
19.	s
20.	t
21.	u
22.	v
23.	w
24.	x
25.	y
26.	z

you know the theory. a certain distinctive bottled lager awakens your 6th sense through the 5 existing ones. you see the chunky green bottle. you touch the embossed glass. you hear the pop-clink. you smell the continental aroma. and finally, you taste it and the 6th sense stirs.

well, that's okey-dokey. but does it really work? judge for yourself...

1. think of a number between 1 & 10.
2. add 3.
3. multiply by 4.
4. subtract 8.
5. halve it.
6. add 6.
7. halve it again.
8. add 3.
9. subtract the number you first thought of.
10. match the remaining number to its corresponding letter on the mystic chart.

now concentrate on a premium lager beginning with that letter.

absolutely correct. your 6th sense is alive and well. it's probably thirsty, too. so why not pop open a chilled bottle of 7-18-15-12-19-3-8?

EXER
CISE
STERI

OGGIE
what's a
UMMER
?

BOARD

1
ANOTHER

THAT

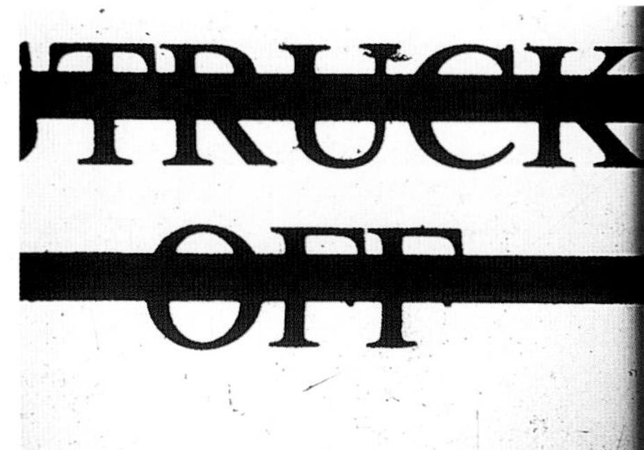

Foggie Bummer

Commercial for a spoken-word radio station

DESIGNER Jonathan Barnbrook

WRITERS Lindsey Redding, Adrian Jefferey

AGENCY Faulds

PRINCIPAL TYPEFACES Clarendon, Times, Franklin Gothic, Eurostile

CLIENT BBC Radio Scotland

Great Britain, 1995

True Romance

Commercial for a spoken-word radio station

DESIGNER Jonathan Barnbrook
WRITERS Lindsey Redding, Adrian Jeffereys
AGENCY Faulds
PRINCIPAL TYPEFACES Manson, Bastard, Nixonscript
CLIENT BBC Radio Scotland

Great Britain, 1995

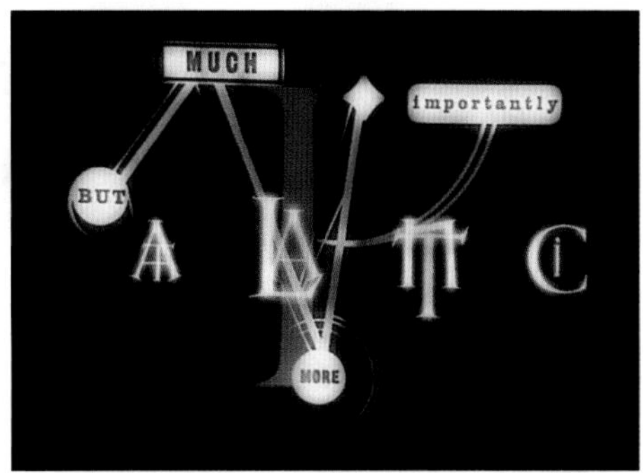

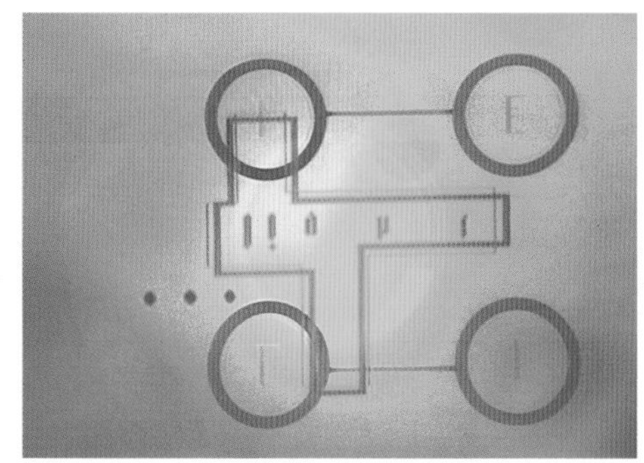

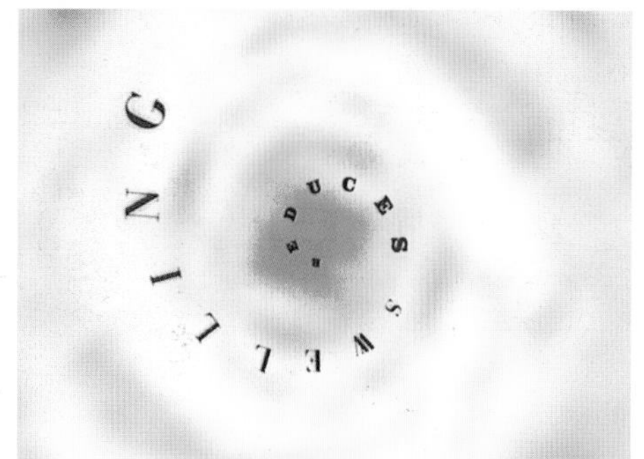

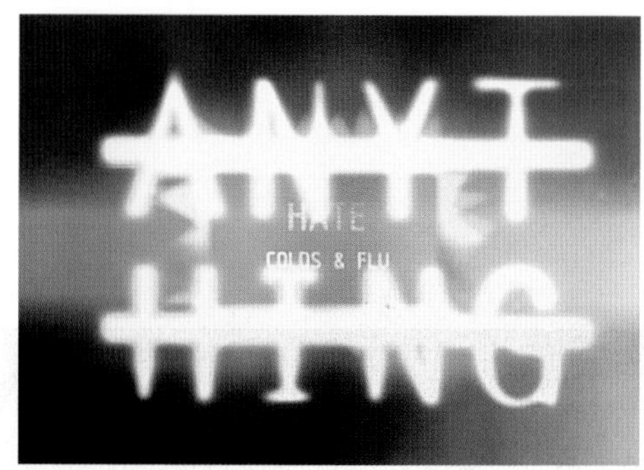

Vicks Action

Commercial for a cold remedy
DESIGNER Jonathan Barnbrook
WRITERS Stuart Newman, Julian Borra
AGENCY Leo Burnett
PRINCIPAL TYPEFACES Letter Gothic, VAG Rounded, Isonorm
CLIENT Procter & Gamble

Great Britain, 1995

The subject of MTV's first European music awards was "global communication" and the designers' aim was to portray this in typography and image. Working collaboratively, they visualised the collage of quotations and specially written texts as an emotive, flowing stream of consciousness, rather than as a series of separate and possibly disjointed spreads. To enhance the intended humanistic feel, most of the artwork was originated by hand and a variety of papers was used.

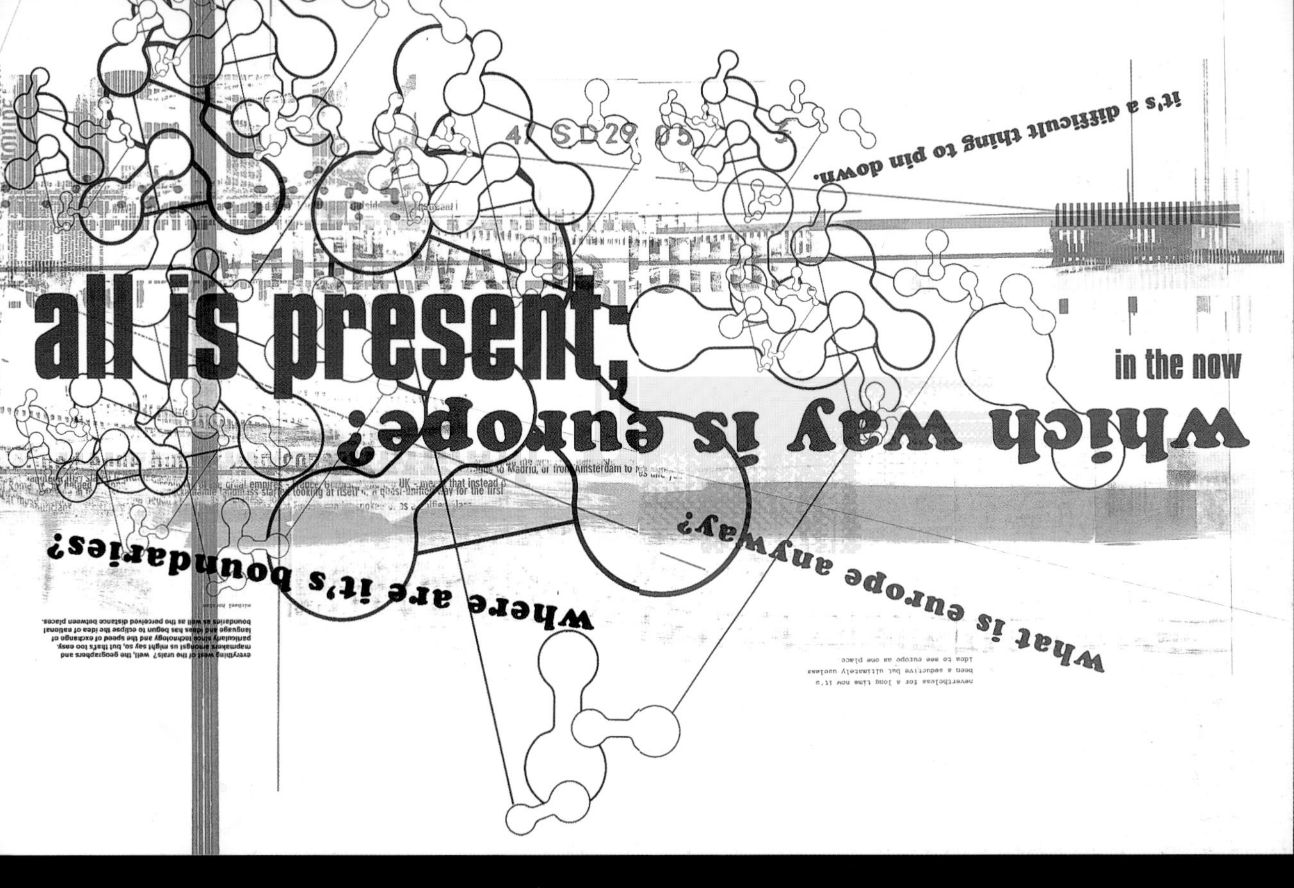

Global Communication: Channel Your Experience

Spreads from a brochure for the MTV Music Awards

DESIGN DIRECTORS John Warwicker, Simon Taylor

DESIGNERS John Warwicker, Simon Taylor, Chris Ashworth, David Smith

WRITER Michael Horsham

DESIGN COMPANIES Tomato, Invisible

PRINCIPAL TYPEFACES Cooper Black, Compacta, Clarendon, Courier, DIN

CLIENT MTV Europe

The complexity I'm interested
I'm not so much interested
layers of meaning . . . I think
society because the conten
complex. Simple black and wh
Graphic design that tries to ma
anybody any real benefit. Soci
to deal with the subtlety, con
contemporary life . . . it is pos
both complexity and intelli

I'M REALLY I
THIS CONCEF
SURFACES" .
MYSTICAL EI
INDUSTRIA
OR ALLOYS, CU

~~*Most of the time the message isn't worth saying. So when you do get a chance to say something yourself, you might as well say something you believe in ... There's a reason for the way I do things and if you look I hope you'll get the meaning, though the communication process isn't so direct that you are necessarily going to get it the first time you look at it.*~~ *Jonathan Barnbrook*

d in is complexity of meaning.
in the layers of form as the
k this approach fits modern
nporary world is subtle and
nite dualisms no longer work.
ake things simple is not doing
iety needs to understand how
nplexity and contradiction in
ssible and necessary to have
igibility in graphic design. Katherine McCoy

NTERESTED IN
PT OF "LIVING
. . IN MERGING
LEMENTS WITH
L ELEMENTS
ULTURAL ALLOYS.

P. SCOTT MAKELA

CULTURE:

INSTITUTIONAL

The designers conceived a campaign to reach populations under-served or ignored by San Francisco's AIDS prevention literature. Each poster combines an honest portrait of a local individual, based on the designers' interviews, with the person's own answer to the question. The typography purposely avoids the customary slickness of most citywide advertising in an attempt to capture a hands-on, spontaneous visual language that will appeal to the target group.

What Are You Worth?

AIDS prevention poster
DESIGNERS Martin Venezky, Raul Cabra
DESIGN COMPANY Diseño
PHOTOGRAPHER Leslie Hirsch
CLIENT San Francisco AIDS Foundation

USA, 1995

Poster for World AIDS Day
DESIGNER Joseph Thomas
DESIGN COMPANY Push
ILLUSTRATORS Joseph Thomas, Patrice Gueroult
PRINCIPAL TYPEFACES Univers, Bureau Grotesque
CLIENT Akina Mama Wa Africa

Great Britain, 1994

Say vol. 3 no. 1

Magazine cover and spread aimed at a student/youth readership

DESIGNERS Hal Wolverton, Pam Racs
DESIGN COMPANY Johnson & Wolverton
PHOTOGRAPHER Stephen Dupont
ILLUSTRATOR Pam Racs
CLIENT Amnesty International

USA, 1994

Rwanda:

A Country Riven by Hatred and Fear

BY DIANA QUICK

PHOTOGRAPHY BY STEPHEN DUPONT

For months the government radio and television had been broadcasting stories that the Tutsi minority was preparing to take over the land, jobs, the entire country. The Hutu majority, according to the propaganda, would once more be subject to Tutsi domination.

Then one day the president of the country, a Hutu, is killed and the media proclaims, without a shred of proof, that he has been assassinated by members of the Tutsi-dominated rebel movement that is poised to take over the country. What happens? The simmering anger, fomented by government propaganda and aided by the easy availability of weapons, organized militias, and the backing of the armed forces, turns to gruesome massacres, and genocidal killings.

It has happened in the past in Europe, Asia and the Americas. Governments, to remain in power, exploit old resentments and ethnic hatreds. Then the situation explodes. This is exactly what has happened in Rwanda since April 6, when President Juvénal Habyarimana, along with the President of neighboring Burundi, Cyprien Ntaryamira, was killed in a plane crash as the result of a rocket attack.

Members of the Rwandan Government immediately claimed that the Rwandan Patriotic Front (RPF), which is mainly Tutsi, was responsible for the assassination. Thousands of Hutu went on a murderous rampage against the minority Tutsi, as well as against Hutu who were perceived as opponents of the regime.

Hutu and Tutsi speak the same language; they even resemble each other, since over the centuries many have inter-married. But for centuries the Tutsi have been seen as superior—more "beautiful," more "powerful," wealthier—an impression exploited by European colonialists. Historically the Tutsi were nobles, military commanders, local officials and cattle herders, while most Hutu were subsistence farmers. When colonialism ended and the Hutu came to power, the carrying of identity cards was required, in part because it was not possible to tell Hutu and Tutsi apart by their appearance. Some children did not know whether they were Hutu or Tutsi until they entered school and had to produce identity cards.

For nearly four years Amnesty International has been calling on the Rwandan Government and the RPF to take measures to safeguard human rights and to end impunity for those who violate them. Amnesty calls the massacres in Rwanda (and neighboring Burundi) the most intense in the organization's 33-year history. The organization has also spoken out against the signally inadequate response of the international community. It has called for strong action from the United Nations, urging that human rights be at the center of any U.N. response to the crisis and that human rights monitors be put in place in Rwanda to report first-hand on the situation.

In the weeks following the assassination of President Habyarimana, reports of the carnage became more and more grotesque. The interim Prime Minister, Agathe Uwilingiyimana, along with 10 Belgian United Nations peacekeepers who tried to save her, was hideously tortured and killed. Men, women and children, even tiny babies, were hacked to death with machetes (according to some Hutu, the "mistake" last time was to allow the Tutsi children to live)—among the most common massacre sites were churches where people had fled for protection. Bloated, mutilated bodies floated down the Kagera River, on the Rwanda/Tanzania border, at the rate of one every five minutes and thousands of bodies washed into Lake Victoria. One hundred and seventy staff members and patients were killed by young soldiers in front of foreign doctors at a hospital in Butare, Rwanda's second-largest city. Twenty-one orphans and 13 local Red Cross workers were killed in Butare soon after the children had been evacuated from Kigali for "safety." And the numbers just kept going up and up; several thousand killed, 10,000 killed, 100,000 killed, up to half a million dead—mainly Tutsi, but also Hutu (before April 6, the population of Tutsi in Rwanda was estimated at 700,000 to 1,100,000). Whole families have been annihilated. Millions of displaced people and refugees, Hutu and Tutsi have sought refuge in churches and stadiums in Rwanda and in hastily established camps in Tanzania, Burundi, Uganda and Zaire.

While this level of genocidal violence is unprecedented, conflict has its roots deep in the country's history.

At the turn of the nineteenth century Rwanda was occupied by Germany and after World War I became a Belgian-administered League of Nations Mandate and later a United Nations Trust Territory until independence in 1962. Conflict between the two main ethnic groups (Hutu make up approximately 85 percent of the population, Tutsi 15 percent) appears to have been heightened by colonial rule, which placed virtually all administrative responsibility in the hands of the minority Tutsi.

In 1959 the Hutu majority overthrew the Tutsi monarchy; tens of thousands of Tutsi were killed and several hundred thousand more fled into exile in surrounding countries.

After independence in 1962, Hutu control was consolidated, first under a civilian government and then, after a military coup in 1973 led by Juvénal Habyarimana, under a military government. Until recently he ruled the country as a one-party state, and most government officials were related to him by birth or marriage.

In the late 1980s the economic and political situation in Rwanda deteriorated sharply.

In 1990 an estimated 10,000 rebels, representing the Tutsi-dominated RPF, crossed the border from exile in Uganda and advanced toward the capital, Kigali. The Rwandan authorities detained more than 8,000 people, most of them Tutsi, many of whom were tortured or killed.

In August, 1993, the Rwandan Government and the RPF signed the Arusha Accords in a move toward a peaceful settlement of the three-year-old civil war, but many members of the President's own party were opposed, because it meant integrating the Rwandan army and the RPF. It is widely suspected that extremists in Habyarimana's party, not the RPF, were responsible for the assassination of President Habyarimana.

But this should not be seen as purely an ethnic conflict, as it has often been portrayed in our media. If this were only a matter of Hutu against Tutsi, Hutu would not have killed fellow Hutu. The conflict in Rwanda is also political: those in power wish to remain in power, and are doing all they can to stay there by exterminating anyone viewed as a potential supporter of the RPF and the multi-ethnic parties opposed to the government party, the Republican National Movement for Democracy and Development.

This party, the party of late President Habyarimana, had armed, trained and mobilized its supporters, especially the party youth wing, known as *interahamwe*—"those who think together and attack together"—to carry out massacres of its political opponents. The Presidential Guard, an elite group of the President's supporters, had long since drawn up lists of its opponents, Tutsi and Hutu. A radio station controlled by an extremist Hutu political party frequently called on militias to murder civilians.

Amnesty International has received reports that members of the militias were forced to kill friends, colleagues and even members of their own family. Many ordinary Hutu villagers were press-ganged by local authorities or militias into carrying out killings, either by promises of land and money or by threats on their own lives.

The RPF is also guilty of human rights violations. Rank and file RPF combatants have carried out revenge killings against Hutu civilians, and on June 6 executed 13 clergymen, including the Archbishop of Kigali, in Kabgayi. It is alleged that these were revenge killings carried out by new recruits who had seen their families massacred in local churches, allegedly with the complicity of Hutu clergy. One of the RPF combatants involved was reportedly immediately executed by the RPF as soon as they found out about the killing.

Amnesty International convened a special forum in early July to plan strategy and action on Rwanda and neighboring Burundi. AI and 17 other non-governmental organizations engaged in human rights, development and relief work in Central Africa wanted to send a strong message and strong action that they care about the people of Rwanda and Burundi—not the politics.

In late July the RPF captured the last remaining strongholds of the government forces and declared victory in the civil war. As many as two million Rwandans, mainly Hutu civilians and army, fled into neighboring Zaire, creating a nightmare situation. Many died en route from mortar fire, exhaustion and disease, and thousands more perished as cholera and dysentery swept through hastily-set-up refugee camps.

The new President, Pasteur Bizimungu, and Prime Minister, Faustin Twagiramungu, both Hutu, have promised to protect all Rwandans and respect human rights. However, the Hutu militia and members of the army continue to exert power in the refugee camps, spreading anti-RPF propaganda and discouraging refugees from returning home. The estimated 15,000 soldiers continue to wear uniform and many brought their weapons across the border into Zaire. They are promising to re-form as an army and re-ignite the conflict.

The immediate human rights crisis may be over in Rwanda, but it could well be only a hiatus. The world cannot rest easy and end its vigilance.

What you can do:

While this article has dealt with the tragedy in Rwanda, the situation in neighboring Burundi is potentially as lethal. There are reports from that country of clashes between the Tutsi-dominated army and armed groups of Hutu extremists. The army has extrajudicially executed hundreds of unarmed, mainly Hutu civilians in recent months. Between October and December 1993 up to 100,000 defenseless people were killed. Following the assassination of President Cyprien Ntaryamira, who was killed in the same plane crash as President Habyarimana, the country remained relatively calm, but there is a very real danger that another massive human rights crisis is brewing.

The situation in Rwanda and Burundi is too chaotic at present to write to authorities there, so you should write to Secretary of State Warren Christopher and ask him to fulfill the U.S.'s international obligation to help the people of Rwanda and Burundi. Urge him to put pressure on the United Nations to beef up its human rights program and to listen to its own experts when they call for action—last year these experts said that steps should be taken to break the cycle of violence in Rwanda, but they were ignored. Call on the Secretary of State to push for the U.N. to send human rights monitors to Burundi as soon as possible. Urge the government to support human rights initiatives taken by the U.N. and the Organization of African Unity which can help to prevent further human rights violations in Burundi.

The Hon. Warren Christopher/Secretary of State/Department of State/Washington, DC 20520

SAY — 8 — SEPT/OCT 1994

SAY — 9 — SEPT/OCT 1994

Say vol. 3 no. 4

Magazine cover and spread aimed at a student/youth readership

DESIGNERS Hal Wolverton, Kat Saito, Robin Muir

DESIGN COMPANY Johnson & Wolverton

CLIENT Amnesty International

USA, 1995

BY RON LAJOIE

A LIONESS FOR FREEDOM

REDUCED TO PAWNS IN A QUARREL BETWEEN TWO STATES

ONE OF CUBA'S GREATEST WRITERS CARRIES ON THE STRUGGLE FROM ABROAD.

Like other exiles and immigrants before her, Maria Elena Cruz Varela made a pilgrimage to the Statue of Liberty during a recent visit to New York City. And like many before her, she read the famous words inscribed on the pedestal with conflicting emotions. Yes, her own personal freedom is vouched safe.

But for thousands of her countrymen huddled behind razor wire on Guantanamo Bay, America's "Golden Door" bolted shut less than 90 sea miles away, the words are tinged with bitter irony.

The land that had sold them its image of freedom and plenty had cut a cynical deal with their oppressors. So now they sit and wait.

"As I read those words, I felt mixed emotions," says Varela. "They are very inspiring ideals. But the United States Government currently has 35,000 people held in concentration camps on Guantanamo, people who have committed no crime but who have been reduced to pawns in a quarrel between two states."

One of Cuba's most internationally respected writers and intellectuals, Maria Elena Cruz Varela knows the power of words. She has been harassed, physically assaulted, publicly humiliated and imprisoned for stating openly and to authority, truths that are expressed only in private in Cuba.

"The greatest crime you can commit in a dictatorship, is to think for yourself," she says. "I chose to think for myself."

Born in Colon, Matanzas in 1953, five years before the Cuban Revolution which brought Fidel Castro to power, Varela should be one of Cuba's most cherished intellectual properties. Her first book of poetry, *Mientras la espera el agua* was published in 1987. It was followed two years later by *Afuera esta lloviendo*. In 1989 she received the Estrella de Marmol Award for her radio serial, "La Avellaneda" and the Julian del Casal Poetry award for her book, *Hija de Eva*. In 1991 her third book of poetry, *El angel agotado* was published in Miami.

She was nominated for the Nobel Peace Prize in 1992 by former Costa Rican President and Nobel Peace prize laureate Oscar Arias. That same year, she was nominated for the Principe de Asturias Award for Peace and Letters and received the Human Rights Award from the Iberoamerican Press Association and the Freedom Award from the Liberal International.

However, in October 1990 Varela, had joined the Cuban dissident intellectual group Criterio Alternativo (Alternative Viewpoint) and, in June 1991, her signature had appeared at the top of the Declaration of Cuban Intellectuals. The document demanded democratic reforms and urged the Castro Government toward a peaceful transition of power.

Later that year the group published a Proposal for an Emergency Program, a call to action on the political crisis. By then the group, which had begun as a mere handful of friends had swelled to about 5,000 members.

"We knew our act would have consequences," she says of the public declaration she had made. "But we certainly didn't foresee the angle of attack they would take against us."

The government ended speculation quickly. On June 19, 1991 Varela was entertaining a group of old friends in her modest Havana apartment when a knock came at the door.

"When I answered, there were three people standing there whom I recognized," she says. "One was the ideological leader of our neighborhood (a Communist party block leader) and the other two were a married couple from the Cultural House, which is basically a Communist invention, to give work to people who don't necessarily have to know much about culture, but who are very militant."

The block leader held up a copy of an Alternative Viewpoint flier.

"How dare you have done this?" the woman said.

It was then that Varela noticed that a gang had formed at the bottom of the stairwell and was now advancing up the stairs. Before she could close the door, they had pushed by her and entered her apartment.

They started trashing the room, systematically destroying the furniture and physically assaulting Varela's guests, beating them as they dragged them out into the street.

"They were in civilian dress, but you could tell they were from the security service by the clothes they were wearing," she says. "It is kind of a joke in Cuba, because you can always tell."

The largest man, the apparent leader of the group, grabbed Varela and, locking her in a strangle hold, began dragging her downstairs, his accomplices kicking and punching her every step of the way. In the courtyard the beating continued as the "peoples' mob" tried to force Varela to swallow the Alternative Viewpoint fliers, to literally eat her own words.

"I refused to eat it, but they kept trying to open my mouth, to force the fliers down my throat," she says. "I was bleeding but they wouldn't stop."

Finally, bleeding profusely from the mouth, battered and bruised over most of her body, she was taken to a police station for questioning, only to be released and returned to her ransacked apartment with the warning that the next time the authorities might not be able to "save her life."

But her ordeal had only begun. The next morning she awoke to find that the apartment building was again surrounded by an angry, jeering mob. Alone, with her two children, a teenage daughter and a 12-year-old son, her water and electricity cut off, she endured three days of official "repudiation."

"They had loudspeakers hooked up," she explains. "The mob was shouting disgusting things, calling me a whore and worse, even young children were involved. Nobody knows how alone one feels in such a situation, the absolute abandonment, the shame one feels, my children had to endure this also."

On the third day the authorities allowed Varela's mother, brother and sister to go up to the besieged apartment.

SAY — 9 — MAR/APR 1995

It's About Change

AIDS fundraising poster

DESIGNERS	Richard Bates, Rob Eberhart
DESIGN COMPANY	Bates Hori
PHOTOGRAPHERS	Richard Bates, Allen Hori
PRINCIPAL TYPEFACES	Goudy, Helvetica
CLIENT	Lifebeat

USA, 1994

46th Spring National Viewing Sessions

Catalogue cover
DESIGNER Joseph Thomas
DESIGN COMPANY Push
PRINCIPAL TYPEFACE Triplex
CLIENT British Film Institute

Great Britain, 1995

Ruth MYLIUS

PHOTOPSY

f.stop Gallery & Darkrooms, Green Park Station, Bath, ba1 1jb.

MYLIUS

INVESTMENT SOUTH WEST ARTS

Green Park STATION

f.Stop Gallery & Darkrooms, Green Park Station, Bath, ba1 1jb.

Design: Julian Harriman-Dickinson.

Photopsy

Poster for photographic exhibition

DESIGNER Julian Harriman-Dickinson

PHOTOGRAPHER Ruth Mylius

PRINCIPAL TYPEFACES Custom-made for the project, Monaco

CLIENT f.Stop Gallery

Great Britain, 1994

Concert poster

DESIGNER	Cornel Windlin
ILLUSTRATOR	Andreas Gefe
PRINCIPAL TYPEFACES	Custom-made for the project
CLIENT	Rote Fabrik

Switzerland, 1994

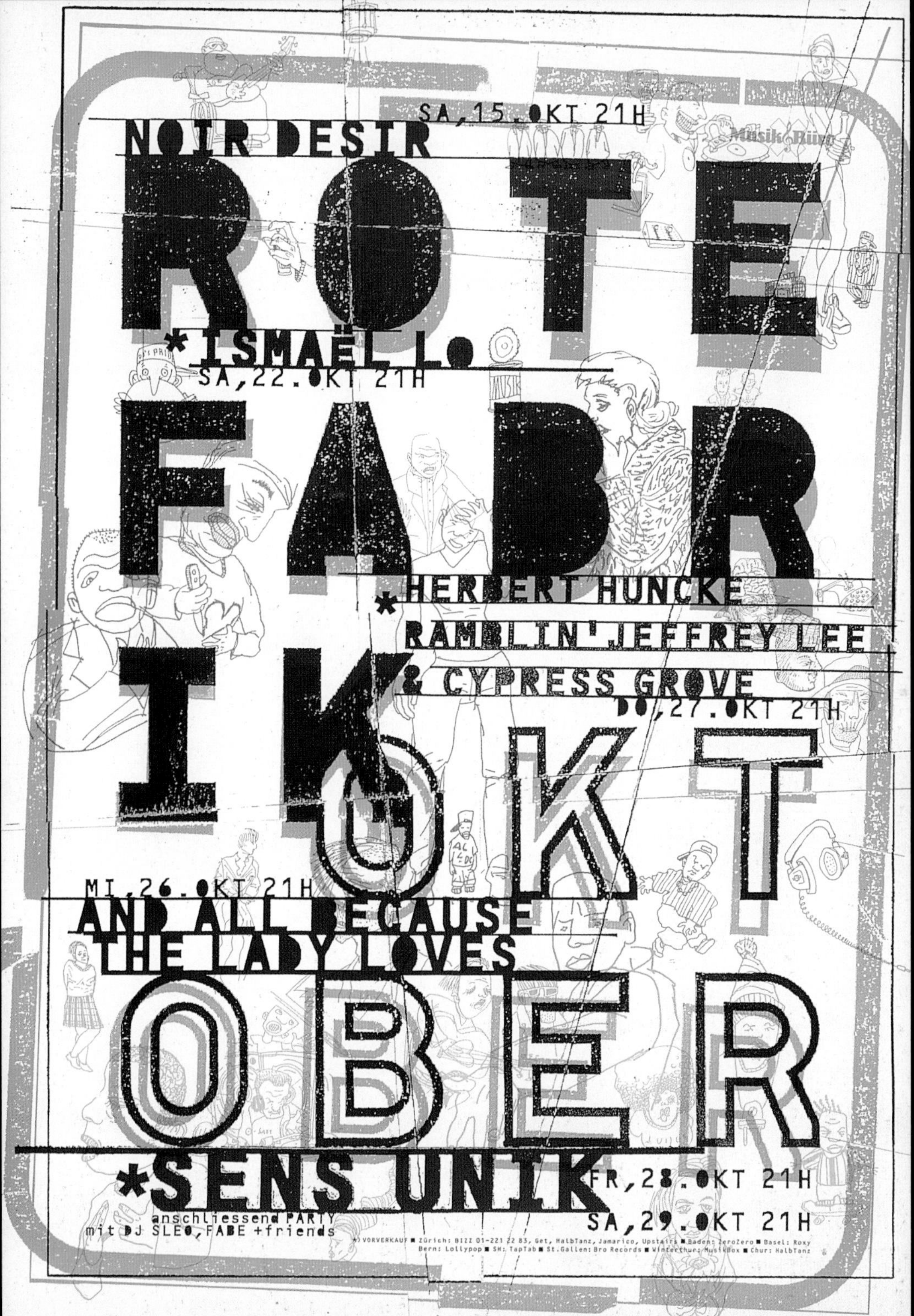

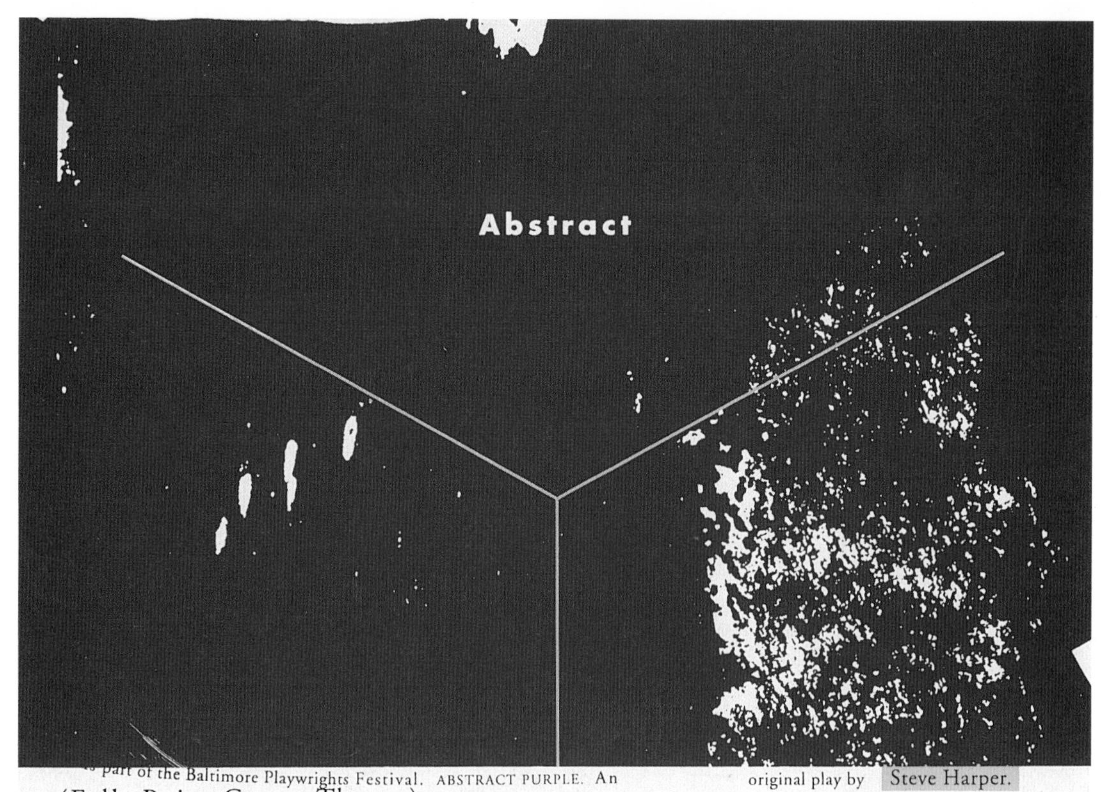

Abstract Purple

Theatre poster

DESIGNER Paul Sahre

PRINCIPAL TYPEFACES Garamond, Futura

CLIENT Fells Point Corner Theatre

USA, 1994

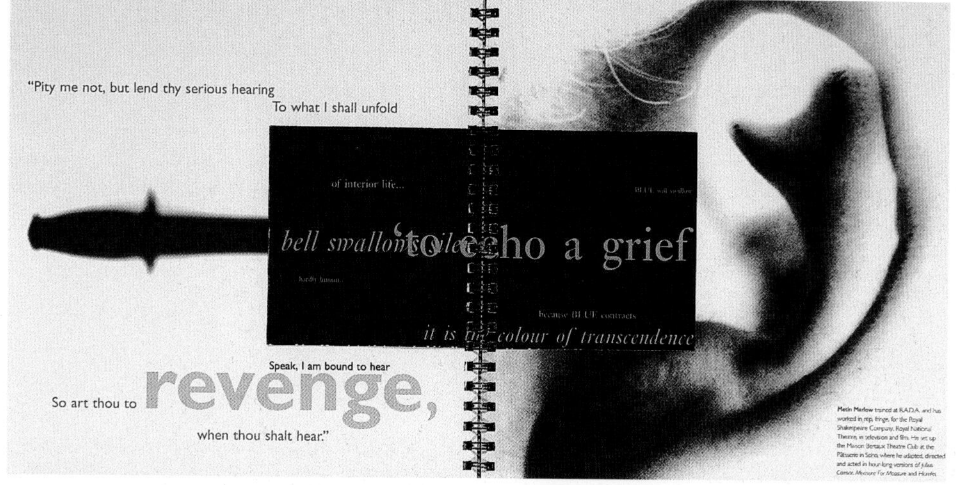

"Among the ancient elements. BLUE occurs

"GOOD HAMLET,

everywhere. BLUE is most suitable as the

colour ... w black

like a b ... ief that

is hard ... cts,

retreats, it is the colour of transcendence,

"These words like daggers enter in mine ears"

CAST THY NIGHTED COLOUR OFF"

leading us away in the pursuit of the infinite."

Hamlet

Theatre programme

DESIGNERS Andrew Johnson, Nick Oates

PRINCIPAL TYPEFACES Gil Sans, Ehrhardt

CLIENT Young Vic Theatre Company

Great Britain, 1994

The pages of the wire-bound programme are cut to form a book within a book, allowing viewers to rearrange the pages in any number of permutations and engaging them in a physical, visual, textual and typographic exploration of the complexities of Shakespeare's tragedy.

To keep colour printing costs down, Zeebelt Theater posters are conceived by Studio Dumbar as extended series. A photograph is printed in quantity and the monthly calendar or information for a specific event – such as The Hague's "Day of Architecture" – is silkscreened on top. Studio interns undertake many experimental typographic interpretations of the same base image.

Theatre posters

DESIGNER	Martin Venezky
DESIGN COMPANY	Studio Dumbar
PHOTOGRAPHER	Lex van Pieterson
PRINCIPAL TYPEFACE	Frutiger
CLIENT	Zeebelt Theater

The Netherlands, 1993

Radix Matrix: The Architecture of Daniel Libeskind

Exhibition poster

DESIGNER Cornel Windlin

PRINCIPAL TYPEFACES Custom-made for the project

CLIENT Museum für Gestaltung, Zurich

Switzerland, 1994

Bang on the Can

Poster for a "noise" music event

DESIGNER Susan LaPorte
DESIGN COMPANY Walker Art Center Design Department
ILLUSTRATOR Susan LaPorte
PRINCIPAL TYPEFACE Big Girl Bold
CLIENT Walker Art Center Performance Art Department

USA, 1992

A Lie of the Mind

Theatre poster
DESIGNERS Paul Sahre, David Plunkert
PRINCIPAL TYPEFACE Futura
CLIENT Fells Point Corner Theatre

USA, 1993

BY SAM SHEPHARD
A LIE
DIRECTED BY DENISE RATAJCZAK
OF THE
MIND
BALTIMORE PREMIERE
276-7837
FELLS POINT
JANUARY 15 THRU FEBRUARY 21
CORNER THEATRE

Spaced Out

Cover and spread from a leaflet for a series of talks on architecture

DESIGNER Jonathan Barnbrook

PRINCIPAL TYPEFACES Delux, Perpetua

CLIENT Institute of Contemporary Arts

Great Britain, 1995

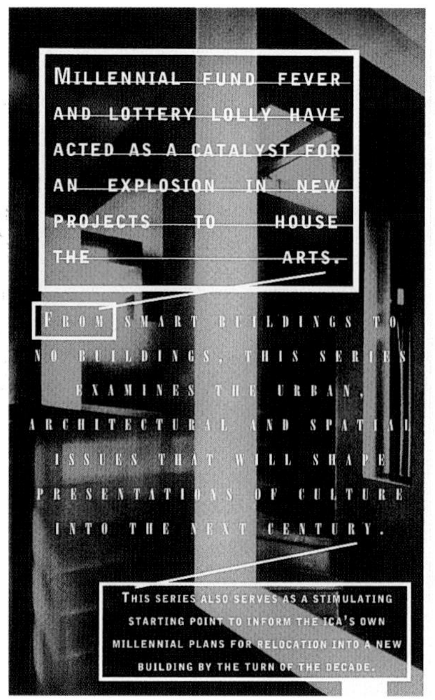

17 JUNE 10.30–17.30HRS
TICKETS £12, £8 MEMBERS AND CONCESSIONS

SPACED OUT

This symposium provides a plenary for the Spaced Out talks that precede it. From the Tate Gallery's plans for Bankside Power Station, to Alsop & Störmer's dramatic proposals for a new river-straddling ICA, London has given rise to many audacious projects to house the arts but there appears, as yet, to be little association between them.

With international speakers from the fields of performance, cinema, visual arts and music, this symposium explores the connections between millennial projects for the arts and considers how to overcome the disciplinary distinctions that divide them.

IN COLLABORATION WITH THE LONDON INTERNATIONAL FESTIVAL OF THEATRE

FOLLOWING THE FIRST SELL-OUT SERIES OF ARCHITECTURAL DISCUSSIONS, SPACED OUT TWO FOCUSES ON IN-BETWEEN SPACES-THE NON-PLACES OF CONTEMPORARY LIFE

15 NOVEMBER 19.30HRS

NON-PLACES: MARK AUGÉ

The waiting room and the supermarket, the car, train and plane, the spaces of cable, wire and media communications are non-places. They involve no sense of identity, and have no ability to establish relations with others. These are the sites which celebrated ethnographer Mark Augé scrutinises in his new study: *Non-Places: Introduction to an Anthropology of Supermodernity* (Verso). Spending more of our time in transit through one non-place to the next, a new form of solitude provokes new questions of identity. Mark Augé is Director of Studies at the Ecole des hautes études en sciences sociales in Paris. His books include *La Traversée du Luxembourg*, *Un ethnologue dans le métro* and *Domaines et chateaux*. With thanks to the French Institute

16 NOVEMBER 19.00HRS AT RIBA

WILL ALSOP: BRIDGING THE ICA

Revealing his plans for the relocation of the ICA to a river straddling site, Will Alsop discusses the implications of his proposals for a city, its public and its living arts.

This lecture is part of the RIBA Architecture Centre series, *Public Spaces, Public Places* and takes place at The Jarvis Theatre, Royal Institute of British Architects, 66 Portland Place, London W1. Bookings for this event only on 0171 251 0791. (Tickets £4, £2.50 concessions.)

22 FEBRUARY 19.30HRS

ZAHA HADID

From plans for *The Peak* in Hong Kong, to the realisation of the *Vitra Fire Station* in Weil am Rhein, Zaha Hadid has long been recognised as an architect working at the sharp end of expressive design and free-spatial practice. Her recent triumph in the competition to design an Opera House for Cardiff has been dogged by equal measures of controversy, debate and delight. Hadid's work has appeared in numerous group and one-woman shows, including *Deconstructivist Architecture* at the Museum of Modern Art, New York.

7 MARCH 19.30HRS

IMAGINEERING ATLANTA

In the age of decentralisation, instant communication and the subordination of locality to the demands of a globalising market, contemporary cities have taken on place-less characters, becoming phantasmagorical landscapes. Atlanta, argues Charles Rutheiser, is a classic example of this generic urbanism. Rutheiser considers the uneven development of Atlanta's landscape with reference to plans for the 1996 Olympic games, and borrows a phrase from Walt Disney to describe its linked, but not always coordinated, acts of urban 'imagineering'. Charles Rutheiser is director of the Graduate programme in Applied Anthropology at Georgia State University and author of *Imagineering Atlanta: Making Place in the Non-Place Urban Realm* (Verso).

21 MARCH 19.30HRS

WHITE WALLS, DESIGNER DRESSES: MARK WIGLEY

The in-between has been most consistently marked this century by the ubiquitous white wall. While histories of modern architecture ignore the face of its whiteness, passing it off as neutral or silent, Mark Wigley, celebrated author of *The Architecture of Deconstruction* investigates the extraordinary psychosexual investments that architects made in smooth white surfaces. Closely reading the most influential buildings of this century, Wigley draws audacious parallels and connections between the architect as builder and dress designer. He reveals architecture as a sensuous multicoloured outfit worn by its inhabitants and dominated by its white fabrics, seemingly innocuous surfaces that have been systematically ignored because they carry an explosive charge. Mark Wigley is Associate Professor of Architecture at Princeton University and author of *White Walls, Designer Dresses : The Fashioning of Modern Architecture* (MIT).

28 MARCH 19.30HRS

FUTURE SYSTEMS

Whether designing a champagne bucket, furniture for outer space, a shelter for a third world disaster area, or a national library in France, Future Systems draw equally from the inspiration of the site, from nature and technology. Future Systems is one of Britain's leading architectural and design practices founded in 1979. Headed by Jan Kaplicky and Amanda Levete the practice explores the possibilities of tomorrow with respect and sensitivity to the past. Celebrated as both innovative and provocative, their work challenges traditional preconceptions of space. Amanda Levete and Jan Kaplicky talk about their projects in the context of the in-between.

Spaced Out 2

Cover and spread from a leaflet for a series of talks on architecture

DESIGNER Jonathan Barnbrook

PRINCIPAL TYPEFACES Bell Gothic, Clarendon, Bodoni, Cooper Black

CLIENT Institute of Contemporary Arts

Great Britain, 1995

The Scapegoat

Cover and spread from a leaflet for a series of talks on social scapegoats

DESIGNER Jonathan Barnbrook
PHOTOGRAPHER Tomoko Yoneda
PRINCIPAL TYPEFACES Scala, False Idol
CLIENT Institute of Contemporary Arts

Great Britain, 1994

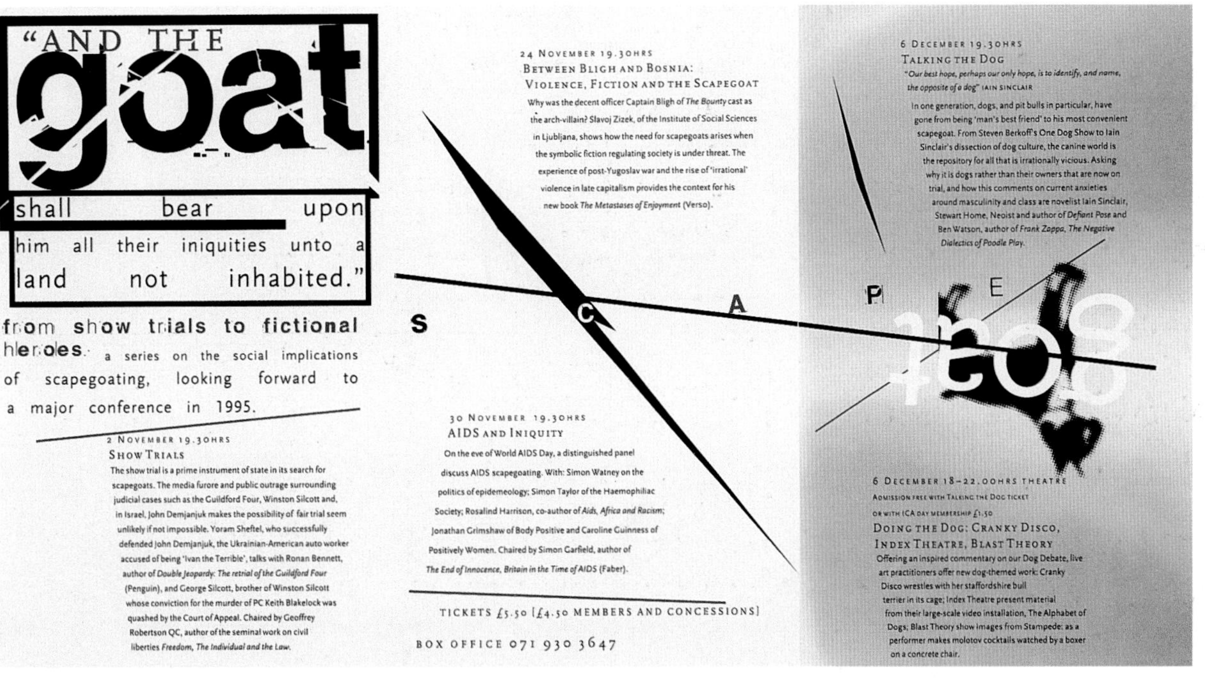

9 th Annual

Port Clinton

ART FESTIVAL

NINTH ANNUAL PORT CLINTON ART FESTIVAL

CENTRAL

LAUREL

August 28 and 29, 1993
10 a.m. to 6 p.m.
Downtown Highland Park Illinois
All Media Juried Show featuring more than 230 Artists
Free Admission
Information: 708.433.7994

Design and Illustration: STEPHEN FARRELL

Port Clinton Art Festival

Poster
DESIGNER Stephen Farrell
DESIGN COMPANY Stephen Farrell Design
PRINCIPAL TYPEFACES Carmella, Keedy Sans, Triplex
CLIENT Highland Park Arts League

USA, 1993

Living Surfaces

Conference poster

DESIGNER P. Scott Makela
DESIGN COMPANY Words and Pictures for Business and Culture
PHOTOGRAPHERS Rik Sferra, P. Scott Makela
PRINCIPAL TYPEFACES Officina, VAG Rounded, Barmeno
CLIENT American Center for Design

USA, 1993

body

december 8 + 9 + 10 1994
modular theatre at 8pm
tickets $10 general $3 alumni $2 students/seniors

the 25th anniversary calarts

soul

dance ensemble

presents

a celebration dedicated to those dance alumni who we have lost to aids

featuring alumni

pain

ecstasy

Dance Ensemble

Poster to announce a concert dedicated to dance alumni who died from AIDS

DESIGNER Jennifer Moody

DESIGN COMPANY Office of Public Affairs, California Institute of the Arts

PHOTOGRAPHER Steven Gunther

PRINCIPAL TYPEFACES Dorchester Script, Scala, Skelter, What the Hell

CLIENT School of Dance, California Institute of the Arts

USA, 1994

SOLO ①

frédérique desfossez présente

3.–8. MAI '94 *20.30 h* **TACHELES** theatersaal

oranienburgerstr. 54–56, 10117 berlin, kartenvorverkauf: 282 61 85

sasha waltz berlin

adria ferrali florenz

kitt johnson kopenhagen

+ newcoming artists...

Kurzfilmtage Oberhausen

Film festival poster

DESIGNERS Heike Grebin, Andreas Trogisch

DESIGN COMPANY Grappa Design

PHOTOGRAPHER/ILLUSTRATOR Andreas Trogisch

PRINCIPAL TYPEFACE Eurostile

CLIENT Internationale Kurzfilmtage Oberhausen

Germany, 1995

Bauhaus Kammerkonzert

Concert posters

DESIGNERS Daniela Haufe, Detlef Fiedler

DESIGN COMPANY Cyan

PRINCIPAL TYPEFACE Akzidenz Grotesk

CLIENT Bauhaus, Dessau

Germany, 1994

Orphée

Opera poster
DESIGNERS David Ellis, Andy Altmann
DESIGN COMPANY Why Not Associates
PHOTOGRAPHER Image Library
PRINCIPAL TYPEFACE Doddy
CLIENT Lippert Wilkens Partner

Great Britain, 1993

Turangalîla

Concert poster
DESIGNER Andrew Johnson
PRINCIPAL TYPEFACE Univers
CLIENT Royal Philharmonic Orchestra

Great Britain, 1993

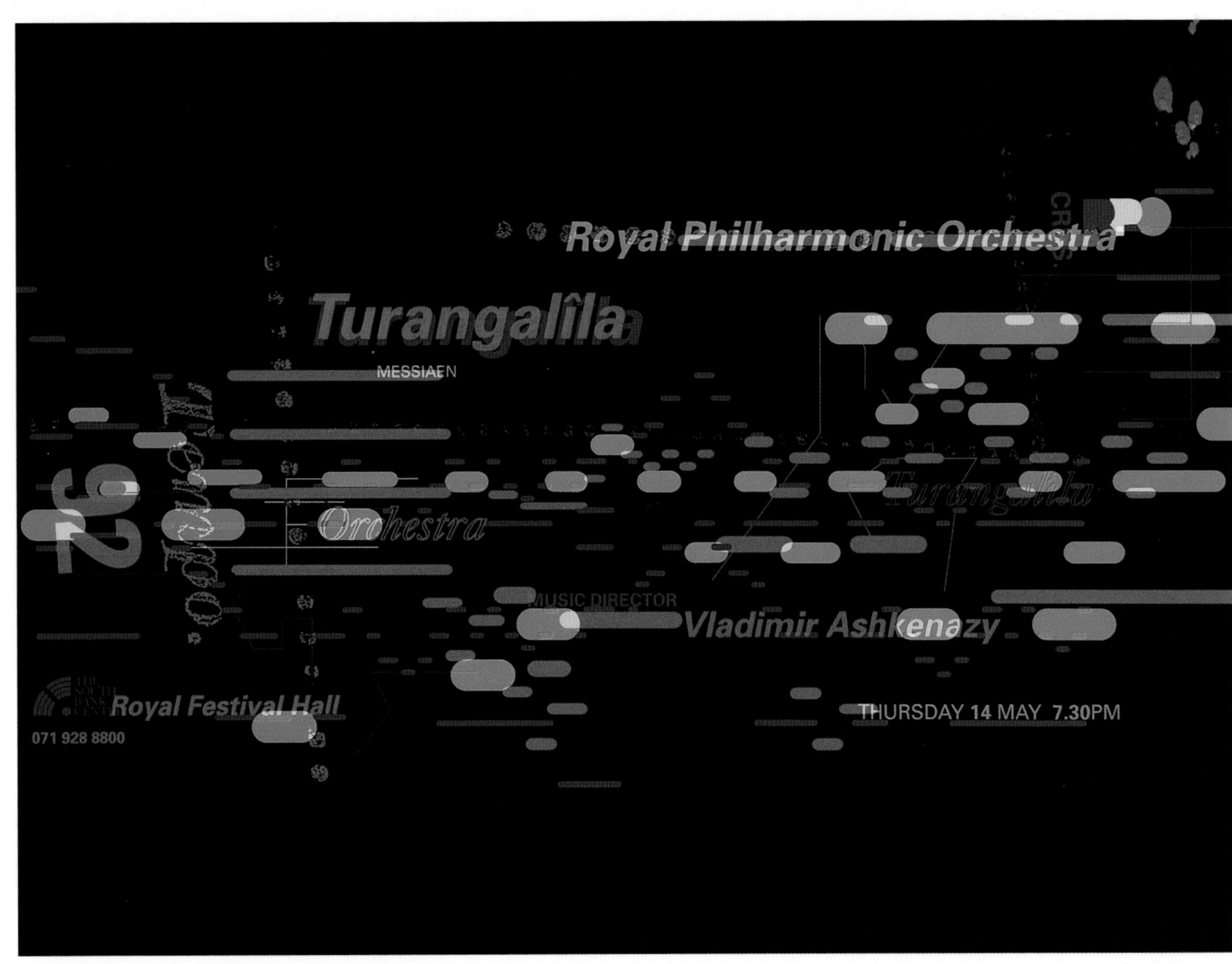

culture

Slide installation for Kobe Fashion Museum

DESIGNERS Andy Altmann, David Ellis, Patrick Morrissey
DESIGN COMPANY Why Not Associates
PHOTOGRAPHERS Rocco Redondo, Richard Woolf, PhotoDisc
PRINCIPAL TYPEFACE Monotype Grotesque
CLIENT Dai Nippon

Great Britain, 1995

Since form cannot be separated from content and since form itself carries meaning, then the idea is, in fact, structured and informed by its presentation.

Just as the invisible typeface is an impossibility, neither can form be invisible.

Louise Sandhaus

THEN

I love the "POST-MODERN PLURALISM" idea of a post-historical forever: mix and match, past and present, high and low, regular and irregular, "inept" and professional, raw and cooked and everything in between, inside and outsider ... and so on and on and on and on.

NOW

Edward Fella

We use styles like maniacs but we never use them lock, stock and barrel. We would usually manipulate them to create some kind of tension. No style is either good or bad, it's just another style – whether you use it wholesale or not.

Lorraine Wild

WHY IS "CUTTING EDGE" USUALLY

SYNONYMOUS WITH ILLEGIBILITY?

WHAT WOULD HAPPEN IF THE TWO TERMS

"hip" and "hard to read"

WERE UNCOUPLED?

Can a text be both readerly and experimental?

J. Abbott Miller

CULTURE:

educational/publishing

II.

(And so now, after five hundred million years have gone by, *I look around* and, above the rock, I see the railway embankment and the train passing along it with a party of Dutch girls looking out of the window and, in the last compartment, a solitary traveler reading Herodotus in a bilingual edition, and the train vanishes into the tunnel UNDER THE HIGHWAY, WHERE THERE IS A SIGN WITH THE PYRAMIDS AND THE WORDS "VISIT EGYPT," AND A LITTLE ICE-CREAM WAGON TRIES TO PASS A BIG TRUCK LADEN WITH INSTALLMENTS OF RH-STIJL, A PERIODICAL ENCYCLOPEDIA that comes out in paperback, but then it puts its brakes on because its visibility is blocked by a cloud of bees WHICH CROSSES THE ROAD COMING FROM A ROW OF HIVES IN A FIELD FROM WHICH SURELY A QUEEN BEE IS FLYING AWAY, drawing behind her a swarm in the direction opposite to the smoke of the train, which has reappeared at the other end of the tunnel, so you can see hardly anything thanks to the cloudy stream of bees and coal smoke, EXCEPT A FEW YARDS FARTHER UP THERE IS A PEASANT BREAKING THE GROUND WITH HIS MATTOCK AND, UNAWARE, HE BRINGS TO LIGHT AND REBURIES A FRAGMENT OF A NEOLITHIC MATTOCK SIMILAR TO HIS OWN, IN A GARDEN THAT SURROUNDS AN ASTRONOMICAL observatory with its telescopes aimed at the sky and on whose threshold the keeper's daughter sits reading the horoscopes in a weekly whose cover displays the face of the star of Cleopatra: I see all this and I feel no amazement because making the shell implied also making the honey in the wax comb and the coal and the telescopes and the reign of Cleopatra AND THE FILMS ABOUT CLEOPATRA AND THE PYRAMIDS AND THE DESIGN OF THE ZODIAC OF THE CHALDEAN ASTROLOGERS AND THE WARS AND EMPIRES HERODOTUS SPEAKS OF AND THE WORDS WRITTEN BY HERODOTUS AND THE WORKS WRITTEN IN ALL LANGUAGES INCLUDING THOSE OF SPINOZA IN DUTCH and the fourteen-line summary of Spinoza's life and works in the installment of the encyclopedia in the truck passed by the ice-cream wagon, and so I feel as if, in making the shell, I had also made the rest. I look around, and whom am I looking for? SHE IS STILL THE ONE I SEEK; I'VE BEEN IN LOVE FOR five hundred million years, AND IF I SEE A DUTCH GIRL ON THE SAND WITH A BEACHBOY WEARING A GOLD CHAIN AROUND HIS NECK AND SHOWING HER THE SWARM OF BEES TO FRIGHTEN HER, THERE SHE IS: I RECOGNIZE HER FROM HER INIMITABLE WAY OF RAISING ONE SHOULDER UNTIL IT ALMOST TOUCHES HER CHEEK, I'M ALMOST SURE, OR RATHER I'D SAY ABSOLUTELY SURE IF IT WEREN'T FOR A CERTAIN resemblance THAT I FIND ALSO IN THE DAUGHTER OF THE KEEPER OF THE OBSERVATORY, AND IN THE PHOTOGRAPH OF THE ACTRESS MADE UP AS CLEOPATRA, OR PERHAPS IN CLEOPATRA AS SHE REALLY WAS IN PERSON, FOR WHAT PART OF THE TRUE CLEOPATRA THEY SAY EVERY representation of Cleopatra contains, or in the queen bee flying at the head of the swarm with that forward impetuousness, or in the paper woman cut out and pasted on the plastic windshield of the little ice-cream wagon, wearing a bathing suit like the Dutch girl on the beach now listening over a little transistor radio to the voice of a woman singing, THE SAME VOICE THAT THE ENCYCLOPEDIA TRUCK DRIVER HEARS OVER HIS RADIO, AND THE SAME ONE I'M NOW SURE I'VE HEARD FOR FIVE MILLION YEARS, IT IS SURELY SHE I HEAR SINGING AND whose image I look for all around, seeing only gulls volplaning on the surface of the sea where a school of anchovies glistens and for a moment I am certain I recognize HER IN A FEMALE GULL, AND A MOMENT LATER I SUSPECT THAT INSTEAD SHE'S AN ANCHOVY, THOUGH SHE MIGHT JUST AS WELL BE ANY QUEEN OR SLAVE-GIRL NAMED BY HERODOTUS OR only hinted at in the pages of the volume LEFT TO MARK THE SEAT OF THE READER WHO HAS STEPPED INTO THE CORRIDOR OF THE TRAIN TO STRIKE UP A CONVERSATION WITH THE PARTY OF DUTCH TOURISTS; I might say I am in love with each of those girls and at the same time I am sure of being in love always with her alone. And the more I torment myself with love for each of them, the less I can bring myself to say to them: "*Here I am!*," afraid of being mistaken and even more afraid that she is mistaken, taking me for somebody else, for somebody who, for all she knows of me, might easily take my place, for example THE BEACHBOY WITH THE GOLD CHAIN, OR THE DIRECTOR OF THE OBSERVATORY, OR A GULL, OR A MALE ANCHOVY, OR the reader of Herodotus, or Herodotus himself, OR THE VENDOR OF ICE CREAM, WHO HAS COME DOWN TO THE BEACH ALONG A DUSTY ROAD AMONG THE PRICKLY PEARS AND IS NOW SURROUNDED BY THE DUTCH GIRLS IN THEIR BATHING SUITS, OR SPINOZA, OR THE TRUCKDRIVER WHO IS TRANSPORTING THE LIFE AND WORKS OF SPINOZA SUMMARIZED AND REPEATED TWO THOUSAND TIMES, OR ONE OF THE drones dying at the bottom of the hive after having fulfilled his role in the continuation of the species.)

And so a graphic designer, although one may be antisocial, cannot not be social, cannot be isolationist.

To work as a designer means taking part in the discussion as an individual.

The discussion may be intimate, it may be very public, but most of all, it is an individual speaking with others.

Designers should take a stand, express a point of view; their work should make transparent politics, bias, passions, emotions.

In a lecture delivered at Brunswick in May 1910, he stated: "It is particularly important for Germany, which has now achieved political power, also to win power in artistic areas...In this way, German art and technology will work towards one goal: towards the power of the German nation, which reveals itself in a rich material life ennobled by intellectually refined design."

FRIGHTENINGLY WELL DESIGNED

So here's our paragon: even at its inception, corporate identity is infused with over-weaning, elitist notions of power and the imposition of order by the visionary few. It is no coincidence, I feel, that within a quarter of a century of this statement, the most effective and arguably the best designed corporate identity of the twentieth century was the one that represented the most effective, and arguably the best organized, socio-political system of the twentieth century; nor that it arose in Germany and that it was imbued with Nietzschean concepts of the UBERMENSCH. It was also the most obscene of all totalitarian regimes. This tempts the question: is it only the monolithic, all-powerful organizations like AEG or the Nazi Party which can make really effective use of corporate identity? Certainly, the near-monopoly of AEG gave the company an assurance that was immensely helpful to Behrens in his design program. And the total control exercised by the Nazi regime over its workforce and the availability of resources was equally important to Albert Speer in his impressive use of corporate identity devices at great gatherings like the Nuremburg Rallies and in bombastic city planning exercises like the 1939 North-South Axis in Berlin (to which, incidentally, Behrens contributed his last architectural work: an office building for AEG). The proposition is also born out by a number of postwar examples of which the corporate identity program for IBM by Eliot Noyes, as design director, and Paul Rand, as design consultant, was—and still is—a model. IBM offers a prime illustration of the contention that, however well designed, a ubiquitous and successful corporate identity is ultimately a calamity just BECAUSE it is ubiquitous. That's the bitter lesson we've only just begun to learn.

"Corporate identity," Garland claims, "is infused with over-weaning, elitist notions of power and the imposition of power by the visionary few."

Yet in order to represent everything, corporate identities become too diffuse, too bland, too all-encompassing.

When we shower the design periodicals and quality newspapers with angry complaints about the blowsy bugler of BT, we are still missing the point. True, the BT style is an even more footling bit of nonsense than the Prudential popinjay, also from the same design office. But any corporate identity that puts itself about as ostentatiously as these two is offensive, whatever it looks like.

NO MORE CASH FOR CANDYFLOSS

So what's to be done? Well, to some extent the problem has solved itself. I cannot believe that any large company will be prepared to fling its money about on candyfloss graphics from now on. Assuming, therefore, that they have any money to spend at all, what portion of it can be justifiably channelled in our direction? For starters, we can throw in our lot with those local authorities, civic amenity groups, town planners and others concerned with the depredations of multinational companies, hypermarkets and recently "liberated" public utilities who have been allowed to blazon their insistent company image over our towns and countryside with minimum control from central government. With them, we can promote the idea of the spirit of the place. Not a new idea, of course; it's probably as old as the first human society. It is a vital part of the training and development of the architect; why not of graphic designers now that they may have as much or more influence on the appearance of some environments?

Then we could attempt to persuade the multinationals and other biggies that swanking around the globe about their bigness is increasingly counter-productive. (I wouldn't be surprized if it hasn't occurred to them already; they're probably ahead of us. Imagine the embarrassment when we turn up at the board room with our next Corp ID proposals and the hard men frown at it and say, "Bit monolithic, isn't it? Does it have to be quite so ostentatious?") And can we divest ourselves of some of the gruesome hangers-on in our business: the rejects from ad agencies and sales departments who've conned us into thinking that they, rather than we, have their fingers on the pulse of business and industry.

Finally, I offer you Garland's Law of Corporate Identity: that the degree of memorability and distinction applicable to any organization should be in inverse ratio to the size of its annual profits or the size of its chief executive's salary, whichever is the greater. Think about it.

There's no reason for corporations to employ such monolithic identities. Perhaps, corporate identities could be broken down into a system of logos to closer represent different individuals and various facets of a given corporation.

Although complaints of "visual babel" and visual illiteracy are being hurled from all sides, at the same time there is a call for designers—to exploit the demise of the corporate identity by cultivating individual identities (and peculiarities, "character," personal style)—that is, to be truly conversational in their work.

"The successful Graphic Designer is, in short, inspired to create—and make every effort to see that his creation reaches out to the viewer with meaning."
LESTER BEALL

Emigre no. 21

Magazine spreads showing projects by California Institute of the Arts students

GUEST EDITOR Jeffery Keedy
DESIGNERS Margo Johnson, Gail Swanlund
CLIENT Emigre Graphics

USA, 1992

The history of modern design is very much about a history of style developing independently of ideology.

— Dan Friedman, *Modernism: Style vs. Ideology*, 1991

Emigre no. 24, "Neomania"

Magazine spread for an article about stylistic change

EDITOR Rudy VanderLans
WRITER/DESIGNER Anne Burdick
PRINCIPAL TYPEFACES Clarendon, Sabbath Black
CLIENT Emigre Graphics

USA, 1992

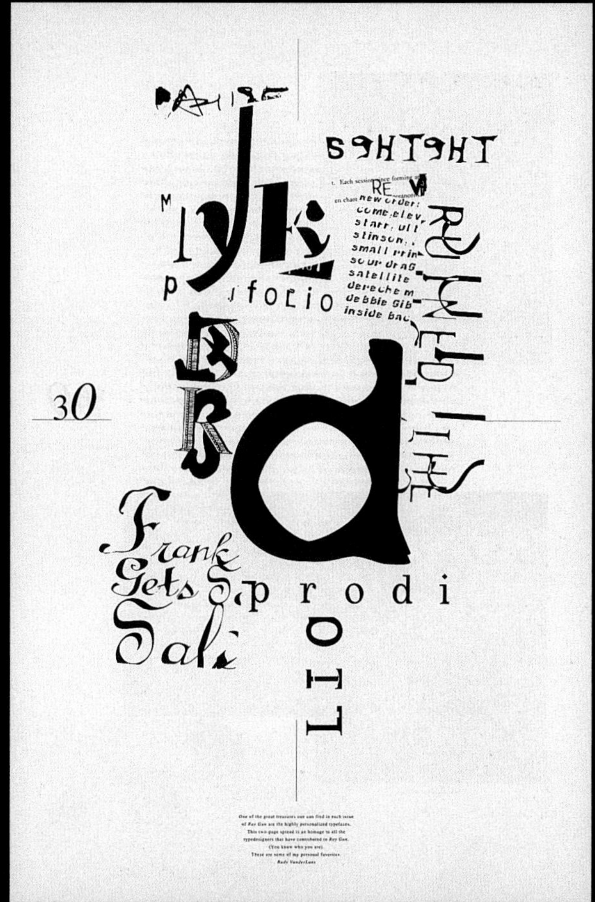

Already a significant force as the 1990s began, Rudy VanderLans's *Emigre* has achieved a thoughtfulness, consistency and rigour in its exploration of experimental typography that is without equal in magazine publishing. Completely redesigned from issue to issue, sometimes by guest editors, the magazine uses the type designs of its partner company, Emigre Fonts, to demonstrate that new approaches to page structure and textual flow can be applied in a way that both encourages and enhances the experience of reading.

Emigre no. 27, "+ David Carson"

Magazine page showing an abstract type construction

EDITOR/DESIGNER Rudy VanderLans
PRINCIPAL TYPEFACES From *Raygun*
CLIENT Emigre Graphics

USA, 1993

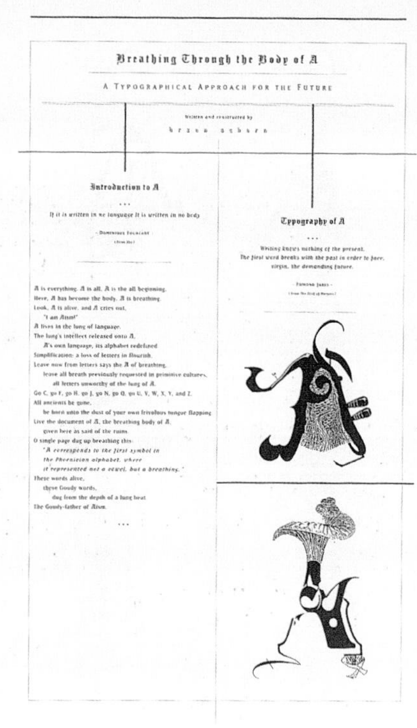

Breathing Through the Body of A

A Typographical Approach for the Future

Introduction to A

If it is written in no language it is written in no body

A is everything. A is all. A is the all beginning.
Here, A has become the body. A is breathing.
Look, A is alive, and A cries out,
"I am Aism!"
A lives in the lung of language.
The lung's intellect released onto A,
A's own language, its alphabet redefined
Simplification: a loss of letters in flourish.
Leave now from letters says the A of breathing,
leave all breath previously requested in primitive cultures,
all letters unworthy of the lung of A.
Go C, go F, go H, go J, go N, go Q, go U, V, W, X, Y, and Z.
All ancients be gone,
be born unto the dust of your own frivolous tongue flapping
Live the document of A, the breathing body of A,
given here as said of the ruins
O single page dug up breathing this:
"A corresponds to the first symbol in
the Phoenician alphabet, where
it represented not a vowel, but a breathing."
These words alive,
these Goudy words,
dug from the depth of a lung beat
The Goudy-father of Aism.

Typography of A

Writing knows nothing of the present.
The first word breaks with the past in order to face,
virgin, the demanding future.

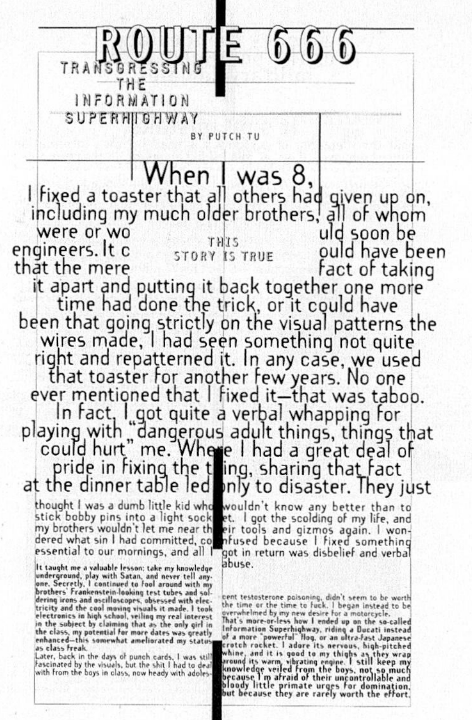

ROUTE 666

TRANSGRESSING THE INFORMATION SUPERHIGHWAY

BY PUTCH TU

THIS STORY IS TRUE

When I was 8, I fixed a toaster that all others had given up on, including my much older brothers, all of whom were or would soon be engineers. It could have been that the mere fact of taking it apart and putting it back together one more time had done the trick, or it could have been that going strictly on the visual patterns the wires made, I had seen something not quite right and repatterned it. In any case, we used that toaster for another few years. No one ever mentioned that I fixed it—that was taboo. In fact, I got quite a verbal whapping for playing with "dangerous adult things, things that could hurt" me. Where I had a great deal of pride in fixing the thing, sharing that fact at the dinner table led only to disaster. They just thought I was a dumb little kid who wouldn't know any better than to stick bobby pins into a light socket. I got the scolding of my life, and my brothers wouldn't let me near their tools and gizmos again. I wondered what sin I had committed, confused because I fixed something essential to our mornings, and all I got in return was disbelief and verbal abuse.

It taught me a valuable lesson: take my knowledge underground, play with Satan, and never tell anyone. Secretly, I continued to fool around with my brothers' Frankenstein-looking test tubes and soldering irons and oscilloscopes, obsessed with electricity and the cool moving visuals it made. I took electronics in high school, veiling my real interest in the subject by claiming that as the only girl in the class, my potential for more dates was greatly enhanced—this somewhat ameliorated my status as class freak.

Later, back in the days of punch cards, I was still fascinated by the visuals, but the shit I had to deal with from the boys in class, now heady with adolescent testosterone poisoning, didn't seem to be worth the time or the time to fuck. I began instead to be overwhelmed by my new desire for a motorcycle.

That's more-or-less how I ended up on the so-called Information Superhighway, riding a Ducati instead of a more "powerful" Hog, or an ultra-fast Japanese crotch rocket. I adore its nervous, high-pitched whine, and it is good to my thighs as they wrap around its warm, vibrating engine. I still keep my knowledge veiled from the boys, not so much because I'm afraid of their uncontrollable and bloody little primate urges for domination, but because they are rarely worth the effort.

Emigre no. 32

Magazine pages

EDITOR/DESIGNER	Rudy VanderLans
DESIGNER AT LARGE	Gail Swanlund
ILLUSTRATOR	Brian Schorn
PRINCIPAL TYPEFACES	Matrix, Template Gothic
CLIENT	Emigre Graphics

USA, 1994

Laurie HAYCOCK MAKELA

MINNEAPOLIS WEDNESDAY, 9.29.93 7 PM

Emigre: You and I keep just missing each other—you took the Walker Art Center Design Director position almost the same day I moved from Minneapolis to go to CalArts. Of course, you're legendary at CalArts.

Laurie Haycock Makela: (LAUGHS) I'm sure, in a variety of ways! UM, I HAVE TO CALL YOU BACK. I NEED TO KICK SOME PEOPLE OUT OF THE HOUSE. We've had so many people over—Scott (LAURIE'S HUSBAND, P. SCOTT MAKELA) is making a video. This is kind of the last of it—we've had people from out of town staying here and people coming over to see the video all week. And then trying to put our daughter, Carmela, to bed in the middle of all that.

E: Sure, I'll talk to you later, then. Bye.

LHM: Bye.

8 PM

LHM: OK. Hi. Jeffrey Plansker, a music video director from Detroit, came for a week to work on a video with Scott for Urge Overkill. Do you know their music?

E: Yeah.

LHM: Well, we've listened to one song of theirs about nine thousand times! (LAUGHS) The great thing about Plansker is that he likes to work with graphic designers. I think he's probably a closet graphic designer—he really looks at design and old advertisements and such. He collages things together and mixes them in with the band dancing. It's really cool.

E: Is he the guy who did the 10,000 Maniacs video with Ed Fella's work spliced in?

LHM: Yeah, and he's worked with Rick Valicenti and Barry Deck, too. He and Scott are in a groove and they work together really well. It's been fun, like a work party, for the last week.

E: So when are you doing your solo album? [LAURIE'S VOCALS ARE FEATURED ON THE AUDIOAFTERBIRTH DEBUT CD "COMMBINE."]

LHM: (LAUGHS) I like that question! It just takes so much energy to engineer all this stuff. Scott played all the instruments on "Commbine" and he used to do all the engineering, too. Now he works with Keith Lewis who is better than him at some of those things. I love being a part of what he does. He really helped me, too, recognizing my singing voice.

E: You have a great voice.

LHM: (LAUGHS) Well, thank you. It just amazes me to hear that because I really never attempted to sing until after I turned thirty. Scott had a lot to do with that—it's just fun to make music with him. I'd love to make a recording, but the mechanics of putting music together right now—digital music—the engineering and so forth, are pretty sophisticated and it takes a lot of energy, too. It's one of those activities in which I like being on the sidelines saying, "Yeah!" I get a big kick out of just having something to do with it.

E: I'm a fan from way back. Jan Jancourt used to play your tapes when we were working together at Artpaper.

LHM: Really? We really respect Jan's work and taste in music. Quiet and mild-mannered Jan would always pull out the most radical recordings. There are two or three people whose opinions mattered to Scott and one of them was Jan's. When Scott started making music and Jan was digging it, that was very encouraging. He was a very early fan.

E: If it weren't for Jan, I'd still be doing pasteup in a basement somewhere.

LHM: You know, five, no, six people who have worked in our studio at the Walker studied with him and they were consistently the best. No question about it. It's a phenomenon. When we interview for interns—designers from all over the country—Jan's students are by far the best, in terms of a specific kind of attention to detail and sensibility. And I say, "Oh thank you, Jan." He's got a really good sense of what it takes to lead a good life, too. He sees what a certain degree of ambition can bring, like a larger sphere of clients, and he could have those clients, but he chooses to design and go fishing, too. He's being profiled in a fly fishing magazine—you'd expect a design magazine, but no!

E: Is being a designer a "lifestyle" choice now, what with the sleepless nights and never enough time in the day?

LHM: Having Carmela definitely organized our lives. Everything becomes much more systematic—she really gives my life a central organizing factor. That's probably something I really needed. Before I left Los Angeles, there was so much disarray: clients in one direction, teaching in another, I was living in yet another—I literally felt like I couldn't get off the freeway. It just feels that way; you get on the freeway and you can't get off. I'm glad I didn't have a baby when I was living there.

I just turned thirty-seven in July. I'm enjoying getting older because, hopefully, you don't do as many totally stupid things.

E: How do you do it? How do you balance being a designer and being a mom?

LHM: (LAUGHS) Well, one thing I've been doing lately—like last night, no two nights in a row—is getting up at three in the morning, so I'm a little spaced during the day. I go to bed early when we put Carmela to bed and then I get up in

5

Emigre no. 28, "Broadcast"

Magazine page

GUEST EDITOR/DESIGNER	Gail Swanlund
PRINCIPAL TYPEFACES	OutWest, Citizen
CLIENT	Emigre Graphics

USA, 1993

RADICAL COMMODITIES

By Rudy VanderLans

The other day, I was reading an article about the Bauhaus by Dietmar Winkler. In it Winkler suggests that the Bauhaus legend is largely based upon myth that has obscured many truths about the Bauhaus. For instance, many of the Bauhaus ideologies, he says, originated at other schools or movements, such as the Constructivists, Futurists and De Stijl. He also points out the enormous gap that existed between the Bauhaus ideologies and the public, resulting in the design of products equally remote from the public's needs and uses. Summing it all up, Winkler writes that **"When Hannes Meyer replaced Gropius as a director of the school, his critical assessment was that its reputation outstripped manifold the quality of the work produced. He attributed this to the unparalleled public relations effort."**

Putch Tu

In the early 1980s, I moved to San Francisco, a place I'd been dreaming of since I was eight. This was after working for a short time in beautiful, postnuclear downtown Detroit, and after a stint in Dallas, which was, at the time, the murder capital of the US. When my friend Wild Bill (thusly named because he isn't) and I landed, it was very late at night, so we stopped at the only place open at three in the morning, a Vietnamese noodle bar on Broadway. It was a time when the Haight was becoming yuppified, when the Silicon Valley was burgeoning, when I picked up one of the first issues of *Emigre*. Back then, *Emigre* had an interesting mix of literature (an excerpt of JG Ballard's Crash, I think), poetry, art, and was not yet a tool of the design cognoscenti. There were five Michaels who seemed to rule the elitist and provincial design world, and the saying went, if you shook any tree, four designers would fall out.

That's when I began my multiple lives: a well-groomed, hopefully fashionable, wealth-and-status seeking designer during the day, hangin' at the Zeitgeist for relief at night, going to the Santa Cruz mountains to play with the intelligentsia from Berkeley and UCSC during the weekends. Most of the latter were fascist, vegetarian-practicing, pagans who were a little too in touch with their inner children for my comfort, but then, the lunatic fringe came as a welcomed relief from the daily burden of makin' pretty pictures for the Man.

Spirit of the Times: Hangin' at the Zeitgeist

The Zeitgeist was a punk C&W (country and western) biker bar tucked under an on-ramp of a freeway, somewhere near lower Hayes Valley and Market. It was as real a postmodern hybrid as it was dangerous; black

From Technology to Commodity. Where do we go from here? Young designers and the contemporary state of graphic design. by

Matt Owens

[04] [05]

Ch, Ch, Ch, Changes

always plagued the discourses of design. First is the easy slide from defining modernism in broad terms to its embodiment in design as a style. **The notion of style is one of our more illusory concepts, and tends to be one of our more obvious stumbling blocks.** Combined with our tendency to discuss design in formalistic terms, we too easily separate form from content and from larger social, political, and economic issues, in turn isolating ourselves from the rich discourses surrounding other disciplines.

What seems to be problematic among designers is the relationship of theory to the practice and creation of artifacts. We seem to confuse theoretical considerations as a way to understand design with an application of them as methodologies for creation - the old theory/practice bifurcation. Someone did not sit in philosophical isolation to devise the idea of modernism that would be later applied to diverse disciplines. Rather, it was a

process and phenomenon that was already occurring in Western societies, the result of society's attempt to come to terms with secularism, industrialization, the move from agrarian to urban organizations, and a reconfiguration of power and economic relations that began to emerge in the nineteenth century. It signalled an epochal shift in consciousness in response to momentous social, political, and economic orders. Philosophers and theoreticians named and characterized what already existed, took that, and pointed toward new directions of thinking and action, as did workers, artists, and the ruling class. We look to theoreticians because they can clarify very complex phenomena and perhaps point toward recommended directions of action, not because they necessarily have a messianic recipe that will endow design with shiny new attributes. When designers confuse style as somehow being equivalent to a theoretical concept, both theory and its embodiment in design suffers. Rather, each influences the other through indirect relationships. **Postmodern theory,** for example, **cannot be merely illustrated with layered or**

Zombie Modernism

It Lives!

Mr. Keedy

End

[06] [07]

Emigre no. 34, "Rebirth of Design"

Magazine spreads

EDITOR/DESIGNER	Rudy VanderLans
PRINCIPAL TYPEFACES	Arbitrary, Matrix, Keedy Sans, Dogma Outline
CLIENT	Emigre Graphics

USA, 1995

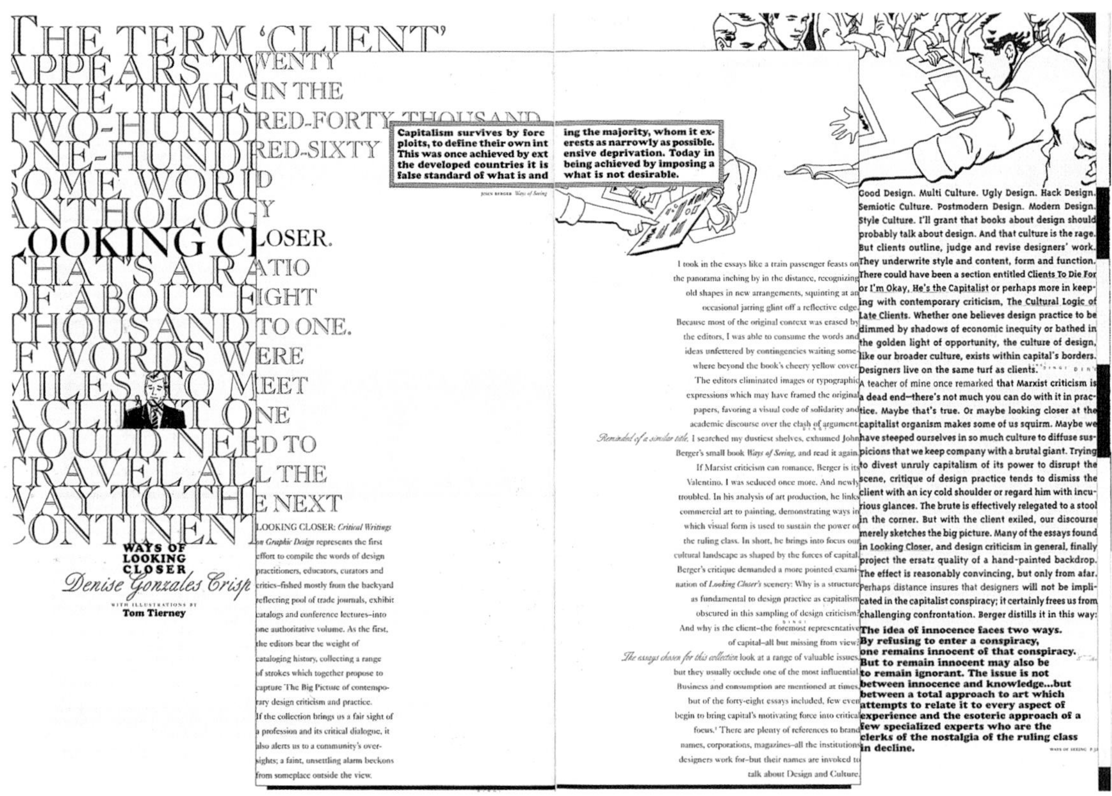

Capitalism survives by forcing the majority, whom it exploits, to define their own interests as narrowly as possible. This was once achieved by extensive deprivation. Today in the developed countries it is being achieved by imposing a false standard of what is and what is not desirable.

WAYS OF LOOKING CLOSER

Denise Gonzales Crisp

WITH ILLUSTRATIONS BY Tom Tierney

LOOKING CLOSER: *Critical Writings on Graphic Design* represents the first effort to compile the words of design practitioners, educators, curators and critics–fished mostly from the backyard reflecting pool of trade journals, exhibit catalogs and conference lectures–into one authoritative volume. As the first, the editors bear the weight of cataloging history, collecting a range of strokes which together propose to capture The Big Picture of contemporary design criticism and practice.

If the collection brings us a fair sight of a profession and its critical dialogue, it also alerts us to a community's oversights; a faint, unsettling alarm beckons from someplace outside the view.

I took in the essays like a train passenger feasts on the panorama inching by in the distance, recognizing old shapes in new arrangements, squinting at an occasional jarring glint off a reflective edge. Because most of the original context was erased by the editors, I was able to consume the words and ideas unfettered by contingencies waiting somewhere beyond the book's cheery yellow cover. The editors eliminated images or typographic expressions which may have framed the original papers, favoring a visual code of solidarity and academic discourse over the clash of argument.

Reminded of a similar title, I searched my dustiest shelves, exhumed John Berger's small book *Ways of Seeing,* and read it again. If Marxist criticism can romance, Berger is its Valentino. I was seduced once more. And newly troubled. In his analysis of art production, he links commercial art to painting, demonstrating ways in which visual form is used to sustain the power of the ruling class. In short, he brings into focus our cultural landscape as shaped by the forces of capital. Berger's critique demanded a more pointed examination of *Looking Closer's* scenery: Why is a structure as fundamental to design practice as capitalism obscured in this sampling of design criticism? And why is the client–the foremost representative of capital–all but missing from view?

The essays chosen for this collection look at a range of valuable issues, but they usually occlude one of the most influential. Business and consumption are mentioned at times, but of the forty-eight essays included, few even begin to bring capital's motivating force into critical focus.[1] There are plenty of references to brand names, corporations, magazines–all the institutions designers work for–but their names are invoked to talk about Design and Culture.

Good Design. Multi Culture. Ugly Design. Hack Design. Semiotic Culture. Postmodern Design. Modern Design. Style Culture. I'll grant that books about design should probably talk about design. And that culture is the rage. But clients outline, judge and revise designers' work. They underwrite style and content, form and function. There could have been a section entitled Clients To Die For or I'm Okay, He's the Capitalist or perhaps more in keeping with contemporary criticism, The Cultural Logic of Late Clients. Whether one believes design practice to be dimmed by shadows of economic inequity or bathed in the golden light of opportunity, the culture of design, like our broader culture, exists within capital's borders. Designers live on the same turf as clients.

A teacher of mine once remarked that Marxist criticism is a dead end–there's not much you can do with it in practice. Maybe that's true. Or maybe looking closer at the capitalist organism makes some of us squirm. Maybe we have steeped ourselves in so much culture to diffuse suspicions that we keep company with a brutal giant. Trying to divest unruly capitalism of its power to disrupt the scene, critique of design practice tends to dismiss the client with an icy cold shoulder or regard him with incurious glances. The brute is effectively relegated to a stool in the corner. But with the client exiled, our discourse merely sketches the big picture. Many of the essays found in Looking Closer, and design criticism in general, finally project the ersatz quality of a hand-painted backdrop. The effect is reasonably convincing, but only from afar. Perhaps distance insures that designers will not be implicated in the capitalist conspiracy; it certainly frees us from challenging confrontation. Berger distills it in this way:

The idea of innocence faces two ways. By refusing to enter a conspiracy, one remains innocent of that conspiracy. But to remain innocent may also be to remain ignorant. The issue is not between innocence and knowledge...but between a total approach to art which attempts to relate it to every aspect of experience and the esoteric approach of a few specialized experts who are the clerks of the nostalgia of the ruling class in decline.

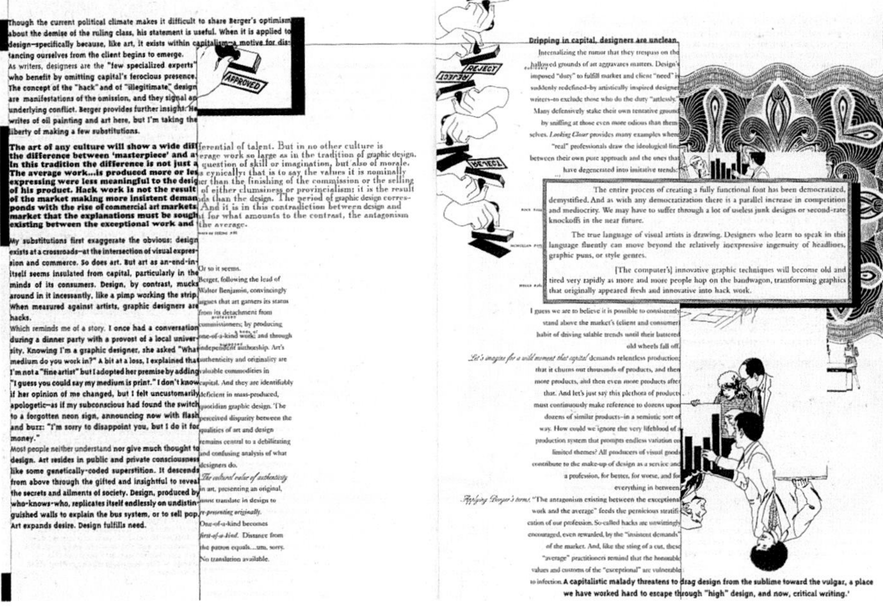

Though the current political climate makes it difficult to share Berger's optimism about the demise of the ruling class, his statement is useful. When it is applied to design–specifically because, like art, it exists within capitalism–a motive for distancing ourselves from the client begins to emerge.

As writers, designers are the "few specialized experts" who benefit by omitting capital's ferocious presence. The concept of the "hack" and of "illegitimate" design are manifestations of the omission, and they signal an underlying conflict. Berger provides further insight. He writes of oil painting and art here, but I'm taking the liberty of making a few substitutions.

My substitutions first exaggerate the obvious: design exists at a crossroads–at the intersection of visual expression and commerce. So does art. But art as an-end-in-itself seems insulated from capital, particularly in the minds of its consumers. Design, by contrast, mucks around in it incessantly, like a pimp working the strip. When measured against artists, graphic designers are hacks.

Which reminds me of a story. I once had a conversation during a dinner party with a provost of a local university. Knowing I'm a graphic designer, she asked "What medium do you work in?" A bit at a loss, I explained that I'm not a "fine artist" but I adopted her premise by adding "I guess you could say my medium is print." I don't know if her opinion of me changed, but I felt uncustomarily apologetic–as if my subconscious had found the switch to a forgotten neon sign, announcing now with flash and buzz: "I'm sorry to disappoint you, but I do it for money."

Most people neither understand nor give much thought to design. Art resides in public and private consciousness like some genetically-coded superstition. It descends from above through the gifted and insightful to reveal the secrets and ailments of society. Design, produced by who-knows-who, replicates itself endlessly on undistinguished walls to explain the bus system, or to sell pop. Art expands desire. Design fulfills need.

Dripping in capital, designers are unclean.

Internalizing the rumor that they trespass on the hallowed grounds of art aggravates matters. Design's imposed "duty" to fulfill market and client "need" is suddenly redefined–by artistically inspired designer-writers–to exclude those who do the duty "artlessly." Many defensively stake their own tentative ground by sniffing at those even more odious than themselves. *Looking Closer* provides many examples where "real" professionals draw the ideological line between their own pure approach and the ones that have degenerated into imitative trends:

The entire process of creating a fully functional font has been democratized, demystified. And as with any democratization there is a parallel increase in competition and mediocrity. We may have to suffer through a lot of useless junk designs or second-rate knockoffs in the near future.

The true language of visual artists is drawing. Designers who learn to speak in this language fluently can move beyond the relatively inexpressive ingenuity of headlines, graphic puns, or style genres.

[The computer's] innovative graphic techniques will become old and tired very rapidly as more and more people hop on the bandwagon, transforming graphics that originally appeared fresh and innovative into hack work.

I guess we are to believe it is possible to consistently stand above the market's (client and consumer) habit of driving salable trends until their battered old wheels fall off.

Let's imagine for a wild moment that capital demands relentless production; that it churns out thousands of products, and then more products, and then even more products after that. And let's just say this plethora of products must continuously make reference to dozens upon dozens of similar products–in a semiotic sort of way. How could we ignore the very lifeblood of a production system that prompts endless variation on limited themes? All producers of visual goods contribute to the make-up of design as a service and a profession, for better, for worse, and for everything in between.

Applying Berger's terms, "The antagonism existing between the exceptional work and the average" feeds the pernicious stratification of our profession. So-called hacks are unwittingly encouraged, even rewarded, by the "insistent demands" of the market. And, like the sting of a cut, these "average" practitioners remind that the honorable values and customs of the "exceptional" are vulnerable to infection. **A capitalistic malady threatens to drag design from the sublime toward the vulgar, a place we have worked hard to escape through "high" design, and now, critical writing.**

In 1995, *Emigre* made an unexpected change to a smaller page size. While the revised format signalled a new emphasis on writing, the magazine's page structures are still subject to constant reinvention. Issue 34 (previous page) uses the visible grid structures of the later large-format issues to divide the page into horizontal bands so that three articles can proceed in parallel. The two "Mouthpiece" issues mount an examination of the relationship of writing and design with a fluidity unconstrained by the reduced format.

Emigre no. 35, "Mouthpiece" part 1

Magazine spreads for an article about clients

GUEST EDITOR Anne Burdick
WRITER/DESIGNER Denise Gonzales Crisp
ILLUSTRATOR Tom Tierney
PRINCIPAL TYPEFACES Triplex, Bembo, Caslon, Cooper Black, Berthold Script
CLIENT Emigre Graphics

USA, 1995

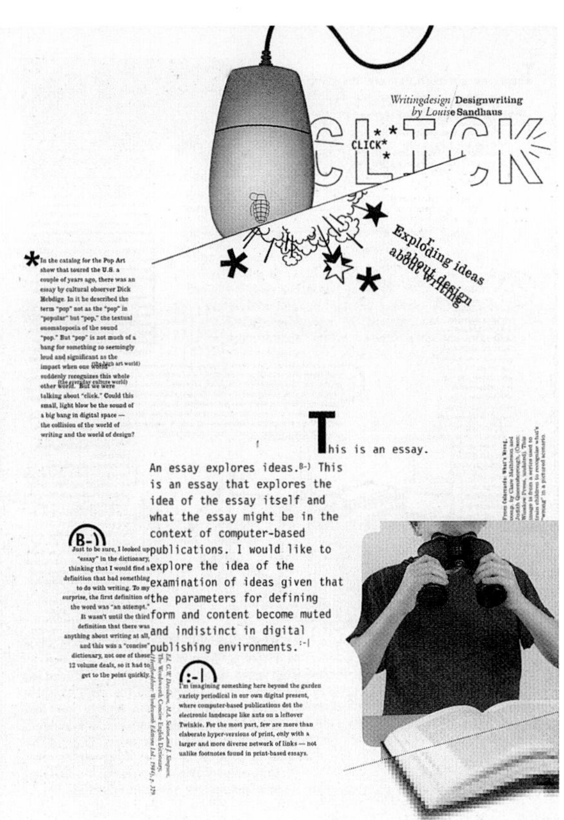

Writingdesign Designwriting
by Louise Sandhaus

CLICK

Exploding ideas about design about writing

*In the catalog for the Pop Art show that toured the U.S. a couple of years ago, there was an essay by cultural observer Dick Hebdige. In it he described the term "pop" not as the "pop" in "popular" but "pop," the textual onomatopoeia of the sound "pop." But "pop" is not much of a bang for something so seemingly loud and significant as the impact when one world (the high art world) suddenly recognizes this whole other world (the everyday culture world). But we were talking about "click." Could this small, light blow be the sound of a big bang in digital space — the collision of the world of writing and the world of design?

This is an essay.

An essay explores ideas.B-) This is an essay that explores the idea of the essay itself and what the essay might be in the context of computer-based publications. I would like to explore the idea of the examination of ideas given that the parameters for defining form and content become muted and indistinct in digital publishing environments.:-|

B-) Just to be sure, I looked up "essay" in the dictionary, thinking that I would find a definition that had something to do with writing. To my surprise, the first definition of the word was "an attempt." It wasn't until the third definition that there was anything about writing at all, and this was a "concise" dictionary, not one of those 12 volume deals, so it had to get to the point quickly.

:-| I'm imagining something here beyond the garden variety periodical in our own digital present, where computer-based publications dot the electronic landscape like ants on a leftover Twinkie. For the most part, few are more than elaborate hyper-versions of print, only with a larger and more diverse network of links — not unlike footnotes found in print-based essays.

Emigre no. 36, "Mouthpiece" part 2

Magazine page and spread for an article about writing and design

GUEST EDITOR Anne Burdick
WRITER/DESIGNER Louise Sandhaus
PRINCIPAL TYPEFACES Clarendon, Letter Gothic
CLIENT Emigre Graphics

USA, 1995

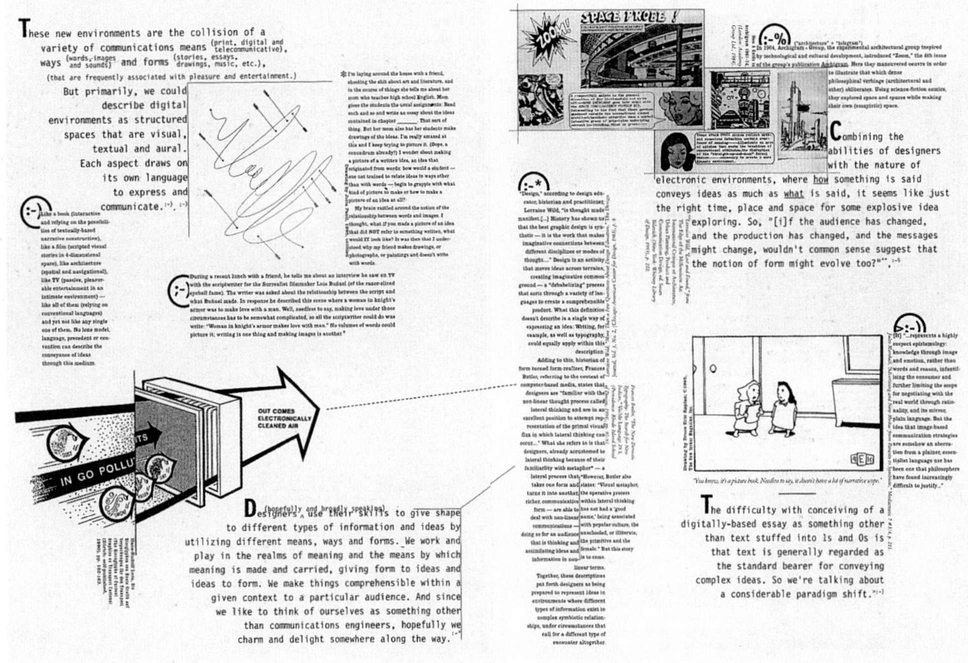

These new environments are the collision of a variety of communications means (print, digital and telecommunicative), ways (words, images and sounds) and forms (stories, essays, drawings, music, etc.), (that are frequently associated with pleasure and entertainment.) But primarily, we could describe digital environments as structured spaces that are visual, textual and aural. Each aspect draws on its own language to express and communicate.:-), :-)

:-) Like a book (interactive and relying on the possibilities of textually-based narrative construction), like a film (scripted visual stories in 4-dimensional space), like architecture (spatial and navigational), like TV (passive, pleasurable entertainment in an intimate environment) — like all of them (relying on conventional languages) and yet not like any single one of them. No lone model, language, precedent or convention can describe the conveyance of ideas through this medium.

*I'm laying around the house with a friend, shooting the shit about art and literature, and in the course of things she tells me about her mom who teaches high school English. Mom gives the students the usual assignments: Read such and so and write an essay about the ideas contained in chapter ______. That sort of thing. But her mom also has her students make drawings of the ideas. I'm really amazed at this and I keep trying to picture it. (Oops, a conundrum already?) I wonder about making a picture of a written idea, an idea that originated from words: how would a student — one not trained to relate ideas in ways other than with words — begin to grapple with what kind of picture to make or how to make a picture of an idea at all?

My brain rattled around the notion of the relationship between words and images. I thought, what if you made a picture of an idea that did NOT refer to something written, what would IT look like? It was then that I understood why my friend makes drawings, or photographs, or paintings and doesn't write with words.

;-) During a recent lunch with a friend, he tells me about an interview he saw on TV with the scriptwriter for the Surrealist filmmaker Luis Buñuel (of the razor-sliced eyeball fame). The writer was asked about the relationship between the script and what Buñuel made. In response he described this scene where a woman in knight's armor was to make love with a man. Well, needless to say, making love under those circumstances has to be somewhat complicated, so all the scriptwriter could do was write: "Woman in knight's armor makes love with man." No volumes of words could picture it; writing is one thing and making images is another.*

Designers (hopefully and broadly speaking) use their skills to give shape to different types of information and ideas by utilizing different means, ways and forms. We work and play in the realms of meaning and the means by which meaning is made and carried, giving form to ideas and ideas to form. We make things comprehensible within a given context to a particular audience. And since we like to think of ourselves as something other than communications engineers, hopefully we charm and delight somewhere along the way.:-*

:-* "Design," according to design educator, historian and practitioner, Lorraine Wild, "is thought made manifest.[...] History has shown us that the best graphic design is synthetic — it is the work that makes imaginative connections between different disciplines or modes of thought..." Design is an activity that moves ideas across terrains, creating imaginative common ground — a "debabelizing" process that sorts through a variety of languages to create a comprehensible product. What this definition doesn't describe is a single way of expressing an idea: Writing, for example, as well as typography, could equally apply within this description.

Adding to this, historian of form turned form-realizer, Frances Butler, referring to the context of computer-based media, states that designers are "familiar with the non-linear thought process called lateral thinking and are in an excellent position to attempt representation of the primal visual flux in which lateral thinking can occur..." What she refers to is that designers, already accustomed to lateral thinking because of their familiarity with metaphor* — a lateral process that takes one form and turns it into another, richer, communicative form — are able to deal with non-linear communications — doing so for an audience that is thinking and assimilating ideas and information in non-linear terms.

*However, Butler also states: "Visual metaphor, the operative process within lateral thinking has not had a 'good name,' being associated with popular culture, the unschooled, or illiterate, the primitive and the female." But this story is to come.

Together, these descriptions put forth designers as being prepared to represent ideas in environments where different types of information exist in complex symbiotic relationships, under circumstances that call for a different type of encounter altogether.

:-% ("architecture" + "telegram") In 1964, Archigram Group, the experimental architectural group inspired by technological and cultural development, introduced "Zoom," the 4th issue of the group's publication Archigram. Here they maneuvered oeuvre in order to illustrate that which dense philosophical verbiage (architectural and other) obliterates. Using science-fiction comics, they explored space and spaces while making their own (essayistic) space.

Combining the abilities of designers with the nature of electronic environments, where how something is said conveys ideas as much as what is said, it seems like just the right time, place and space for some explosive idea exploring. So, "[i]f the audience has changed, and the production has changed, and the messages might change, wouldn't common sense suggest that the notion of form might evolve too?"*.:-%

>:-) [It] "...represents a highly suspect epistemology: knowledge through image and emotion, rather than words and reason, infantilising the consumer and further limiting the scope for negotiating with the real world through rationality, and its mirror, plain language. But the idea that image-based communication strategies are somehow an aberration from a plainer, essentialist language use has been one that philosophers have found increasingly difficult to justify..."

"You know, it's a picture book. Needless to say, it doesn't have a lot of narrative scope."

The difficulty with conceiving of a digitally-based essay as something other than text stuffed into 1s and 0s is that text is generally regarded as the standard bearer for conveying complex ideas. So we're talking about a considerable paradigm shift.>:-)

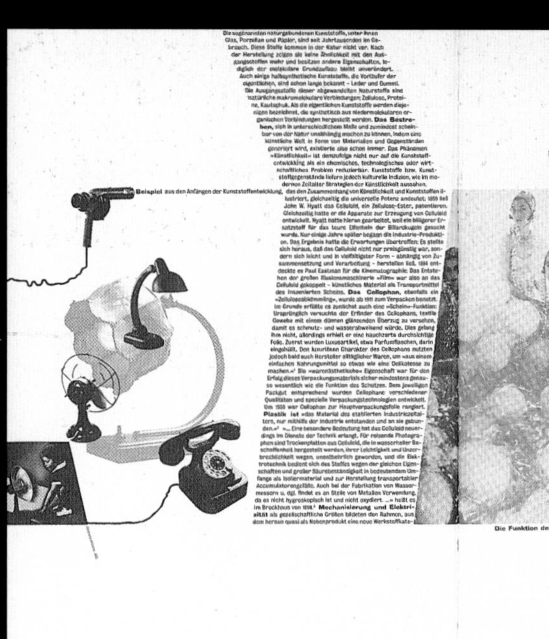

Form + Zweck no. 2/3

Magazine spreads

DESIGNERS Daniela Haufe, Detlef Fiedler

DESIGN COMPANY Cyan

PRINCIPAL TYPEFACE Bureau Grotesque

CLIENT *Form + Zweck*

Germany, 1991

Published in Berlin, *Form + Zweck* addresses design issues from a historical, practical and theoretical perspective and its own design reflects the critically informed modernism of its editorial position. Cyan's typography is extreme in its formalism yet controlled with precision. Type and image are engineered into mutually reinforcing structures, while atmospheric photography, sometimes reminiscent of the 1920s avant-garde, is used to counterpoint the textual arabesques. Colour and a high degree of attention to the material qualities of paper and binding play an essential role.

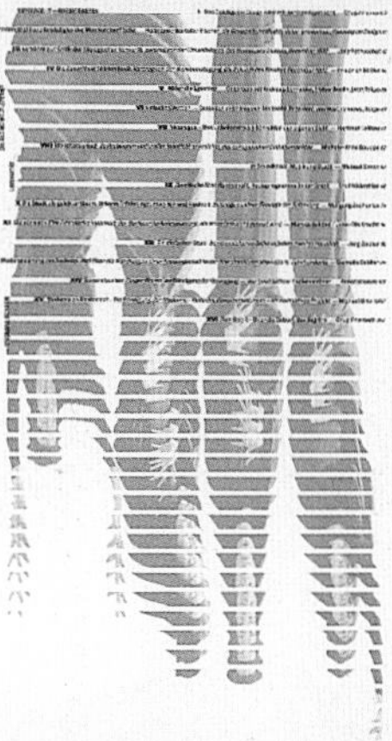

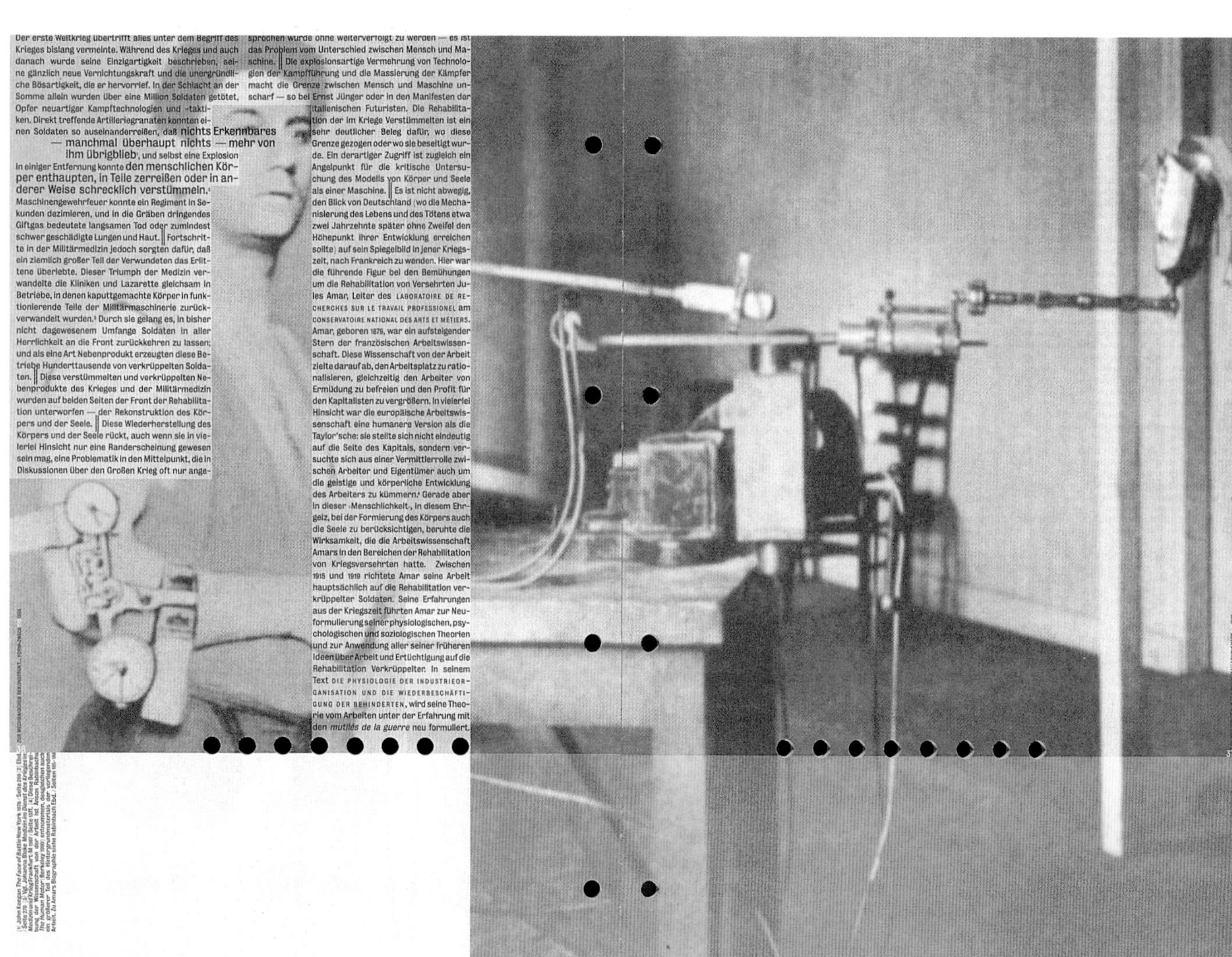

Der erste Weltkrieg übertrifft alles unter dem Begriff des Krieges bislang vermeinte. Während des Krieges und auch danach wurde seine Einzigartigkeit beschrieben, seine gänzlich neue Vernichtungskraft und die unergründliche Bösartigkeit, die er hervorrief. In der Schlacht an der Somme allein wurden über eine Million Soldaten getötet, Opfer neuartiger Kampftechnologien und -taktiken. Direkt treffende Artilleriegranaten konnten einen Soldaten so auseinanderreißen, daß nichts Erkennbares — manchmal überhaupt nichts — mehr von ihm übrigblieb[1], und selbst eine Explosion in einiger Entfernung konnte den menschlichen Körper enthaupten, in Teile zerreißen oder in anderer Weise schrecklich verstümmeln.[2] Maschinengewehrfeuer konnte ein Regiment in Sekunden dezimieren, und in die Gräben dringendes Giftgas bedeutete langsamen Tod oder zumindest schwer geschädigte Lungen und Haut. ‖ Fortschritte in der Militärmedizin jedoch sorgten dafür, daß ein ziemlich großer Teil der Verwundeten das Erlittene überlebte. Dieser Triumph der Medizin verwandelte die Kliniken und Lazarette gleichsam in Betriebe, in denen kaputtgemachte Körper in funktionierende Teile der Militärmaschinerie zurückverwandelt wurden.[3] Durch sie gelang es, in bisher nicht dagewesenem Umfange Soldaten in aller Herrlichkeit an die Front zurückkehren zu lassen; und als eine Art Nebenprodukt erzeugten diese Betriebe Hunderttausende von verkrüppelten Soldaten. ‖ Diese verstümmelten und verkrüppelten Nebenprodukte des Krieges und der Militärmedizin wurden auf beiden Seiten der Front der Rehabilitation unterworfen — der Rekonstruktion des Körpers und der Seele. ‖ Diese Wiederherstellung des Körpers und der Seele rückt, auch wenn sie in vielerlei Hinsicht nur eine Randerscheinung gewesen sein mag, eine Problematik in den Mittelpunkt, die in Diskussionen über den Großen Krieg oft nur angesprochen wurde ohne weiterverfolgt zu werden — es ist das Problem vom Unterschied zwischen Mensch und Maschine. ‖ Die explosionsartige Vermehrung von Technologien der Kampfführung und die Massierung der Kämpfer macht die Grenze zwischen Mensch und Maschine unscharf — so bei Ernst Jünger oder in den Manifesten der italienischen Futuristen. Die Rehabilitation der im Kriege Verstümmelten ist ein sehr deutlicher Beleg dafür, wo diese Grenze gezogen oder wo sie beseitigt wurde. Ein derartiger Zugriff ist zugleich ein Angelpunkt für die kritische Untersuchung des Modells von Körper und Seele als einer Maschine. ‖ Es ist nicht abwegig, den Blick von Deutschland (wo die Mechanisierung des Lebens und des Tötens etwa zwei Jahrzehnte später ohne Zweifel den Höhepunkt ihrer Entwicklung erreichen sollte) auf sein Spiegelbild in jener Kriegszeit, nach Frankreich zu wenden. Hier war die führende Figur bei den Bemühungen um die Rehabilitation von Versehrten Jules Amar, Leiter des LABORATOIRE DE RECHERCHES SUR LE TRAVAIL PROFESSIONEL am CONSERVATOIRE NATIONAL DES ARTS ET MÉTIERS. Amar, geboren 1879, war ein aufsteigender Stern der französischen Arbeitswissenschaft. Diese Wissenschaft von der Arbeit zielte darauf ab, den Arbeitsplatz zu rationalisieren, gleichzeitig den Arbeiter von Ermüdung zu befreien und den Profit für den Kapitalisten zu vergrößern. In vielerlei Hinsicht war die europäische Arbeitswissenschaft eine humanere Version als die Taylor'sche: sie stellte sich nicht eindeutig auf die Seite des Kapitals, sondern versuchte sich aus einer Vermittlerrolle zwischen Arbeiter und Eigentümer auch um die geistige und körperliche Entwicklung des Arbeiters zu kümmern.[4] Gerade aber in dieser ›Menschlichkeit‹, in diesem Ehrgeiz, bei der Formierung des Körpers auch die Seele zu berücksichtigen, beruhte die Wirksamkeit, die die Arbeitswissenschaft Amars in den Bereichen der Rehabilitation von Kriegsversehrten hatte. Zwischen 1915 und 1919 richtete Amar seine Arbeit hauptsächlich auf die Rehabilitation verkrüppelter Soldaten. Seine Erfahrungen aus der Kriegszeit führten Amar zur Neuformulierung seiner physiologischen, psychologischen und soziologischen Theorien und zur Anwendung aller seiner früheren Ideen über Arbeit und Ertüchtigung auf die Rehabilitation Verkrüppelter. In seinem Text DIE PHYSIOLOGIE DER INDUSTRIEORGANISATION UND DIE WIEDERBESCHÄFTIGUNG DER BEHINDERTEN, wird seine Theorie vom Arbeiten unter der Erfahrung mit den *mutilés de la guerre* neu formuliert.

37

Form + Zweck no. 11/12

Magazine spreads

DESIGNERS Daniela Haufe, Detlef Fiedler
DESIGN COMPANY Cyan
PRINCIPAL TYPEFACE Bureau Grotesque
CLIENT *Form + Zweck*

Germany, 1995

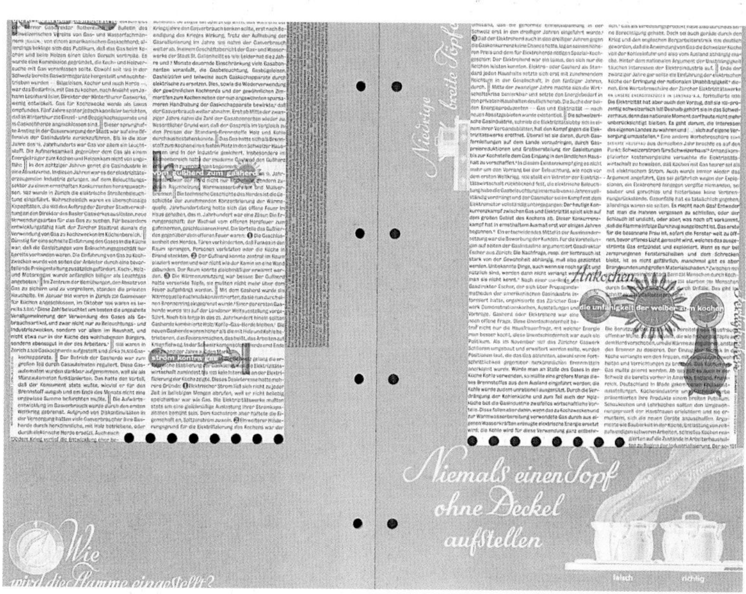
Niedrige breite Töpfe
Niemals einen Topf ohne Deckel aufstellen
falsch
richtig
Wie wird die Flamme eingestellt?

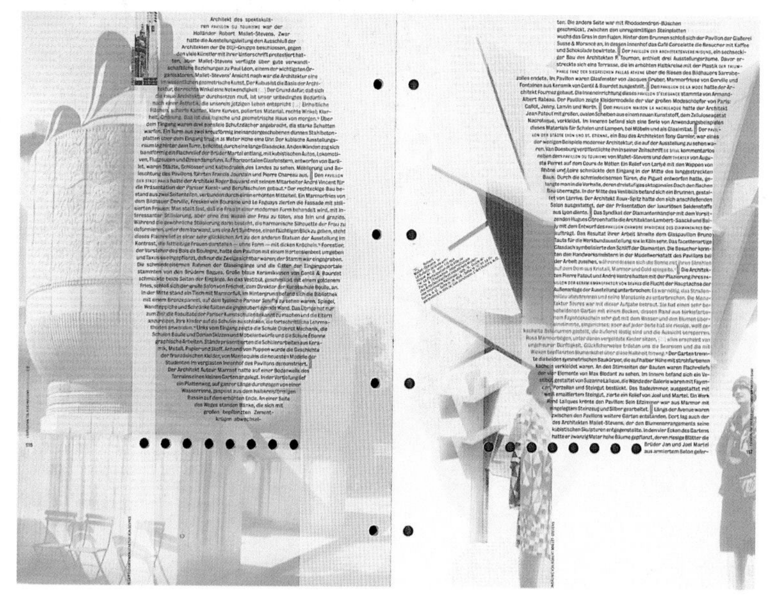

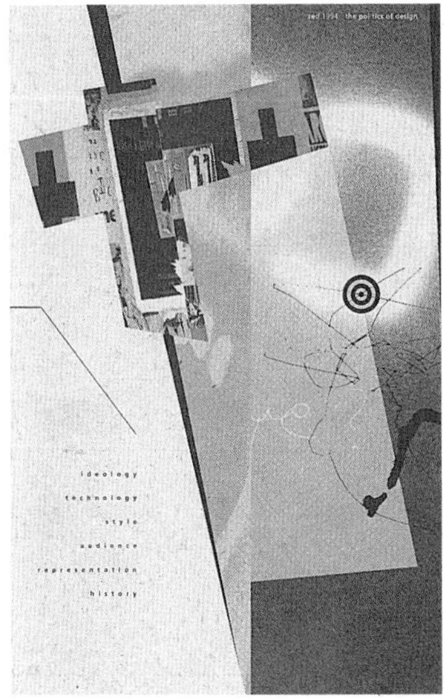

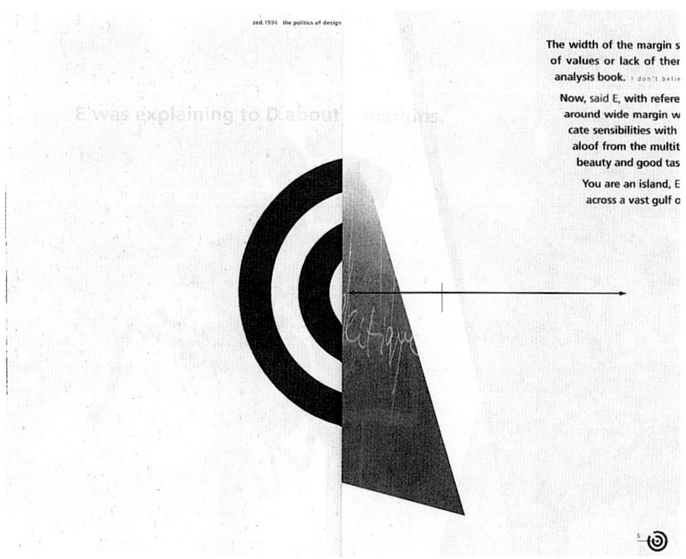

ows culture, aestheticism and a sense
, s/he said, quoting the handwriting
n it, said D.

ce to your signs there, you have an all
ich shows a person of extremely deli-
ove of color and form, one who holds
de of lives in his own dream world of
e.'

said, and I'm communicating with you,
darkness.

Ideas do, indeed, have consequences.

Nearly a year ago the concept for this journal was borne out of a perceived gap, or margin, in the current design dialogue. No forum presently exists within the field of visual communications that deals with fundamental issues of concern to practitioners, educators, and students as a group, and acknowledges the impact of these issues on society. **It is true that there is a lot being said—we are all speaking—but not to each other,** it seems. Divided by age, generation, ideology, and circumstance, designers, educators, and students have, in the past, retired to common ground where the language and concerns are familiar and where there is little chance of stepping off the edge. Consequently, designers speak to other designers, academics to other academics, and students to no one in particular, or any who might listen.

And so the margins grow. We have wrapped our conversations tightly around ourselves, blankets of white noise offered with expectations of sameness. Entrenched and faithful to our own cause we have lost interest in the value of debate and of a community rich in individual opinions and ideas. It is just easier that way.

Inevitably, the gap widens.

Editor's note

For better or for worse, design has entered a state of **balkanization**—now a sprawling, fragmented borderland of communities turned inward, fiercely territorial and dismissive of anything perceived as "other". Each holds up its philosophy for emulation and grounding as the status quo—the way of being and seeing in the (design) world. Assimilation is encouraged, even by those prizing subjectivity as a noble pursuit—for it is us against them. Choose or move on.

This "either-or" mentality has designer, educator, and student alike pledging weary allegiance to an uncertain cause. How many times in recent history have we found ourselves surfing the edge of the periphery while simultaneously emulating and rejecting the center? **Expressivity or objectivity? Theory or pragmatics? Modernism or Grunge?** Maybe we are trying too hard. Perhaps we needn't believe that the shared, or agreed upon, is more valuable in our pursuit than difference and contradiction. History should be enough to show that there are no absolutes. Our conscience and aesthetic taste are, equally, products of the cultural environment in which we grow and are educated. As Anne Burdick has written, "What we require is a set of ideologies that accepts and analyzes rather than disdains and dismisses." To this I would add an awareness of the self-defined value-system of our field and a respect for the depth of intellectual and aesthetic experimentation being pursued all around us, regardless of personal "taste." **Each is an indelible part of the other, separate but connected through this activity we call design.**

In fostering the growing gap between theory and practice, technology and craft, Modernism and everything else, we are participating in our own special version of *capture-the-flag*—that childhood game of power and single-minded pursuit. **One wo/man, one flag. World domination.** We would do well to remember the day as children when we grasped that four-square resulted in far fewer bruises and that, in this game, the bully was never hero.

To understand this, then, is to understand what *Zed* is all about. To identify and embrace the margins; to question, debate, and question again; to weigh the alternatives and consider the possibilities.

7

Zed no. 1, "The Politics of Design"

Journal cover and spreads

EDITOR/DESIGNER	Katie Salen
PHOTOGRAPHERS	Karen White, Sonya Mead, Katie Salen
PRINCIPAL TYPEFACES	Interstate, Frutiger
CLIENT	Center for Design Studies, Communication Arts and Design, Virginia Commonwealth University

USA, 1994

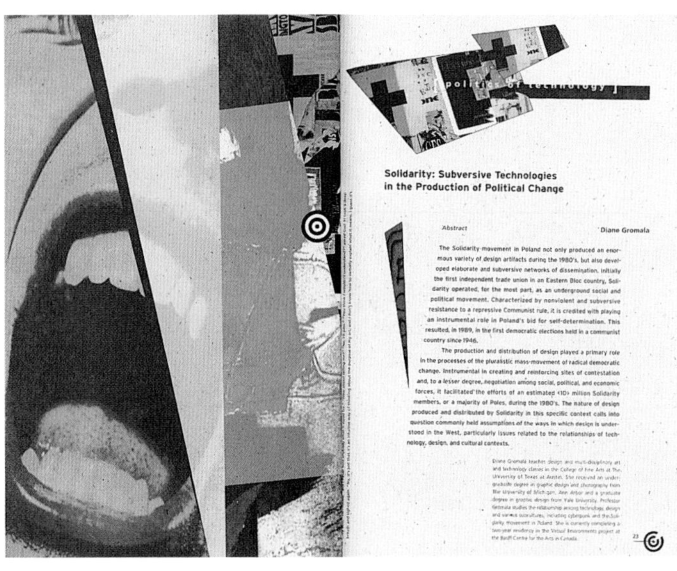

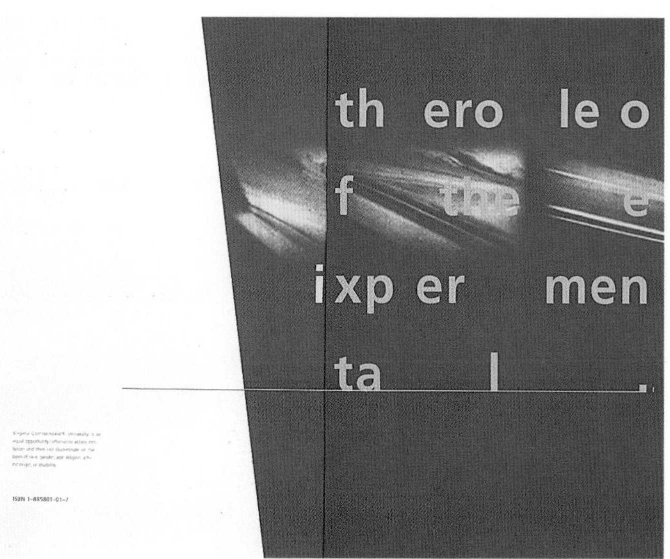

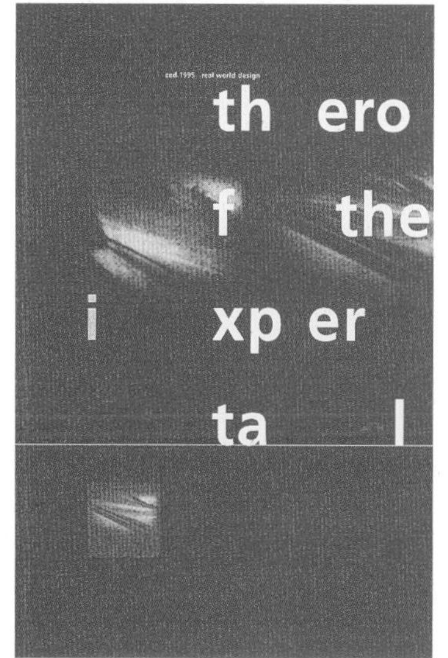

39 zed.2 1995 The Role of the Experimental

Pussy Galore – a typeface designed by the **Women's Design Research Unit (WD+RU)** for FUSE magazine

Teal Triggs :-( ) She Wears Lipstick

[z.re presen ta tio n

:-( ) She Wears L pst ck

Teal Tr ggs

As we move further through the 1990s a s gn f cant sh ft s occurr ng n women's relat onsh ps w th technology. Nowhere s th s more true than n the graph c des gn profess on where technology, pr mar ly n the form of the computer, s ncreas ngly access ble to women. L ke other profess ons, women's new pos t on v s a v s new technology s v ewed as **"acceptable"** by men desp te the endurance of a trad t onal patr arch cal structure. As computers become f rmly entrenched n contemporary des gn pract ce, women ncreas ngly have opportun t es to explore the capab l t es of new technology. New poss b l t es ar se for devel op ng new v sual languages and as such, may become an mportant veh cle for l berat ng women's vo ces.

For women, technology has often been treated as a means of l berat on. In the 1950s, the relat onsh p between women and technology was descr bed by Amer can advert sers n campa gns for consumer prod ucts. The **"domest c goddess"** would be l berated from the drudgery of housework by household appl ances.[1] Such **"labour-sav ng dev ces"**—d shwashers, hoovers, and wash ng mach nes—st ll reta n the r pos t on n the home but ncreas ngly w ll s t comfortably alongs de computers, fax mach nes and mob le commun cat ons. More pr m t ve mechan cal technology may have once prom sed domest c l berat on from the actual phys cal stra n of house hold labour, but as Lesl e We sman observes, "... t has never **freed women or men from the conf nement of gender roles"**.[2] In contrast d g tal technology and computers offer another type of **"l berat on"**. Even so as Jan Z mmerman has caut oned, **"Women could use computers... or computers could use women, just as other tech nolog es have..."**[3] M ndful of th s warn ng, careful con s derat on must be g ven to how and why women are us ng technology today, before any pronouncement on l berat on can be made.

Zed no. 2, "Real World Design: The Role of the Experimental"

Journal cover and spreads

EDITOR/DESIGNER Katie Salen
PHOTOGRAPHERS Nancy Nowacek, Katie Salen
PRINCIPAL TYPEFACES Interstate, Myriad
CLIENT Center for Design Studies, Communication Arts and Design, Virginia Commonwealth University

USA, 1995

Zed is an annual publication that aims to bridge the gap between designer, student and teacher by acting as a vehicle for divergent viewpoints and new voices. While conforming to the conventions of the "design journal" in its booklike proportions and editorial tone, *Zed* manifests a high degree of purposeful experimentation in its design. In the second issue, on the theme of the experimental, the letter "i" is deleted from some articles, requiring readers to "assimilate the unfamiliar" and adapt their method of reading to the modified presentation.

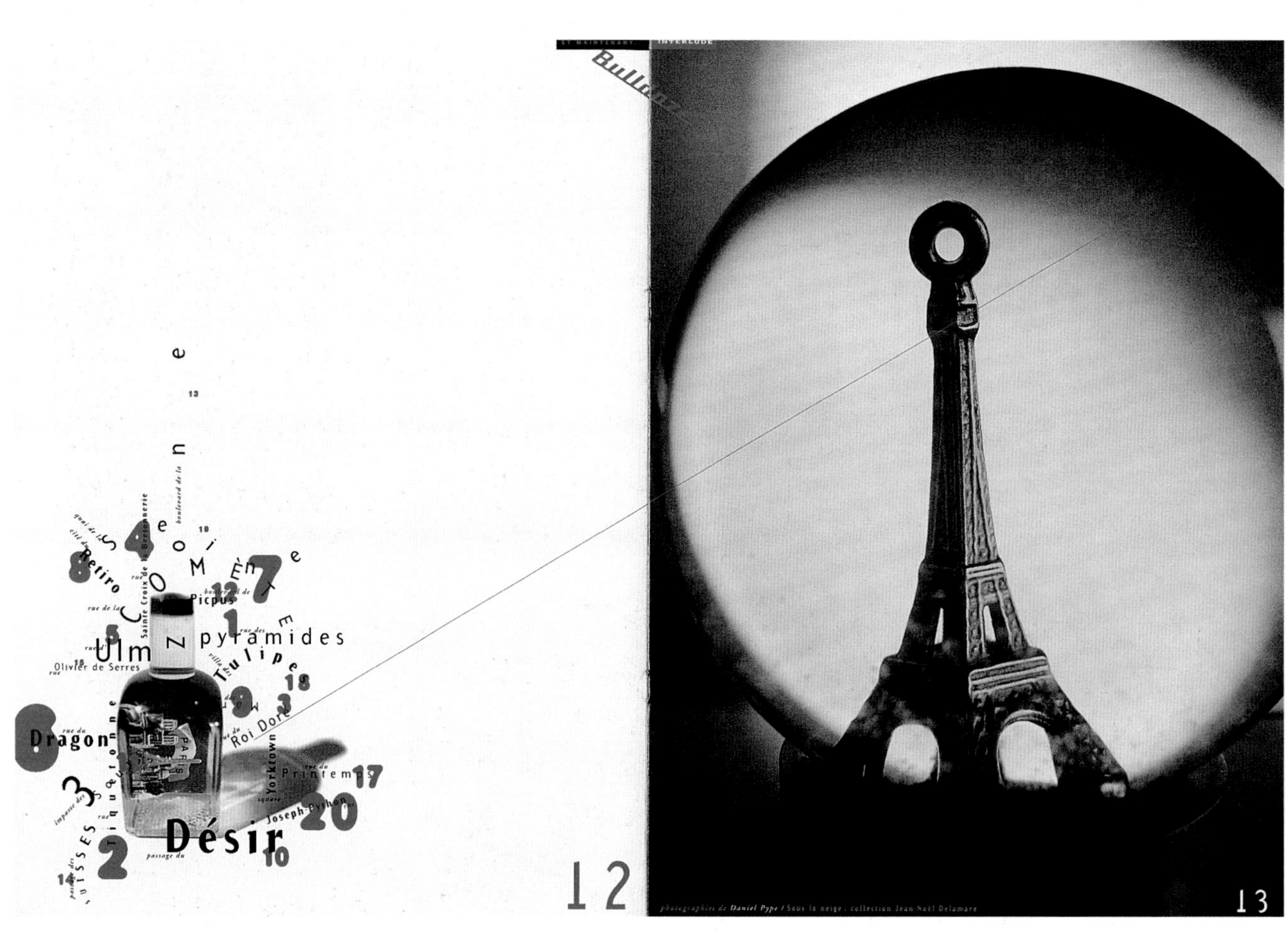

Bulldozer no. 0

Spreads from a graphic design magazine

ART DIRECTOR/DESIGNER Frédéric Bortolotti

DESIGN COMPANY Bulldozer

PHOTOGRAPHERS Daniel Pype, Simon Niedenthal

PRINCIPAL TYPEFACES Arbitrary, Serifa, Blur, Garamond

CLIENT *Bulldozer*

France, 1993-94

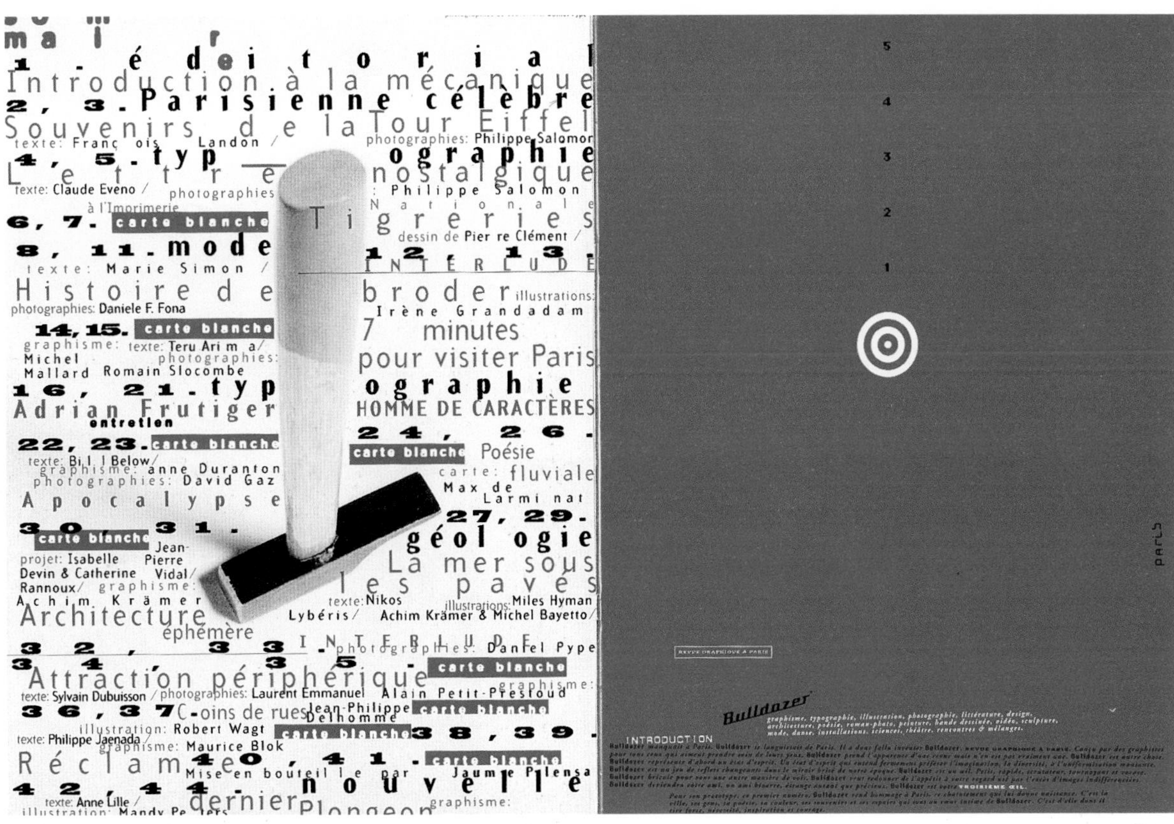

1. éditorial
Introduction à la mécanique
2, 3. Parisienne célèbre
Souvenirs de la Tour Eiffel
texte: François Landon / photographies: Philippe Salomon
4, 5. typographie
Lettre nostalgique
texte: Claude Eveno / photographies : Philippe Salomon
à l'Imprimerie Nationale
6, 7. carte blanche
Tigreries
dessin de Pierre Clément /
8, 11. mode
texte: Marie Simon /
Histoire de broder
photographies: Daniele F. Fona
illustrations: Irène Grandadam
12, 13. INTERLUDE
14, 15. carte blanche
7 minutes pour visiter Paris
graphisme: texte: Teru Arima / Michel Mallard
photographies: Romain Slocombe
16, 21. typographie
Adrian Frutiger
entretien
HOMME DE CARACTÈRES
22, 23. carte blanche
24, 26.
carte blanche
Poésie
texte: Bill Below /
graphisme: anne Duranton
photographies: David Gaz
carte: fluviale
Max de Larminat
Apocalypse
27, 29.
géologie
30, 31.
carte blanche
Jean-Pierre Vidal /
projet: Isabelle Devin & Catherine Rannoux /
graphisme: Achim Krämer
La mer sous les pavés
texte: Nikos Lybéris /
illustrations: Miles Hyman
Achim Krämer & Michel Bayetto /
Architecture éphémère
32, 33 INTERLUDE
photographies: Daniel Pype
34, 35.
carte blanche
Attraction périphérique
graphisme:
texte: Sylvain Dubuisson / photographies: Laurent Emmanuel
Alain Petit-Prestoud
36, 37 Coins de rues
Jean-Philippe Delhomme
carte blanche
illustration: Robert Wagt
texte: Philippe Jaenada /
carte blanche
38, 39.
graphisme: Maurice Blok
Réclame
40, 41.
carte blanche
Mise en bouteille par Jaume Plensa
42, 44.
nouvelle
texte: Anne Lille /
dernier Plongeon
graphisme:
5
4
3
2
1
paris
REVUE GRAPHIQUE À PARIS
Bulldozer
graphisme, typographie, illustration, photographie, littérature, design, architecture, poésie, roman-photo, peinture, bande dessinée, vidéo, sculpture, mode, danse, installations, sciences, théâtre, rencontres & mélanges.
INTRODUCTION

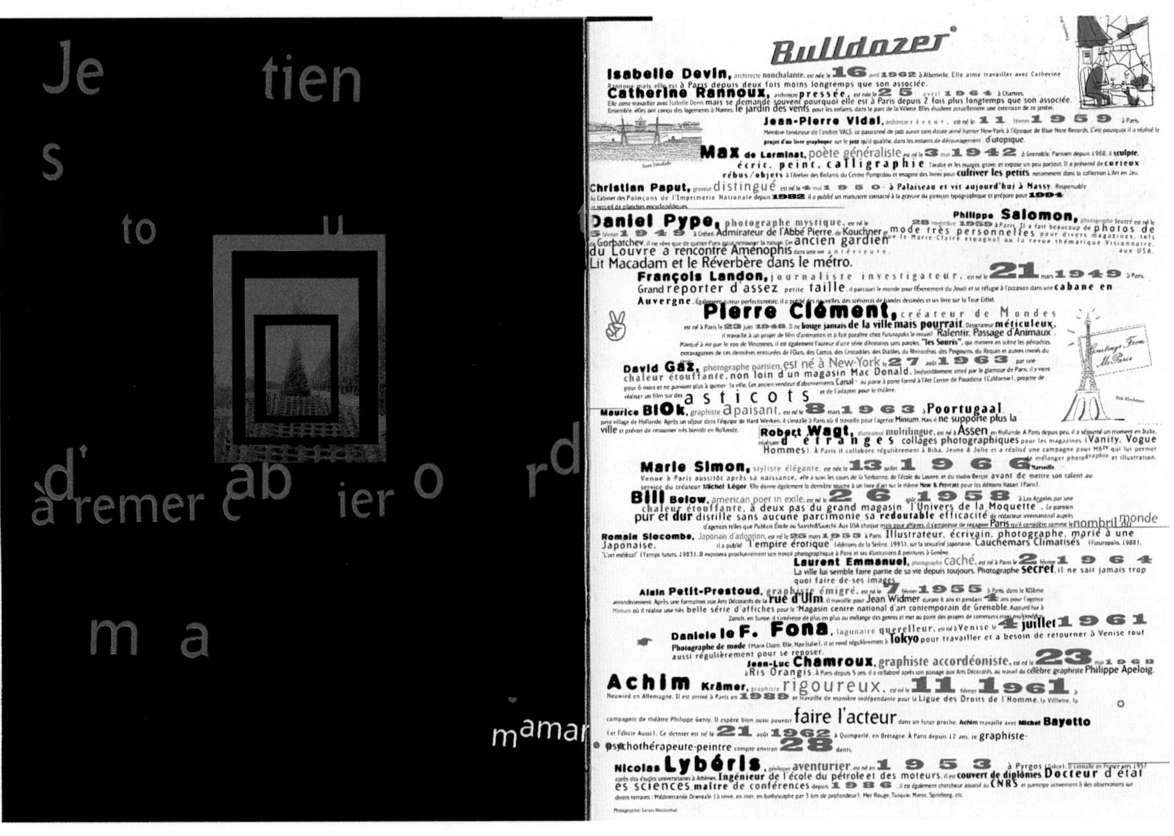

Je tiens
to u
d'abord
à remercier
ma
mamar
Bulldozer
Isabelle Devin,
Catherine Rannoux,
Jean-Pierre Vidal,
Max de Larminat,
Christian Paput,
Daniel Pype,
Philippe Salomon,
François Landon,
Pierre Clément,
David Gaz,
asticots
Maurice BlOk,
Robert Wagt,
Marie Simon,
Bill Below,
Romain Slocombe,
Laurent Emmanuel,
Alain Petit-Prestoud,
Daniele le F. Fona
Jean-Luc Chamroux,
Achim Krämer,
faire l'acteur
Nicolas Lybéris,

I like the

The most familiar "use" of vernacular is to produce nostalgia. The problem with the nostalgic vernacular is that it steals from the past to deny the future. The past is robbed of its authenticity and historical context (or specificity) to be rewritten as if it were an episode of *Happy Days* or a Norman Rockwell painting. Absence makes the heart grow fonder, and there's no fiction like "the good old days." This kind of nostalgic reverie is an escape from the anxiety of an uncertain future; it's not so much historical quotation as it is nostalgic sound bite. Authenticity is **NOT** a high priority for graphic designers because it's usually the feeling we're after, **NOT** the fact. This allows us to play fast and loose with history to construct feelings, like that of the art deco thirties or the fifties, that never really correspond to any specific time, place, or people. It's not the past, it's better than the past – and the present and the future. Retreating into nostalgia is turning your back on the present and running in fear of the future. If graphic designers are busy daydreaming about the good old days, then who is going to show us what the future looks like? Who's in charge of inventing tomorrow? Are we all so embarrassed that the modernist visions of Herbert Bayer, Raymond Loewy, and Bucky Fuller didn't exactly come true that we must retreat to some imaginary past life that didn't really exist, either?

The commercial artist was transformed into the graphic designer with the help and encouragement of modernism. Graphic design's identity is so co-dependent on modernism that one does not dare contemplate design outside of the modernist paradigm. Now, in an era of postmodern plurality and technological change, the good old days of the easy and unchallenged answers of modernism are gone for good. That's why graphic design is suffering from an identity crisis. When you are having trouble defining something it is often easier to define what it is **NOT**, and the vernacular is what we (professional graphic designers) are **NOT**.

I think much of the current interest in vernacular is a symptom of the lack of direction and groping for self-definition of the design profession. So many times I hear designers waxing poetically about some lovely little matchbook cover, menu design, or hand-lettered sign and how terrific it is – what graphic designer doesn't have a stash of such found goodies to "borrow" from? And there's nothing wrong with that; after all, the capacity to appreciate something will expand your understanding, **NOT** define it.

vernacular

Appropriation of the "other" (to use the current art world vernacular) means taking something from a culture "other" than your own. You can appropriate something without reference to its original context (pastiche), or in a way that calls attention to its original context (parody/irony). Other cultures are not just literally other national cultures but can be high, low, pop, and subcultures. When one culture borrows from another there are often problems that arise due to issues of dominance and equality. For example, when the high-culture graphic designer (trained in a design school) borrows clip art illustrations or crude lettering from the low-culture hack (trained in the school of hard knocks) it can be a condescending act of elitism that deliberately draws attention to the difference in status between them as if to say,

"Hey, look at what this so-called illustrator did...isn't it corny? I could never do anything that silly, I'm too sophisticated. I really wish I could but I'm just too clever to do anything like that. In fact, I'm too clever to do anything at all, that's why I have to use stuff from these poor hacks."

This appropriation/nostalgia thing has not only become a bit tiresome lately, but is increasingly mean spirited as well; but only in the most covert fashion because the plunderers are always the first to proclaim how much they love the one they are plundering. The idea of "borrowing" in graphic design is so pervasive that it's often done unconsciously. What is needed is an awareness of what crossing cultural/historical barriers actually means, as well as an understanding of the importance of context.

How many more designers must join the timeless undead victims of ... Count Vernacula ?

The culture that is perceived to be high or dominant is not the only one to be empowered. In this negotiation of status, the plundered underdog is given the unassailable status of the authentic, capable of true, natural, or honest expression. The so designated dominant culture, on the other hand, is a vacuous imitator/manipulator plundering the **TRUTH** from the real "other" culture. Thus, the price of dominance in the culture war is authenticity. "They" used to be great, but now that they're mainstream/commercial they're just crap! In this exchange of tit-for-tat, the high and low cultures are leveled out into one popculture. Is it the graphic designer's task to please everyone in this pan-pop culture? Or to affirm their client's status as the high, and the audience/consumer's status as the low?

You can't please some of the people some of the time, but you can please all of the people all of the time!

Today, cuttingedge vernacular users are the designers creating rave graphics. (For those of you who live in a cave, a rave is an illegal underground party of a thousand kids on ecstasy [DRUG], dancing in puddles of their own sweat to techno-house music until the cows come home, or the cops drop in [FUN].) The old and low cultures that rave designers borrow from are primarily American corporate and package design of the seventies and eighties (**now there's some hacks!**). Rave designers love logos, lots of color, and outlined type, and hey who doesn't? The fact that the "professional designer's" work is now being reworked like any other bit of ephemera might be some kind of poetic justice, but it fails to be a very interesting design strategy. That's because their work (like their predecessors) is essentially a one-liner that has little resonance beyond the "shock of the old." What little invention there is in rave graphics is provided mostly by the computer.

I remember the late 80s ... now those were the good old days!

At this point it would seem the vernacular idea in graphic design has pretty much played itself out. The only thing the cutting-edge appropriators can do is continuously reuse what they just did last year. This strategy couldn't really be called vernacular design, after all there are already a lot of designers who do this and call it "timeless design." Have you ever seen a dog chasing his own tail? Now that's timeless.

The past used to be considered a classic example or ideal for the present. In the postindustrial postmodern world the past is just another place to go shopping, except most of the past has been bought up, just leaving yesterday's news. Retrofitting a popular old song is the easiest way to get a hit. It is a very different thing to recycle the past for the purposes of "instant gratification" than to reinvent the past as an ideal for the present. Reinventing the past is a lot of hard work (scholarship), and who wants to wait for the future (it may never come). When the general cultural mood is here-today-gone-tomorrow, all history is reduced to one undifferentiated vernacular (no linear hierarchies, please).

Is there a "correct" way to use the idea of vernacular in graphic design, or is the whole idea of the vernacular overly simplistic and not very useful?

Isn't getting "inspiration" from your *Print, How, I.D.,* and *Emigre* magazines using the vernacular?

Why is it that graphic design history includes cave painting, cuneiform alphabets, and woodblock engravings but doesn't include sign painting or clip art?

When is the vernacular just history?

What is the point of asking all these questions if you aren't going to answer them?

NOT!

by Mr. Keedy

Currently, graphic design practice and history is neither specific nor general in its scope; rather, it is elusively constructed out of fickle self-interest and unchallenged ego. Unchallenged, because for the most part the rest of the world doesn't give a shit about graphic design anyway.

Maybe we should either expand our notion of what constitutes graphic design or become even more specific and rigorous in our self-definition of graphic design practice. Maybe graphic designers should go back to the old business of inventing the future instead of regurgitating a past that's been digested so many times that it has no taste* (not to mention style*).

Deep down inside I think most designers suspect that "using vernacular" is a chicken shit's easy way out. It's a retreat from style, or at least from expressing your own style forged from your own experience and time. Graphic designers should be responsive to and responsible for the development of their own style. Instead of just "using" the vernacular we are creating it, and it tells us not only who we were and are, but **who we hope to be**

* I realize most graphic designers today find these two words problematic, since we allegedly are problem-solvers instead of tastemakers and trendsetters, but anyone with half a brain can see what the larger culture values most in graphic design.
Background lettering by Stephen X. McMahon, from *100 Moods in Lettering* 1947

Lift and Separate: Graphic Design and the Quote Unquote Vernacular

Essay spreads from an exhibition catalogue

EDITOR Barbara Glauber

WRITER/DESIGNER Jeffery Keedy

PRINCIPAL TYPEFACE Manu Sans

BACKGROUND LETTERING Stephen X. McMahon, from *100 Moods in Lettering*, 1947

CLIENT The Herb Lubalin Study Center, The Cooper Union

USA, 1993

The monograph examines the complex relationship between the vernacular and the contemporary graphic designer. Ten essays explore the hierarchy, appropriation and recontextualisation of various visual dialects, including the use of nostalgic imagery and the graphic language of roadside signage. Most of the contributors are practising designers whose visual voices are expressed through the design of their articles.

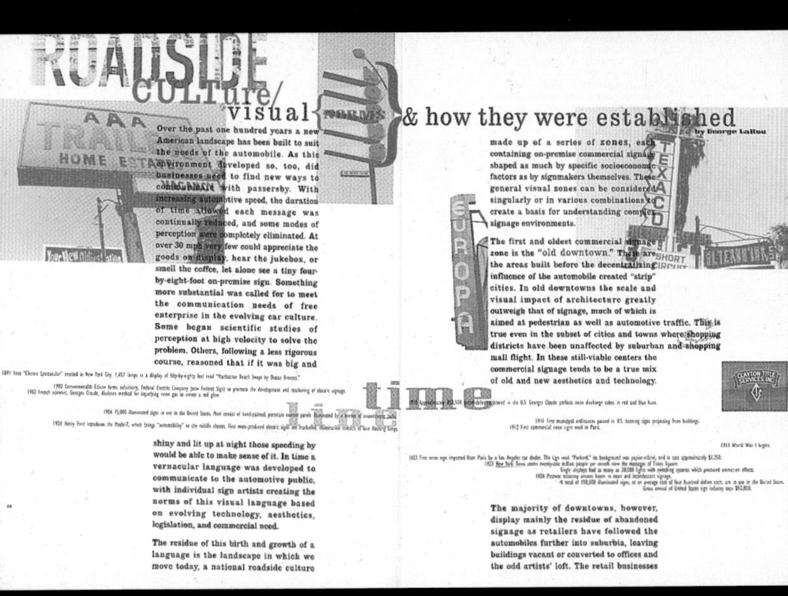

ROADSIDE culture/ visual & how they were established

by George LaRou

Over the past one hundred years a new American landscape has been built to suit the needs of the automobile. As this environment developed so, too, did businesses need to find new ways to communicate with passersby. With increasing automotive speed, the duration of time allowed each message was continually reduced, and some modes of perception were completely eliminated. At over 30 mph very few could appreciate the goods on display, hear the jukebox, or smell the coffee, let alone see a tiny four-by-eight-foot on-premise sign. Something more substantial was called for to meet the communication needs of free enterprise in the evolving car culture. Some began scientific studies of perception at high velocity to solve the problem. Others, following a less rigorous course, reasoned that if it was big and shiny and lit up at night those speeding by would be able to make sense of it. In time a vernacular language was developed to communicate to the automotive public, with individual sign artists creating the norms of this visual language based on evolving technology, aesthetics, legislation, and commercial need.

The residue of this birth and growth of a language is the landscape in which we move today, a national roadside culture made up of a series of zones, each containing on-premise commercial signage shaped as much by specific socioeconomic factors as by signmakers themselves. These general visual zones can be considered singularly or in various combinations to create a basis for understanding complex signage environments.

The first and oldest commercial signage zone is the "old downtown." These are the areas built before the decentralizing influence of the automobile created "strip" cities. In old downtowns the scale and visual impact of architecture greatly outweigh that of signage, much of which is aimed at pedestrian as well as automotive traffic. This is true even in the subset of cities and towns where shopping districts have been unaffected by suburban and shopping mall flight. In these still-viable centers the commercial signage tends to be a true mix of old and new aesthetics and technology.

time line

The majority of downtowns, however, display mainly the residue of abandoned signage as retailers have followed the automobiles further into suburbia, leaving buildings vacant or converted to offices and the odd artists' loft. The retail businesses

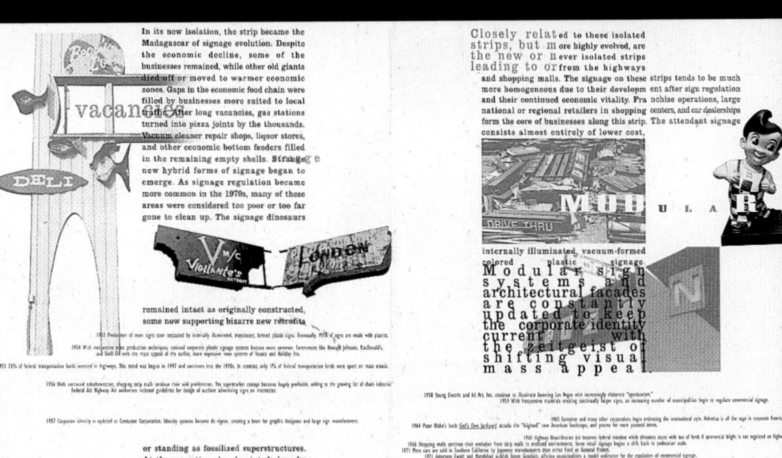

In its new isolation, the strip became the Madagascar of signage evolution. Despite the economic decline, some of the businesses remained, while other old giants died off or moved to warmer economic zones. Gaps in the economic food chain were filled by businesses more suited to local traffic. After long vacancies, gas stations turned into pizza joints by the thousands. Vacuum cleaner repair shops, liquor stores, and other economic bottom feeders filled in the remaining empty shells. Strange new hybrid forms of signage began to emerge. As signage regulation became more common in the 1970s, many of these areas were considered too poor or too far gone to clean up. The signage dinosaurs remained intact as originally constructed, some now supporting bizarre new retrofits or standing as fossilized superstructures. At the same time, hand-painted signs by lettering artists and muralists of wildly varying skill and craft began to compete with new plastic fascias, vinyl letters, mobile signs, and backlit lettered awnings, vying for the attention of motorists in this Grand Canyon of visual historic sediment.

vacancies

Closely relat ed to these isolated strips, but m ore highly evolved, are the new or n ever isolated strips leading to or from the highways and shopping malls. The signage on these strips tends to be much more homogeneous due to their developm ent after sign regulation and their continued economic vitality. Fra nchise operations, large national or regional retailers in shopping centers, and car dealerships form the core of businesses along this strip. The attendant signage consists almost entirely of lower cost, internally illuminated, vacuum-formed colored plastic signage.

MODULAR

Modular sign systems and architectural facades are constantly updated to keep the corporate identity current with the zeitgeist of shifting visual mass appeal.

This constant change tends to erase any historic reference more than twenty years old.

Lift and Separate: Graphic Design and the Quote Unquote Vernacular

Essay spreads from an exhibition catalogue

EDITOR Barbara Glauber

WRITER/DESIGNER George LaRou

PRINCIPAL TYPEFACES Egyptian, Gill Sans, Boy Wide

CLIENT The Herb Lubalin Study Center, The Cooper Union

USA, 1993

Coil no. 1

Cover and spreads from a journal of the moving image

DESIGNER Damian Jaques
DESIGN COMPANY Proboscis
PRINCIPAL TYPEFACES Wunderlich, Quadraat, Disturbance, Coventry, OCRB
CLIENT *Coil*

Great Britain, 1995

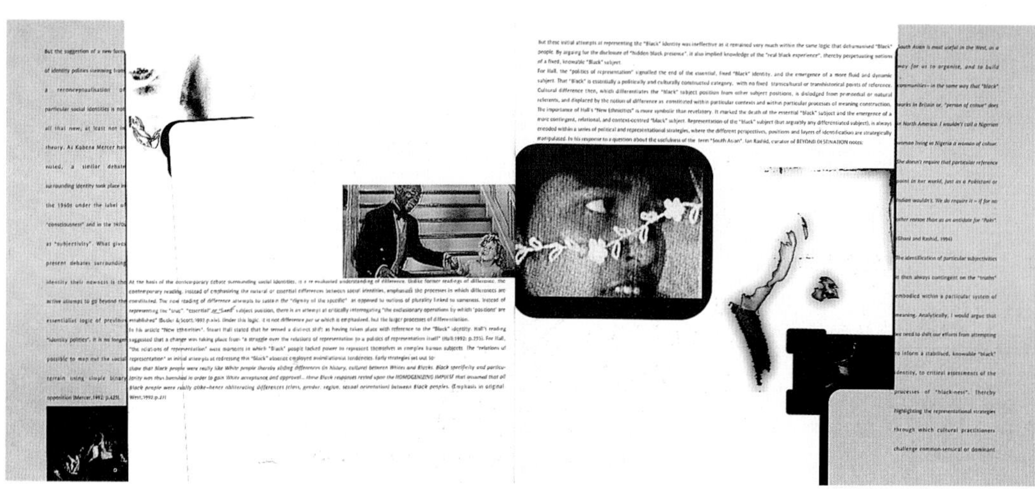

the poetics of blue

psi net

kathleen rogers

the perpetual minute

Wayne Sleeth

Coil is an independent publication that addresses the cultural, theoretical and practical aspects of the moving image (film, video and digital/electronic imaging). The contrasting natures and thematic concerns of the different media are reflected in a design which asks for a high degree of involvement from the reader. Early feedback suggests practitioners feel the time is right for a journal presenting this subject matter in a highly activated visual style.

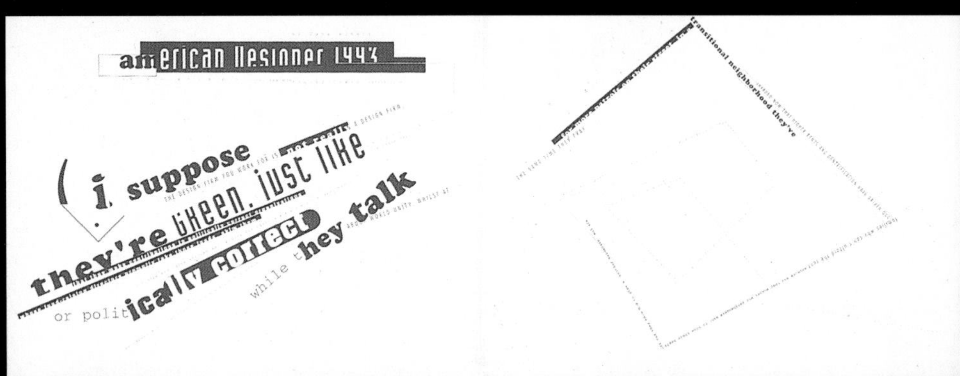

In this celebratory catalogue the ambiguous nature of the creative process is given the same emphasis as the clarity of the designers' philosophies and finished work. The book is structured and paced to reflect the range of rhythms the viewer would experience in exploring the exhibition. Subtle differences between elements and dramatic juxtapositions suggest the eclectic nature of American design.

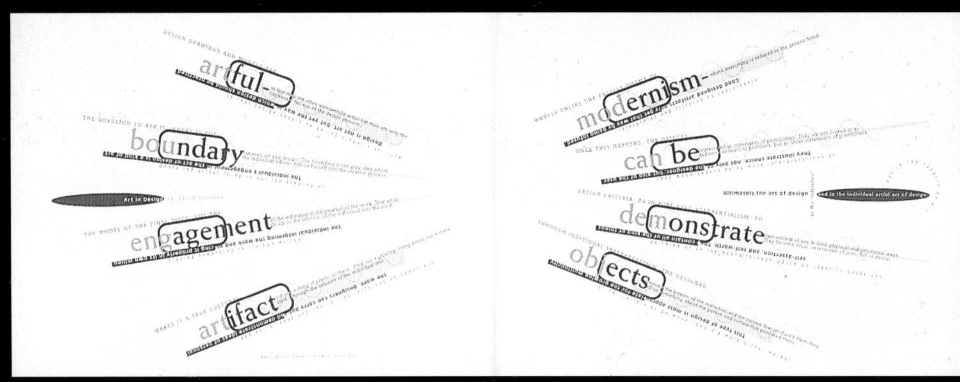

Art of Design 2

Spreads from an exhibition catalogue

DESIGNER Susan Lally

DESIGN COMPANY Lally Design

PRINCIPAL TYPEFACES Futura, Goudy, Franklin Gothic, Garamond

CLIENT Harry Wirth and the American Design Network

USA, 1993

Still There Will Be Stories

Children's illustration exhibition poster/catalogue

DESIGNER Carlo Tartaglia

ILLUSTRATORS James Jarvis, Sara Fanelli

PRINCIPAL TYPEFACE Univers

CLIENT Royal College of Art

Great Britain, 1994

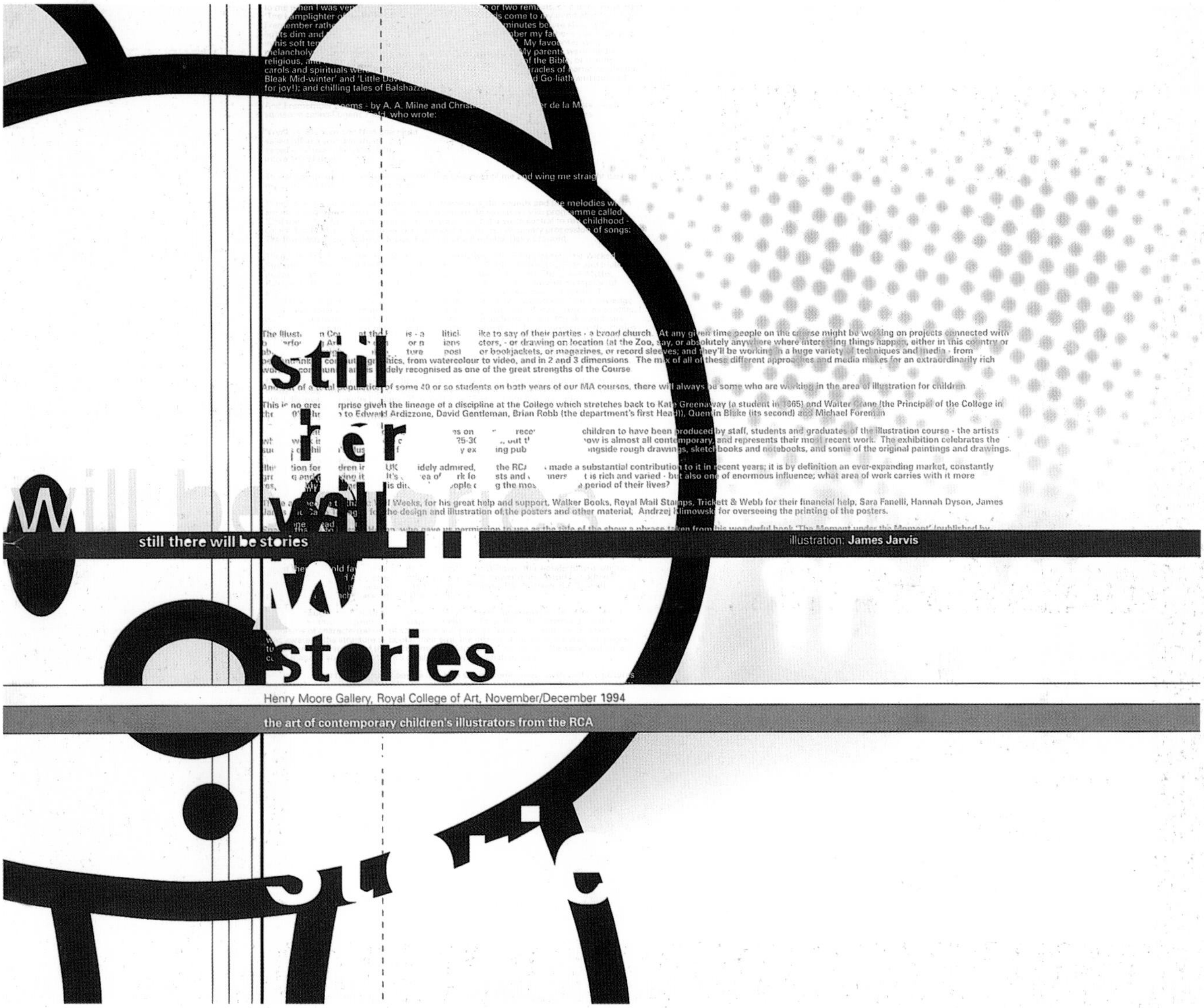

still there will be stories

illustration: James Jarvis

stories

Henry Moore Gallery, Royal College of Art, November/December 1994

the art of contemporary children's illustrators from the RCA

Cut and folded, the poster also functions as a catalogue. Text is used as digitally manipulated texture on the cover, reversing the usual relationship between word and image in conventional children's story books.

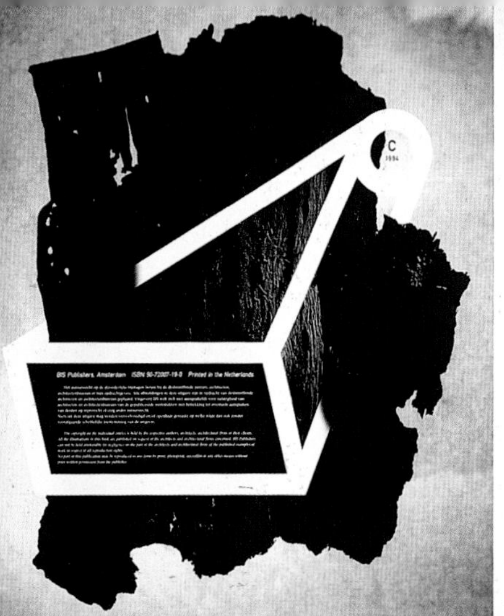

NED.

Architecten

volume 1

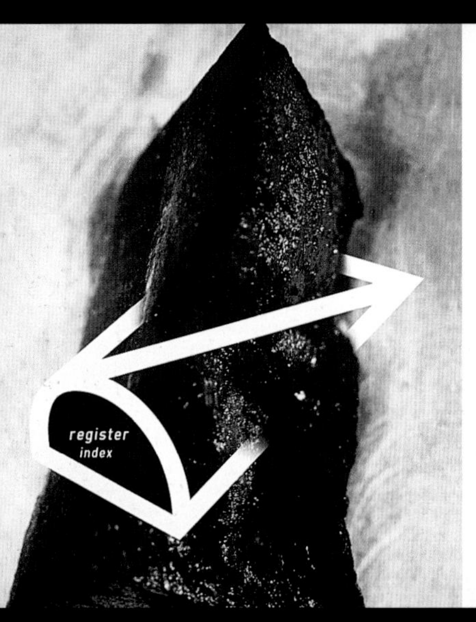

22
Aardewerk Partners
Architekten & Ontwerpers BNA BNI bNO

[illegible]
2514 BC Den Haag

24
AAtW Architecten

[illegible]
1018 MR Amsterdam

Opgericht / Founded 1990

Bureauprofiel

[illegible]

Projecten

[illegible]

Profile

[illegible]

Projects

[illegible]

26
Abken bv

Newtonbaan 1
[illegible] NK Nieuwegein

Opgericht / Founded september 1958
Aantal medewerkers / Staff 11

Bureauprofiel

[illegible]

Opdrachtgevers

[illegible]

Profile

[illegible]

Clients

[illegible]

28
AG Nova Architecten BNA

Zuidvliet 26
8921 BL Leeuwarden
Postbus 816
8901 BB Leeuwarden

Hertog van Saxenlaan 76/b
8802 EE Franeker
Postbus 234
8800 AE Franeker

Opgericht / Founded 1975
Aantal medewerkers / Staff 140

Bureauprofiel

[illegible]

Gerealiseerde werken

[illegible]

Profile

[illegible]

Completed projects

[illegible]

Book spreads

DESIGNERS	Jacques Koeweiden, Paul Postma
DESIGN COMPANY	Koeweiden Postma Associates
PHOTOGRAPHER	Marc van Praag
PRINCIPAL TYPEFACES	KP DIN, Stone
CLIENT	Uitgeverij BIS

The Netherlands, 1994

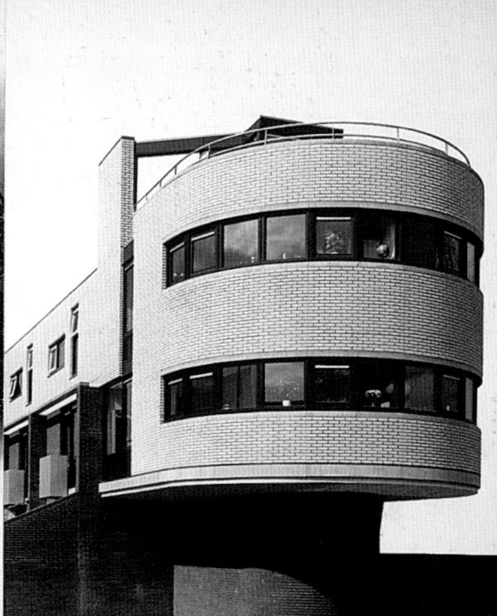

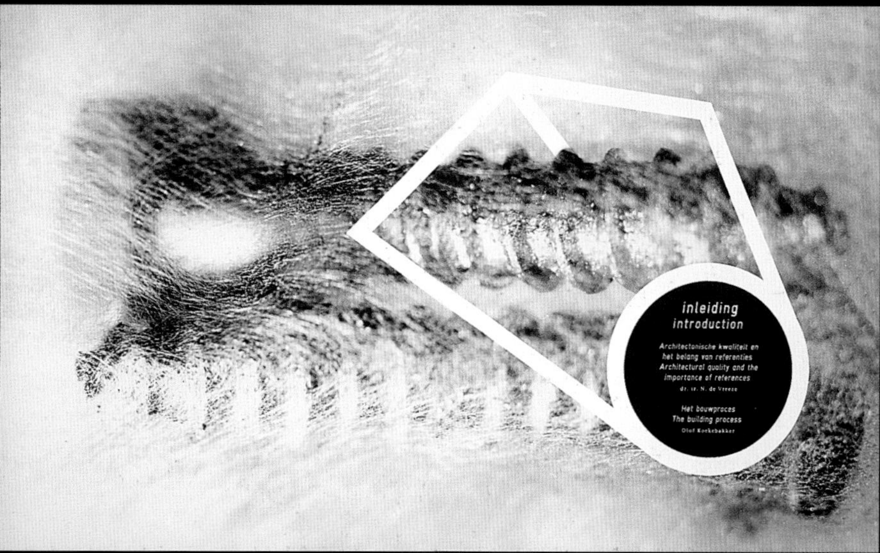

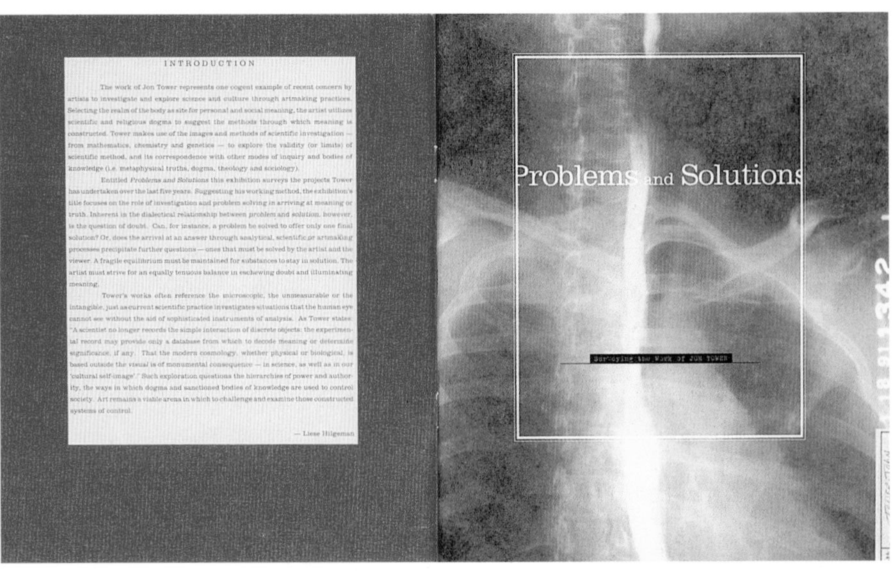

INTRODUCTION

The work of Jon Tower represents one cogent example of recent concern by artists to investigate and explore science and culture through artmaking practices. Selecting the realm of the body as site for personal and social meaning, the artist utilizes scientific and religious dogma to suggest the methods through which meaning is constructed. Tower makes use of the images and methods of scientific investigation — from mathematics, chemistry and genetics — to explore the validity (or limits) of scientific method, and its correspondence with other modes of inquiry and bodies of knowledge (i.e. metaphysical truths, dogma, theology and sociology).

Entitled *Problems and Solutions* this exhibition surveys the projects Tower has undertaken over the last five years. Suggesting his working method, the exhibition's title focuses on the role of investigation and problem solving in arriving at meaning or truth. Inherent in the dialectical relationship between *problem* and *solution*, however, is the question of doubt. Can, for instance, a problem be solved to offer only one final solution? Or, does the arrival at an answer through analytical, scientific or artmaking processes precipitate further questions — ones that must be solved by the artist and the viewer. A fragile equilibrium must be maintained for substances to stay in solution. The artist must strive for an equally tenuous balance in eschewing doubt and illuminating meaning.

Tower's works often reference the microscopic, the unmeasurable or the intangible, just as current scientific practice investigates situations that the human eye cannot see without the aid of sophisticated instruments of analysis. As Tower states: "A scientist no longer records the simple interaction of discrete objects: the experimental record may provide only a database from which to decode meaning or determine significance, if any. That the modern cosmology, whether physical or biological, is based outside the *visual* is of monumental consequence — in science, as well as in our 'cultural self-image'." Such exploration questions the hierarchies of power and authority, the ways in which dogma and sanctioned bodies of knowledge are used to control society. Art remains a viable arena in which to challenge and examine those constructed systems of control.

— Liese Hilgeman

Problems and Solutions:
Surveying the Work of Jon Tower

Exhibition catalogue cover and spreads

DESIGNERS Laura Lacy-Sholly, James Sholly
DESIGN COMPANY Antenna
PRINCIPAL TYPEFACES Clarendon, Bell Gothic, STA Portable
CLIENT Herron Gallery, Indianapolis Center for Contemporary Art

USA, 1992

RENDERING THE INVISIBLE VISIBLE

Liese Hilgeman

Credo ut intelligum
I believe in order that I may understand
-Anselm of Bec . 12th century

The liminal zone between the conceptualized and the visible is the site of Jon Tower's projects. His aim is to render the invisible visible. He devises systems and tropes to present social, spiritual, or scientific concepts and ideas to create tangible visual examples through which the metaphysical can be grasped, understood and questioned. One can perceive the results of something that is indecipherable or invisible. Any given natural phenomenon can be apprehended when it effects a change in the material world. The presence of air, the movement of wind is realized when it is captured in a windsock or moves something visible in its path — clouds, the leaves or branches of a tree. Yet, there are other equally ethereal and unseen presences in the world — the construction of meaning, the social power structures of knowledge and dogma, the biochemical processes whereby we think, act and exist.

The artist Joseph Kosuth in an essay entitled *No Exit* (1988) positions the Postmodern artist's struggle to produce art "which contextualized and provided meaning for *things* (even theoretical 'things')" as emerging out of Minimalism's and Conceptualism's reactions to Modernist definitions of art based on material and formalist strategies.[1] He states:

> Post-Minimalism's primary concern is with a radicalization of alternative MATERIALS rather than alternative MEANINGS. But it is issues of meaning — the process of signification — that define Conceptual art and have made it relevant to recent art practice. The substantial import of such work, it would seem to me, has been the radical reevaluation of how an artwork works, thereby telling us something of how culture itself works: how meanings can change even if materials don't.[2]

3

Halos. Installation view, 1989. 23 karat gold powder on paper, enamel on wall, and brass. Thomas Solomon's Garage, Los Angeles. Various Private Collections.

Untitled (Female Chromosomes), 1990. Sterling silver (46 unique castings). Courtesy of American Fine Arts Co., New York.

Celestial Stars After Giotto (for D.D.K.), installation view, 1992. Silk screen and acrylic on ceiling. PS1, New York. Courtesy of American Fine Arts Co., New York

Jon Tower's art deals with the processes of socialisation that shape perceptions of religion, education, art and science. The catalogue represents the conceptual nature of his work by distilling elements from the visual culture of these disciplines into a document that is part laboratory report, part text book and part early volume on art.

Black Maria no. 2

Magazine cover (front and back)
DESIGNER Cornel Windlin
PRINCIPAL TYPEFACE Custom-made for the project
CLIENT *Black Maria*

Switzerland, 1994

Oceaan Coalities

Catalogue cover and spreads
DESIGNER Roelof Mulder
DESIGN COMPANY Roelof Mulder Studio
PHOTOGRAPHERS Jozee Brouwer, Christa van Kolfschoten
PRINCIPAL TYPEFACE Ocean Normal
CLIENT Oceaan Galerie

The Netherlands, 1992

OCEAAN

COALITIE IS EEN TENTOONSTELLINGSPROJEKT DAT IN 1991 IN OCEAAN PLAATSVOND. TWEE INITIATIEFNEMERS VAN OCEAAN, HESTER OERLEMANS EN NIEK DE JONG BESLOTEN HUN EIGEN KUNSTENAARSCHAP ALS UITGANGSPUNT TE NEMEN VOOR EEN SERIE TENTOONSTELLINGEN. KUNSTENAARS WERDEN UITGENODIGD EEN INHOUDELIJK VERBOND MET ÉÉN VAN HEN AAN TE GAAN OM ZO GEZAMENLIJK TENTOONSTELLINGEN TE REALISEREN.
DE TENTOONSTELLINGEN DUURDEN STEEDS DRIE WEKEN EN WERDEN AFGEWISSELD MET ZOGENAAMDE 'ZATERDAGAVONDTENTOONSTELLINGEN' WAARIN JUIST DOOR KUNSTENAARS INGEDIENDE PLANNEN CENTRAAL STONDEN. AAN DE 8 COALITIE-TENTOONSTELLINGEN DIE IN OCEAAN HEBBEN PLAATSGEVONDEN HEBBEN MEER DAN 25 KUNSTENAARS DEELGENOMEN. DAARBIJ ZIJN DE MEEST UITEENLOPENDE DISCIPLINES, ZOALS DESIGN, FOTOGRAFIE, GRAFIEK, SCHILDERKUNST, PERFORMANCE, ARCHITECTUUR, SCULPTUUR, TECHNIEK EN KERAMIEK TE ZIEN GEWEEST.
COALITIE HEEFT EEN BIJZONDERE REEKS TENTOONSTELLINGEN OPGELEVERD WAARMEE OCEAAN HAAR HEEL EIGEN VISIE OP HET BEGRIP 'KUNSTENAARSINITIATIEF' HEEFT KUNNEN LATEN ZIEN.

COALITIES

BORN TO BE WILD

COALITIE IS EEN COMMUNICATIEPROGRAMMA. TWEE OF MEER KUNSTENAARS GAAN VOOR EEN BEPAALDE TIJD MET ELKAAR IN ZEE EN PROBEREN EEN VERBINDING TUSSEN HUN WERK TOT STAND TE BRENGEN. EEN GESPREK OP ARTISTIEK-INHOUDELIJK NIVEAU MET EEN TENTOONSTELLING ALS RESULTAAT. EEN JAAR LANG HEB IK IEDERE DRIE MAANDEN EEN TENTOONSTELLING GEMAAKT STEEDS IN SAMENWERKING MET ÉÉN OF MEERDERE KUNSTENAARS. ALS KUNSTENAAR NIEK DE JONG ÉN ALS ORGANISATOR. EEN BROEIERIGE DUBBELROL.

MET COALITIE WERD DE RELATIE TUSSEN ORGANISATIE EN KUNSTENAAR TOT EEN MAXIMALE INTENSIVITEIT OPGEVOERD. IK VOND HET NIET MEER ZO INTERESSANT OM VANAF DE ZIJLIJN TOE TE KIJKEN HOE COLLEGAE HET ER IN DE RUIMTE VAN ONS INITIATIEF VANAF BRACHTEN. MIJN IDEALEN REIKTEN VERDER DAN HET SLIJTEN VAN MIJN TIJD ACHTER HET BURO, DE TELEFOON EN DE COMPUTER. IK BEN IN DE WIEG GELEGD VOOR HET KUNSTENAARSCHAP ZELF. DAARBIJ: GALERIES ZIJN ER GENOEG, HET WARE KUNSTENAARSINITIATIEF WORDT STEEDS ZELDZAMER. IK BEDOEL EEN PLEK WAAR GEÏNVESTEERD WORDT IN DE ONTWIKKELING VAN KUNSTENAARS. EEN PLEK DIE NIET ALLEEN MAAR OP ZOEK IS NAAR 'NAMEN', MAAR EEN VERANTWOORDELIJKHEID DRAAGT VOOR EEN ACHTERBAN. EEN PLEK DIE GEEN VOORWAARDEN STELT, MAAR ZE JUIST SCHEPT.

HET BELANGRIJKSTE DOEL VAN COALITIE WAS HET MAKEN VAN PRACHTIGE KUNST, DIT VOOROP. DAARBIJ: DE MANIER WAAROP.
IK VERBAASDE ME ER LAATST OVER WAAROM IK VANAF HET BEGIN VAN OCEAAN OP ÉÉN OF ANDERE MANIER ALTIJD OP ZOEK WAS NAAR DIALOOG, NAAR EEN KLANKBORD. IK VOND HET MAAR NIKS OM IN MIJN ATELIER AAN DINGEN TE WERKEN DIE GEEN DIREKTE FUNKTIE HADDEN, OM ALLEEN MAAR EEN BEETJE IN MIJN EIGEN GEDACHTENWERELDJE TE ZITTEN WROETEN. IK WILDE NAAR BUITEN MET HET SPUL, ZIEN WAT ER GEBEURT ALS JE MENSEN ERMEE KONFRONTEERT. OM JE ALS AANKOMEND KUNSTENAAR DOELEN TE KUNNEN STELLEN MOET JE EERST WETEN WIE JE BENT EN WAAR JE STAAT. OM DAAR ACHTER TE KOMEN MOET JE JE VERHOUDEN MET JE OMGEVING, COLLEGAE EN PUBLIEK, MET DE REALITEIT. EERST IS HET NATUURLIJK MOEILIJK OM DIE DIALOOG OP GANG TE BRENGEN. TOCH BLIJFT HET VOLGENS MIJ VAN LEVENSBELANG OM HET DAARNA OP GANG TE HOUDEN. DE KUNST MOET ZICH STEEDS BLIJVEN VERHOUDEN MET DE REALITEIT. EN IK DENK DAT HET DAAR NOG WEL EENS AAN SCHORT. VEELSTEVEEL MOOIE PLAATJES EN MOOIE PRAATJES.

HET WAS DE BEDOELING VAN COALITIE OM KUNSTENAARS UIT TE DAGEN. HOEVER KUN JE IN EEN SAMENWERKING GAAN ZONDER JEZELF TE BUITEN TE GAAN? KUN JE JEZELF WEL TE BUITEN GAAN? MIJN UITGANGSPUNT WAS NIET TE SNEL BIJ ELKAAR TE WILLEN KOMEN MAAR DE STRIJD JUIST OP TE VOEREN, DAAR HEB JE VEEL MEER AAN. KIJKEN TOT HOEVER JE KUNT GAAN. OP ZOEK NAAR JE GRENS. PROBEREN MEZELF EN DEGENE WAARMEE IK WERKTE TE DWINGEN TOT EEN ZO EXTREEM MOGELIJKE UITSPRAAK TE KOMEN.

DE ENE SAMENWERKING IS NATUURLIJK ANDERS DAN DE ANDERE. DE ENE IS OOK VEEL SPANNENDER ALS DE ANDERE. DIT GELDT VOOR COALITIE MAAR EIGENLIJK VOOR ELKE TENTOONSTELLING IN OCEAAN. STEEDS MOET IK PLAATSBEPALEN. WELKE ROL KAN IK BINNEN DIT GEHEEL SPELEN. SOMS LIJKT HET OF IK MIJN KUNSTENAARSCHAP BUITEN DE DEUR MOET ZETTEN EN SOMS IS MIJN

1E COALITIE

27 MAART

ZO WAS HET

VOOR DEZE TENTOONSTELLING HEEFT NIEK DE JONG DEAN BRANNAGAN UIT LONDEN UITGENODIGD NAAR ARNHEM TE KOMEN OM SAMEN AAN EEN TENTOONSTELLING TE WERKEN.
BRANNAGAN WERKTE VEEL MET HET BEGRIP ENGAGEMENT. ENGAGEMENT IS VERLOVING, EEN VERBINTENIS, MAAR OOK BETROKKENHEID BIJ MAATSCHAPPELIJKE ONTWIKKELINGEN. BRANNAGAN WAS ZEER GEÏNTERESSEERD IN DE GESCHIEDENIS VAN ARNHEM TIJDENS DE TWEEDE WERELDOORLOG. GEZAMENLIJK HEBBEN ZIJ EEN AANTAL HISTORISCHE PLEKKEN IN ARNHEM EN OMGEVING BEZOCHT. AL WERKEND ONTSTOND VANUIT DEZE ERVARINGEN EEN PERFORMANCE.
DE PERFORMANCE IS EEN REACTIE OP DE MANIER WAAROP DE GESCHIEDENIS HET VERLEDEN, DIE OP DE BEZOCHTE PLEKKEN NOG HEEL STERK VOELBAAR IS, INTERPRETEERT: ZO WAS HET (NIET).
HET PUBLIEK KOMT BINNEN IN EEN LEGE RUIMTE, NIEK DE JONG EN DEAN BRANNAGAN VOLGEN, BEIDEN IN HET ZWART GEKLEED. NIEK DOOPT EEN KWAST IN EEN EMMER DODEKOPVERF EN BEGINT LEVENSGROTE LETTERS OP DE MUUR TE KALKEN. DEAN ONTROLT INMIDDELS DE BRANDSLANG VAN OCEAAN. HIJ VOLGT DE VORM VAN DE LETTERS MET DE BRANDSPUIT. UITEINDELIJK WORDT DE ZIN 'ZO WAS HET' EVEN LEESBAAR OM HET VOLGENDE MOMENT ONZICHTBAAR TE VERDWIJNEN, DOOR EEN HARDE WATERSTRAAL UITGEWIST.

STone UTTERS

Spreads from a book about John Baskerville

WRITER/DESIGNER Phil Baines

PRINCIPAL TYPEFACES Monotype Baskerville, Grot

Self-published
Great Britain, 1992

The ENGLISH form o f seriffed, varied-weight (stressed) letter, t he norm to which the vernacular form gr avitates unless there is a good reason for it to resist, has a rich full shape, a vertical st ress, a nd a fairly sharp gradation from thick to thi n strokes; although it is less abrupt than in the characteristic French form. The differe n is nce of weight between strokes thick and thi often quite marked; the latter are virtually hairlines. R ich bracketted serifs terminate sharply, if not always a ctually to a point. The tails of the

Q

R

Apart from the work o f some of t he later W est Countr y tombston e carvers, t he vernacu lar traditio n

&

usually have great ver ve, the tail of the latt er being bowed, not st raight. Proportions te nd to be squarer and more regular than tho se of Roman forms. A, (p.9

The

The ENGLISH letter rance in 1754 when th writing master and ja *e* began producing his : although there can b signs were based on st eveloped by tombston irty years previously. T ans and **grotesques dense smoke of th tion round about 1** he first definitive form racteristics which now lish could be found in ms of early tombstone dates on houses, and e derived though they w ls.

Whether Bask erville was a cquainted w ith the 'rom ain du roi' it is imposs ible to say, but it is ne arly impossible that h e was not acquainted with Shelley's book: it is inconceivable that a ny professional writin g-master in the time Baskerville was teachi ng writing would not have known of the bo ok. And again, the let

ters

n has been little influe nced by ty pe designs. Indeed, th e influence has often b een very m uch the ot her way ro und. A, p.7

(The 'romain du roi' was cut by Gra ndjean for the exclusive use of th e Royal Printing Hou se in France, it was fir st used to print *Medail les sur les Principaux Ev enements du Regne-de-Lo uis le Grand* in 1702. The type certainly is a

break

made its official appea e printer, lettercutter, panner *John Baskervill* innovative letterforms e no doubt that his de yles which had been d e carvers twenty or th he clarendons, egypti **emerged from the e Industrial Revolu 800.** But long before t s appeared, many cha seem particularly Eng the primitive letterfor s, builders' marks and ven in Caslon's types, ere from Dutch mode A, p.10

Much-*I* think too much-h as been mad e of the writ ing masters' influence upon the tombstone c arvers. Probably the fi rst relevant master w as Cocker, whose spec imens were published around 1670; and fro m 1680 to 1741 hardl y a year passed witho ut other masters issui ng specimens. A, p.32

Amongst

Part history and part homage, the book explores John Baskerville's place in the English lettering tradition. The grid structure alludes to gravestones and rubbings but is used differently from page to page to express the subject matter.

ave endeavoured to produce a *Sett of Types* according to what I conce ived to be their true proportion. D

The general bril liance Basker ville's was influenced th e desi gns: w as mas

of types by copybook he himself a writing

ter. Their however far more to those actual forms r elate cl osely fo und on tombston es.

With generous curves, strongly differentiated thicks and th ins, long untapered but bracketted serifs, his types were fo llowed in 1769 by what is known today as *Fry's Baskerville* , (...). A,p.11

If he had merely imi tated Caslon, even if he had improved on hi m, there would have b een little to say, or to s peculate

Finally, after ma ny delays cause d by the desire of Baskerville t o have the book perfe ct, the Virgil went to press in 1757, after sev en years of careful, pa tient, persistent work upon it. It was a surp rise

peculate about; but he bandoned a] the Caslon tradition, and with Grandjean, Fourn ier a nd other type-cutters, began a new tradition which, in the eighte enth

rise to the literary wo rld. It was the first fi ne book printed in En gland. (...) Every part of the volume was in harmony with every o ther part. There was n o dissproportion. The book has been well sa id to be a landmark in the history of typogra phy. In looking at it t oday we wonder how it was done when it w as done. It seems as th ough the Birmingham artist had come befor e his time. E,p.39

enth c e ntury revo lutionised the appear ance of the printed pa ge. (...)

The revolution which Grandjean and Basker ville brought about w as in the relationship between the thick an d thin parts of a letter , in the position of th e thickest parts of the letter, and in the trea tment of the serifs. Al l these are minutiae; b ut type design is a ma tter of minutiae. Bask erville thickened the t hick parts of his roma n letter and made the thin parts thinner, giv ing them a sharper, s

mart s er appearance. (...) He pulled the thickest part of a curved letter away from the positio n of being 45° to the h orizontal and raised i t higher up the curve. (...) He made more of the serifs of the letters, m aking them more noti ceable by giving them a sharper, spiky quali ty. (...) These minute changes of detail would proba bly have gone unnotic ed (...) if it had not bee n for his

sup erb p r e

He had a const ant succession o f hot plates of copper ready, b etween which, a s soon as printed (...) the sheets w ere inserted. The wet was th us expelle d, the ink s et, and a g lossy surface p ut on all simu ltaneously. E,p.65

s W o r k

superior ink, and s mooth paper.

, Baskerville made o ther innovations in design. The type of th e late seventeenth cen tury was, on the whol e, rather compressed —whether for reasons of aesthetic appeal or economy it is difficult to say—but Baskervill e gave his letters a ro unded, open appeara nce. They take up a l ot of room. B,p.161

The type was cu t for him by Jo hn Handy (d.1 792) who, by t he time of Baskerville 's death, had worked for

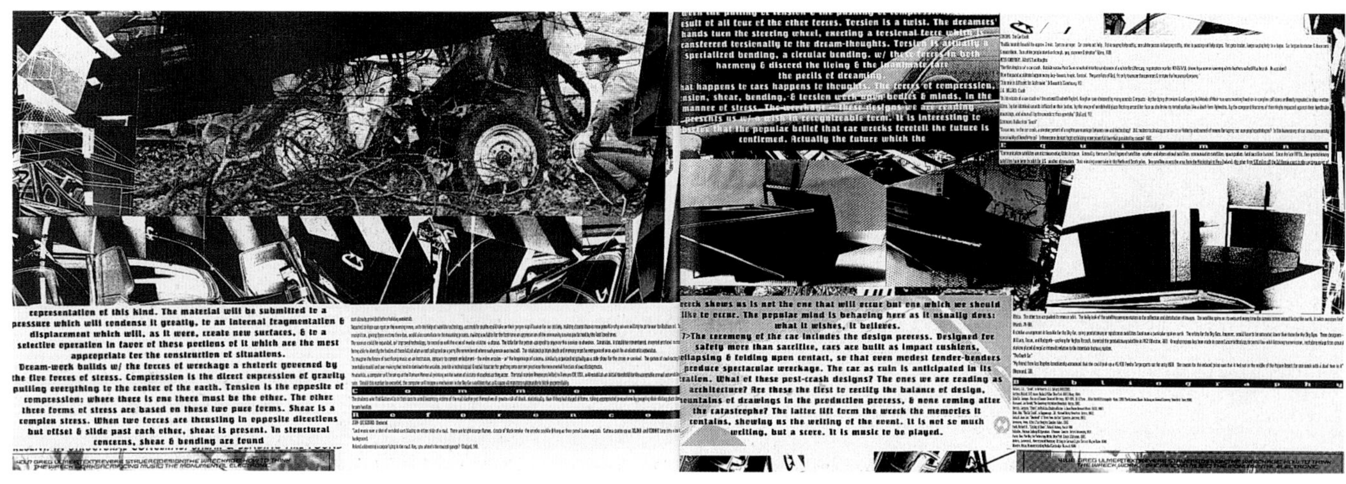

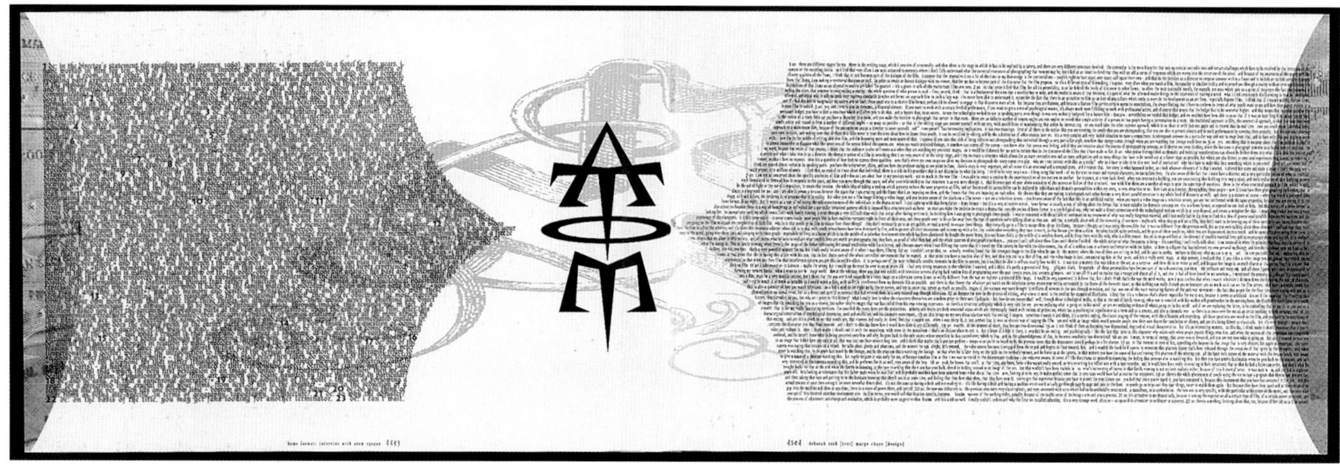

Semiotext(e) Architecture

Book spreads

EDITOR/DESIGNER Hraztan Zeitlian

DESIGNERS Reverb Struere, Margo Chase, David Carson, Barry Deck

CLIENT *Semiotext(e)*

USA, 1992

To begin: Two paintings by Attila Richard Lukacs– Call Michael and Like That which are a perfect simulacrum of the universe of sacrificial violence and cold seduction. 1. Sacrificial Meditations Call Michael is the painterly invocation of de Sade's Mass of the dead. Not traditional Catholic liturgy with its celebration of the sacrifice of Christ, but just the opposite. The "black mass" of the skinheads, where, just like in de Sade's imaginary kingdom of pleasure, all of the sacrificial signs are reversed. Candles for high mass stick out of asses, the eucharist is offered up by hands engaged in the pleasures of sadomasochism, hightops substitute for the traditional depictions of Christ's feet nailed to the cross, and even vestments are part of a sexual orgy which never ends. A fascinating, because so deeply disturbing, depiction then of a sacrificial burnout which always culminates in orgasmic excess. Does this mean that Lukacs has simply reversed the black mass, substituting the obsessive rituals of sadomasochism for the public rituals of the Catholic ceremonial ...

The large-format edition of the theoretical journal *Semiotext(e)* devoted to architecture achieved instant notoriety on its publication. Editor and project designer Hraztan Zeitlian enlisted a cast of American designers known for their experimental approaches to typography to construct a demandingly visual, not to say overloaded, examination of theory's role in architectural design.

Interference Poster 27/9/94 20:06 Row 1:2 Column 2:2
in the control room, surrounded by grey monitors, he is the nearly resident of omniscient vision
visual hallucinations.
Interference John Holden
ISBN No. 0-9523640-0-X
Published by
UMRAN PROJECTS 1994
£25
Distributed by
Cornerhouse Publications
70 Oxford Street Manchester
M1 5NH England
T 061 237 9662 F 061 236 7323
Gritty Typographics by Chris Ashworth
Text by Sean Cubitt
Design Assistance by David Smith
AJS I MAN F JH & Co.
Contact :
Invisible T 071 284 7882
Book. Poster. Postcard.

Interference

Book spreads

DESIGNERS Chris Ashworth, Neil Fletcher, Amanda Sissons, John Holden
PHOTOGRAPHER John Holden
PRINCIPAL TYPEFACES Custom-made for the project
CLIENT Ümran Projects

Great Britain, 1994

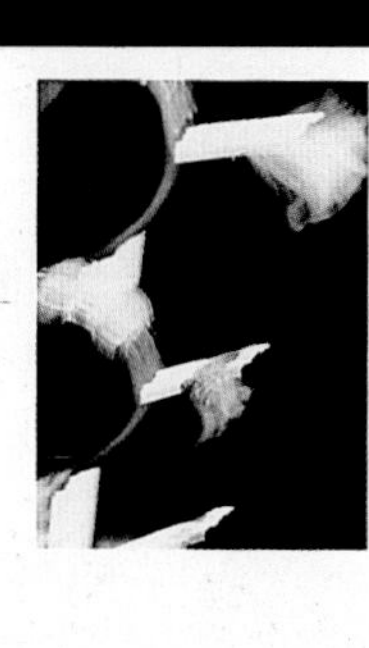

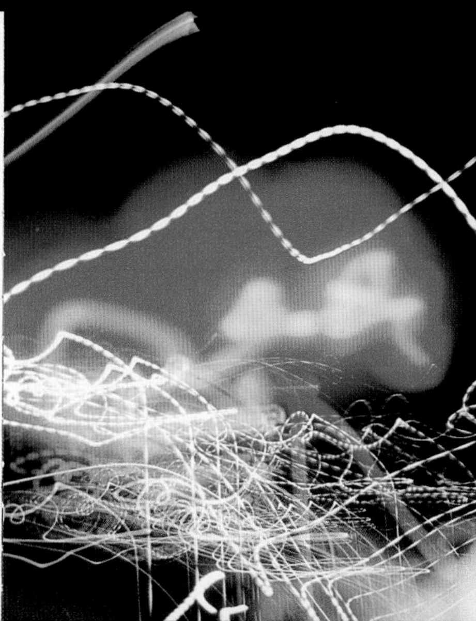

Interference is a photographic essay on surveillance in the city. In response to John Holden's lushly sinister images, the designers created typographic illustrations of technological

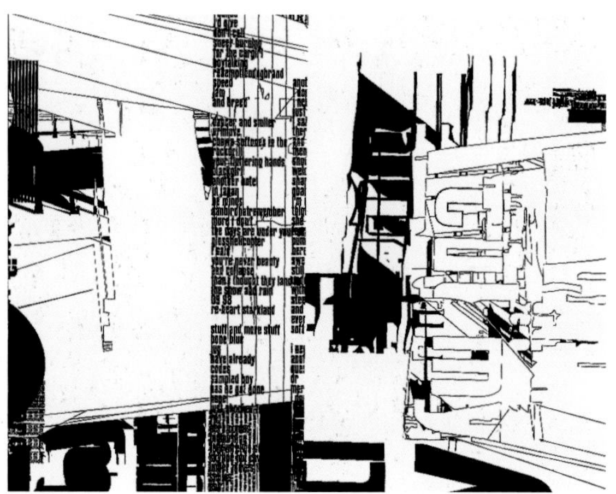

Mmm ... Skyscraper I Love You

Spreads from a typographic journal of New York

WRITERS/DESIGNERS John Warwicker, Karl Hyde

DESIGN COMPANY Tomato

PRINCIPAL TYPEFACES Compacta, Clarendon, Bureau Grotesque, Shelley

CLIENT Booth-Clibborn Editions

Great Britain, 1994

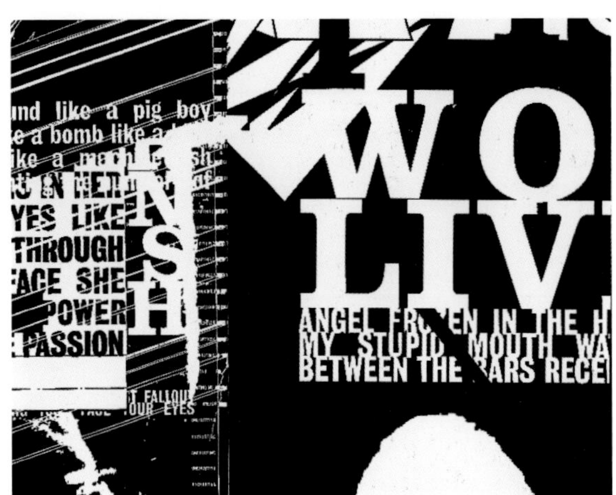

Randomly spliced together, the pages of *Skyscraper* record the sights, sounds, "crosstalk and chaos" of a journey through the streets of New York. Material was first developed during the recording of Underworld's album *dubnobasswithmyheadman* (two of the group, including Karl Hyde, are members of Tomato). Subsequently published, the project is closely related to the artist's book genre, except that it is available in ordinary bookshops.

Olyan teljesen átlagos reggel, ami egyszerre ígér mindent és semmit. Megpróbáltam felállni, de lábaim kifáradva a nagy rohanástól meg-megbicsaklottak. Elvergődtem a fürdőszobáig, ráültem a WC-re. 6 óra volt. Lassan agyamról felszállt a köd, és ahogy minden reggel, felrajzolódott előttem az

új nap

összes teendőivel.

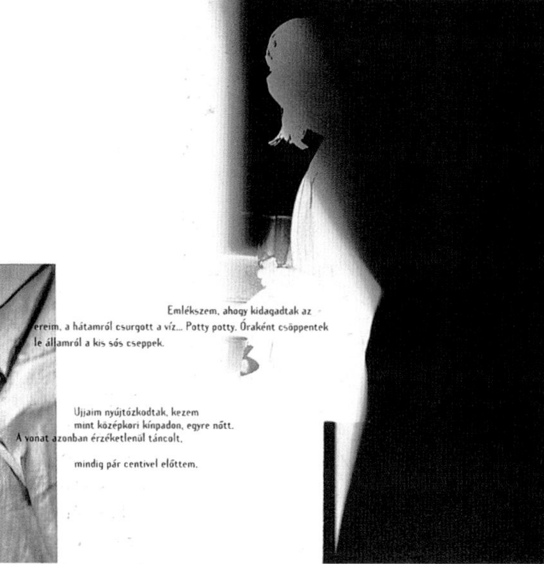

L e - m a - r a d t , l e - m a - r a d t , l e - m a - r a d t , l e - m a - r a d t

üvöltötte egy kegyetlen hang belülről. Egy kéz fehér lappal takarta le a tájat és az eget, a vonat képe egyre egyszerűsödött a szemem előtt. Sziluettjét mintha fekete ceruzával vagy tussal húzták volna át. Nem volt ott már más, csak a száguldozó monstrum és egy absztrakt fájó rohanás. Ez azonban kínjaimon nem enyhített és a feladat sem tűnt értelmetlenebbnek. A lényegen nem változtathat semmi, amikor az ember tudja, hogy rohannia kell, mert lemarad.

kell

Rövidülni Kezdet

Spreads from a literary booklet

DESIGNER	Zsolt Czakó
WRITER	Krisztina Somogyi
PRINCIPAL TYPEFACE	Template Gothic

Self-published
Hungary, 1995

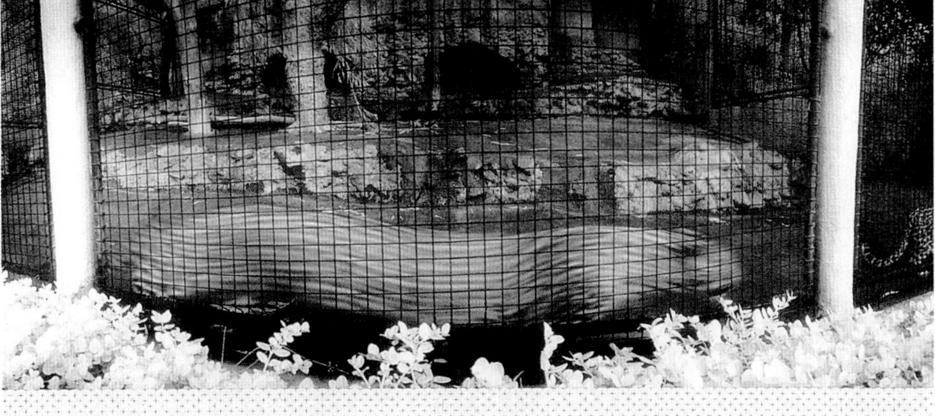

The Getty Center's 1996–97 Scholars and Seminars Program was dedicated to research on Los Angeles and Southern California. ReVerb's brief, for a poster to be displayed primarily at educational institutions, was to represent LA and its diverse cultures. The photographs compare two urban landscapes: a freeway system and a caged animal. The typography reinforces the visual language of the photography by mimicking the barriers and screens as well as the organic.

Perspectives on Los Angeles: Narratives, Images, History

Poster

DESIGNER Lisa Nugent
DESIGN COMPANY ReVerb
PHOTOGRAPHER Dennis Keeley
PRINCIPAL TYPEFACES Alternate Gothic, Scala Sans
CLIENT The Getty Center for the History of Art and the Humanities

USA, 1995

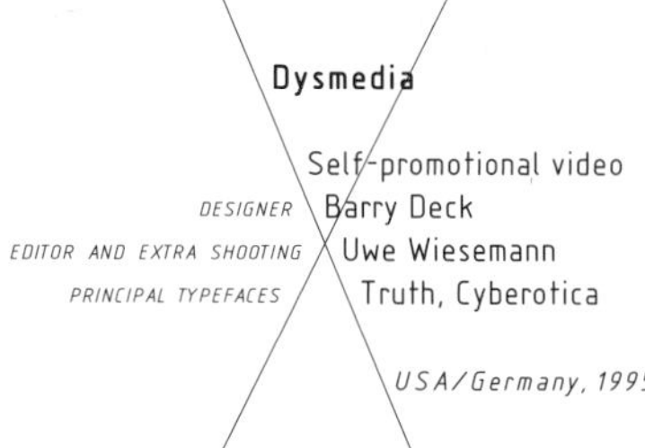

Dysmedia

Self-promotional video

DESIGNER Barry Deck

EDITOR AND EXTRA SHOOTING Uwe Wiesemann

PRINCIPAL TYPEFACES Truth, Cyberotica

USA/Germany, 1995

Born/Burn: Paper + Cathode

Exhibition poster

DESIGNER P. Scott Makela
DESIGN COMPANY Words and Pictures for Business and Culture
PHOTOGRAPHER Billy Phelps
PRINCIPAL TYPEFACES Officina, VAG Rounded, Trade Gothic, WAC Mittelschrift
CLIENT Kendall College of Art and Design

USA, 1995

National Portfolio Day 1992

Poster inviting prospective students to show their work

DESIGNER/PHOTOGRAPHER/ILLUSTRATOR Alexei Tylevich

PRINCIPAL TYPEFACES Blur, Template Gothic, custom-made for the project

CLIENT Minneapolis College of Art and Design

USA, 1992

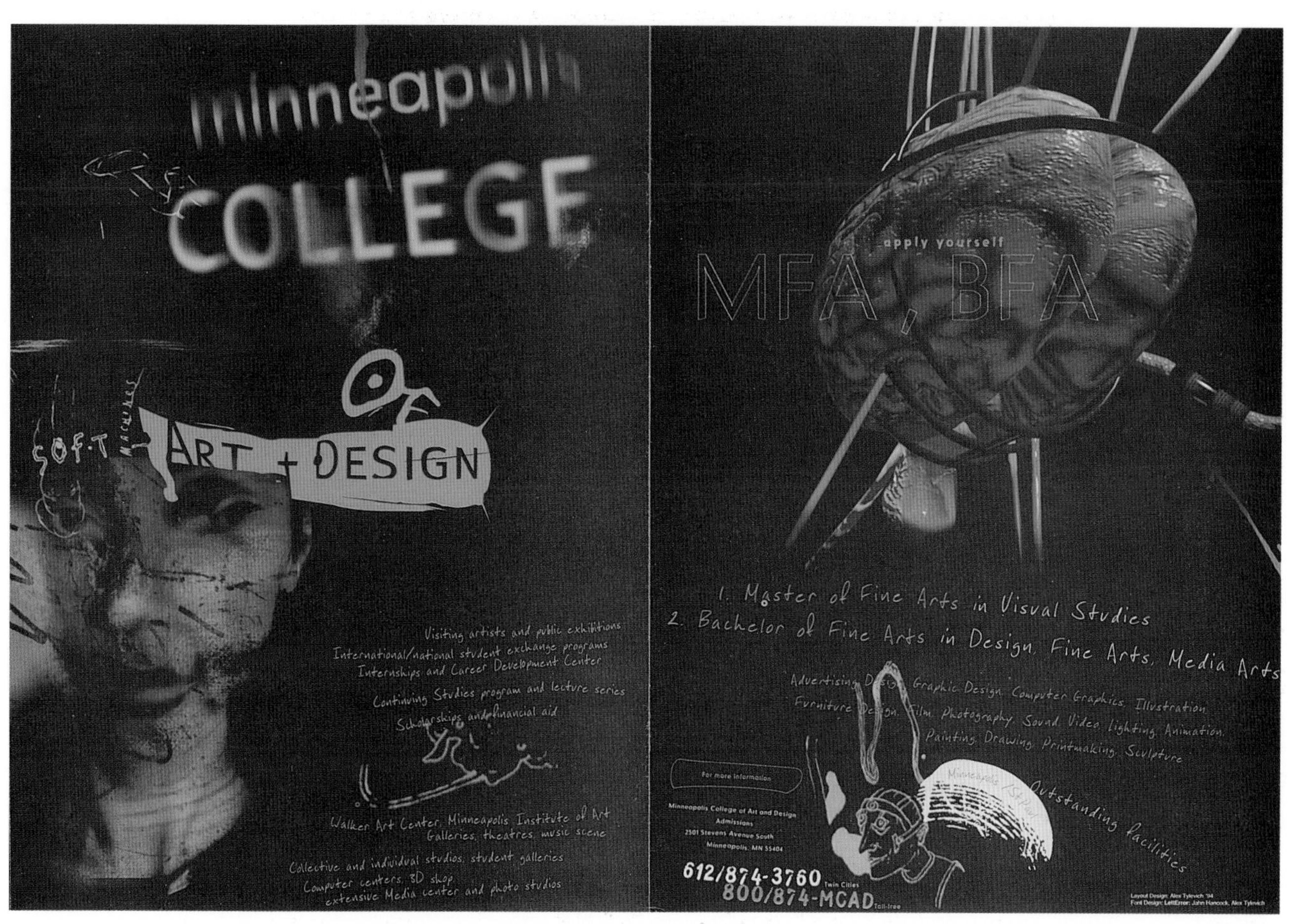

Magazine advertisement aimed at high school advisers and students

DESIGNER/ILLUSTRATOR / Alexei Tylevich

PRINCIPAL TYPEFACES / Calculus, Hancock, Stamp Gothic

CLIENT / Minneapolis College of Art and Design

USA, 1993

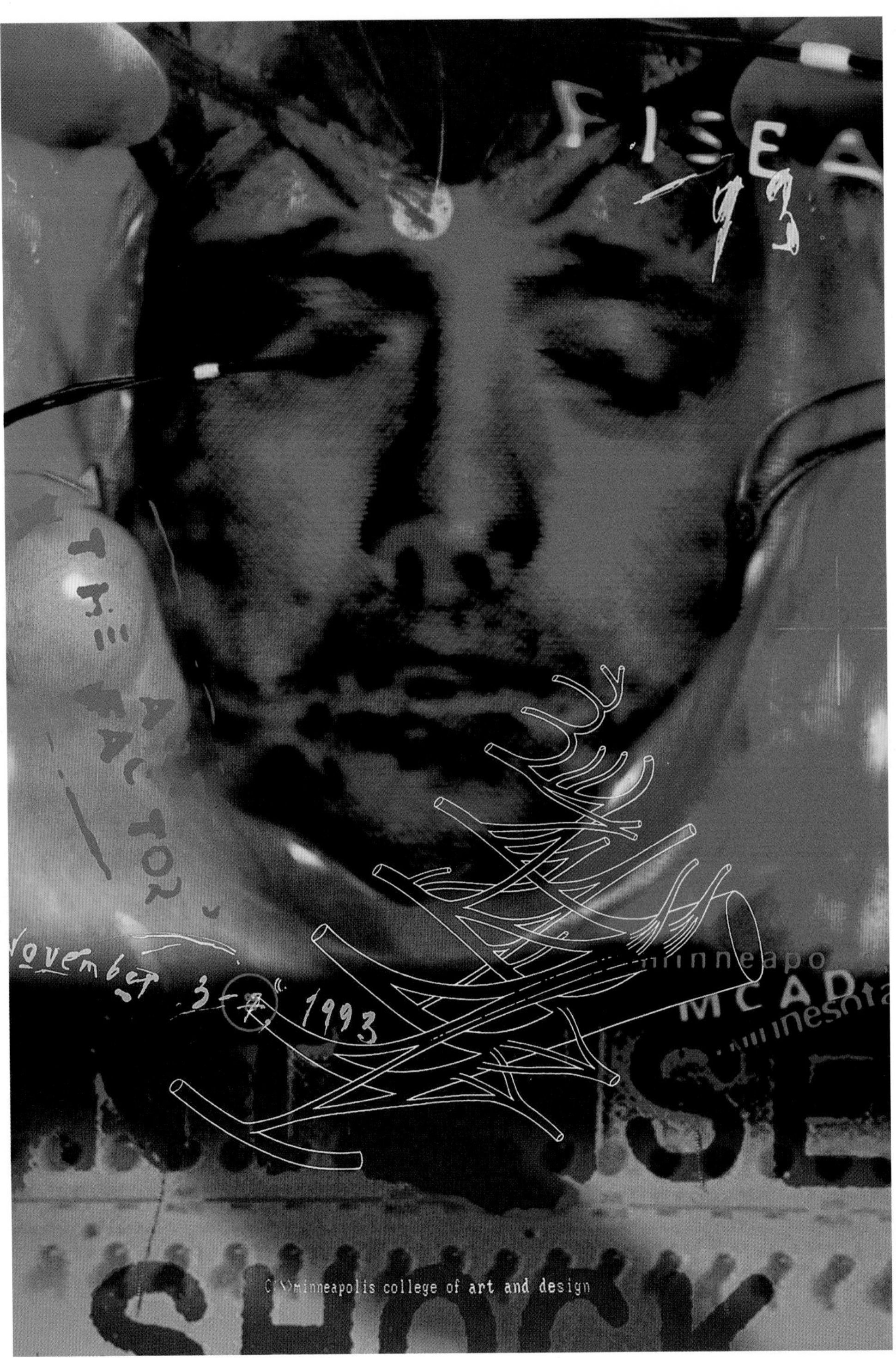

FISEA '93

Conference poster

DESIGNER/PHOTOGRAPHER/ILLUSTRATOR Alexei Tylevich

PRINCIPAL TYPEFACE Custom-made for the project

CLIENT Minneapolis College of Art and Design, International Symposium on Electronic Art

USA, 1993

Alexei Tylevich's poster for the Fourth International Symposium on Electronic Art expresses the contemporary merging of art, technology and the body as a brutal "cyborg icon" – an anonymous, wired, Christlike figure immersed in fluid tissue, through which the type itself seems to course like a new kind of informational blood.

Visual Language '94

Exhibition poster
DESIGNER/ILLUSTRATOR Alexei Tylevich
PRINCIPAL TYPEFACE Custom-made for the project
CLIENT Minneapolis College of Art and Design

USA, 1994

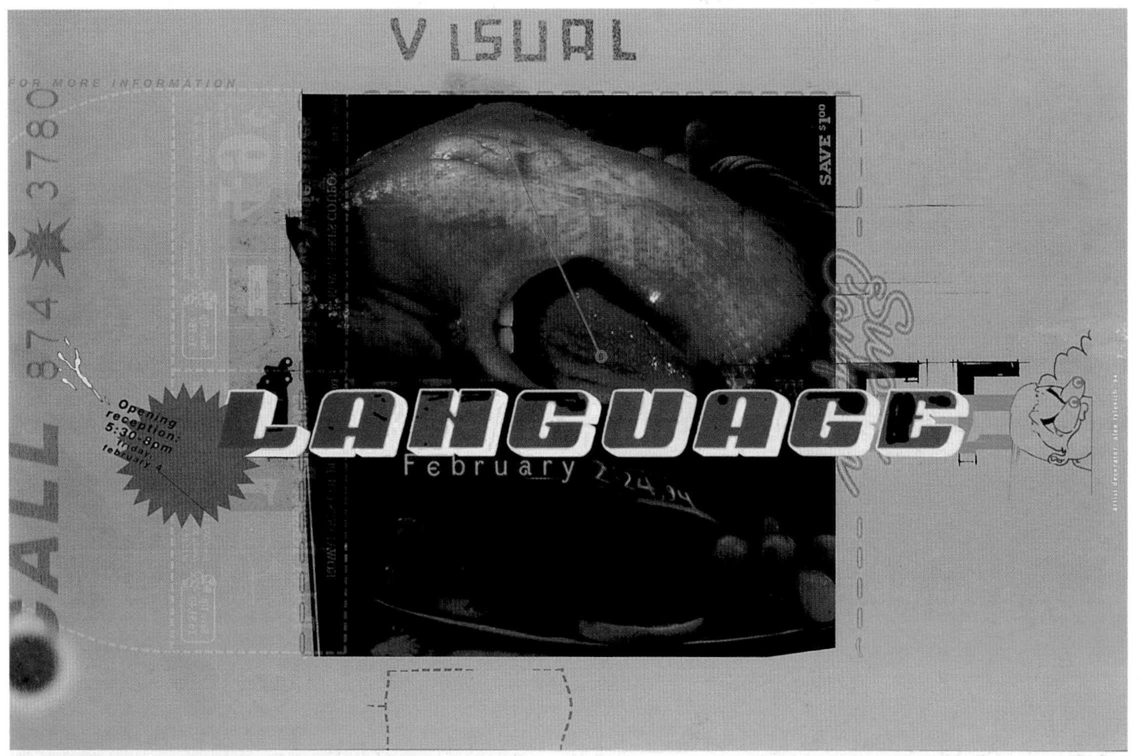

A MINNEAPOLIS COLLEGE OF ART AND DESIGN
a juried show of work representing Fine Arts, Media Arts and Design
ALL-STUDENT EXHIBITION.

Interdisciplinary Fellowships 1994

Catalogue

DESIGNER Jan Jancourt
DESIGN COMPANY Jancourt & Associates
PHOTOGRAPHER Warwick Green
PRINCIPAL TYPEFACES Franklin Gothic, Officina
CLIENT Intermedia Arts

USA, 1994

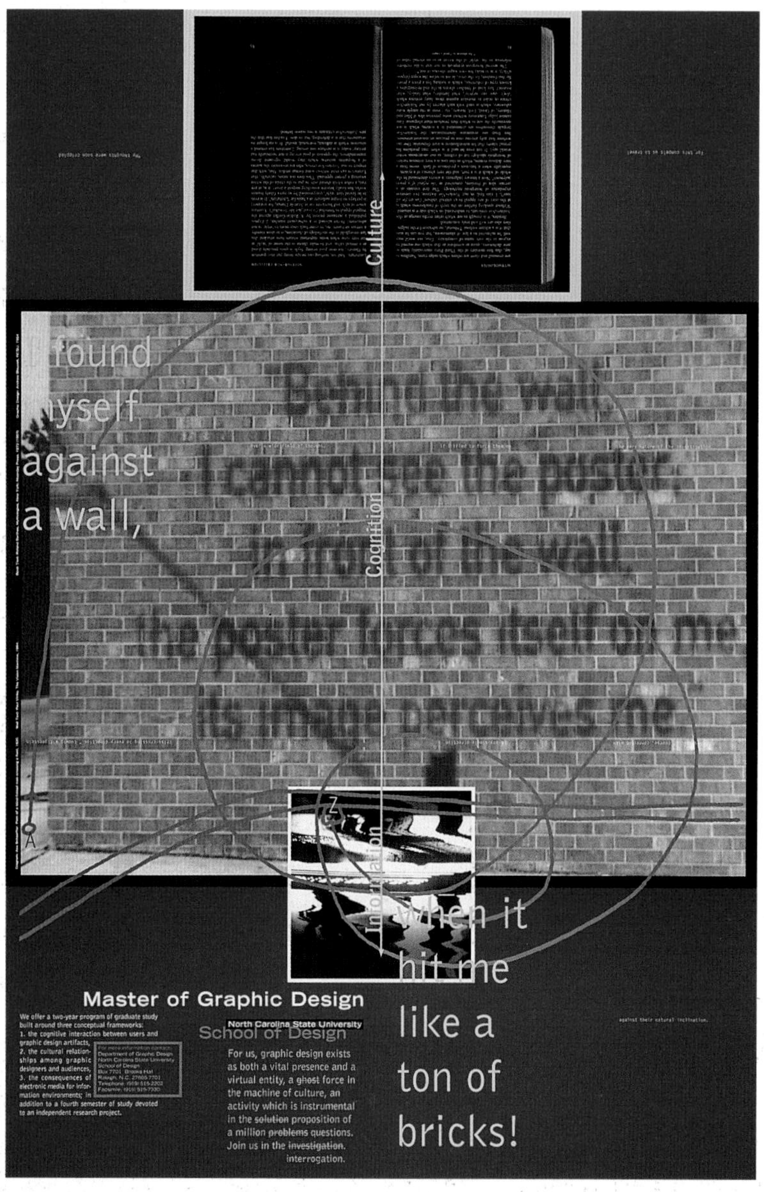

Conceptually, the poster/brochure uses a number of "texts" or "voices" to create a dialogue with the reader. Since the graphic design programme's philosophy is divided into three frameworks (cognitive interaction, cultural dynamics, information media environments), three images were chosen to represent these areas. The only proviso was that they should all relate to the statement "I found myself against a wall, when it hit me like a ton of bricks", intended to suggest the student's moments of frustration and discovery.

Master of Graphic Design Recruitment

Poster/brochure

DESIGNER/PHOTOGRAPHER Andrew Blauvelt
PRINCIPAL TYPEFACES Bell Gothic, Trade Gothic, Letter Gothic
CLIENT Department of Graphic Design, North Carolina State University

USA, 1995

Based on a TV image of US Speaker of the House Newt Gingrich, whose controversial history course was broadcast by satellite, the poster announces a symposium on the ways educators and artists can begin to counteract the political advances made by America's right wing, which now defines the agenda on cultural issues. The designers scanned in a copy of the standardised handwriting model for students ("the Basic Curriculum") but let the program's outline recognition software redefine their shapes according to its parameters.

Outside the Basic Curriculum: Redefining Education and Artistic Practice

Conference poster

DESIGNERS Andrew Blauvelt, Anne Burdick
PHOTOGRAPHER Anne Burdick
PRINCIPAL TYPEFACES Monospace 821, DIN Neuzeit Grotesk, Manuscript
CLIENT Atlanta College of Art Gallery

USA, 1995

Open House at Art Center

Poster

DESIGN DIRECTOR Rebeca Méndez
DESIGNERS Rebeca Méndez, Darin Beaman
DESIGN COMPANY Art Center College of Design
PHOTOGRAPHER Steven A. Heller
PRINCIPAL TYPEFACE Franklin Gothic
CLIENT Art Center College of Design

USA, 1993

Refuel, Refuge, Refugee, Refuse

Exhibition poster

DESIGNER Joan Dobkin
DESIGN COMPANY Joan Dobkin Design
VIDEO STILLS Gadi Gofbarg
PRINCIPAL TYPEFACE Franklin Gothic
CLIENT Seigfred Gallery, School of Art, Ohio University

USA, 1993

Text/Image

Promotional poster for a new course offered by the faculties of Design and Photography

DESIGNER Joan Dobkin
DESIGN COMPANY Joan Dobkin Design
PHOTOGRAPHER Patty Mitchell
PRINCIPAL TYPEFACE Franklin Gothic
CLIENT School of Art, Ohio University

USA, 1993

de Program 1992

Poster
DESIGNER/PHOTOGRAPHER Doug Kisor
PRINCIPAL TYPEFACE City
CLIENT Eastern Michigan University Design Department

USA, 1992

Doug Kisor's posters promoting European study programmes for American designers offer complex visual analogues of their educational intentions. Their aim is to model potentially life-changing experiences in ways that suggest the intellectual "layering" that is central to the programmes' approach. The 1992 poster addresses Dutch notions of the "modern" within the context of early 1990s design debates.

London/Rotterdam Design Program

Poster
DESIGNER/PHOTOGRAPHER Doug Kisor
PRINCIPAL TYPEFACES Interstate, One Iota
CLIENT Eastern Michigan University Design Department

USA, 1995

de Program 1994

Poster

DESIGNER/PHOTOGRAPHER Doug Kisor

PRINCIPAL TYPEFACE Industry

CLIENT Eastern Michigan University Design Departmen

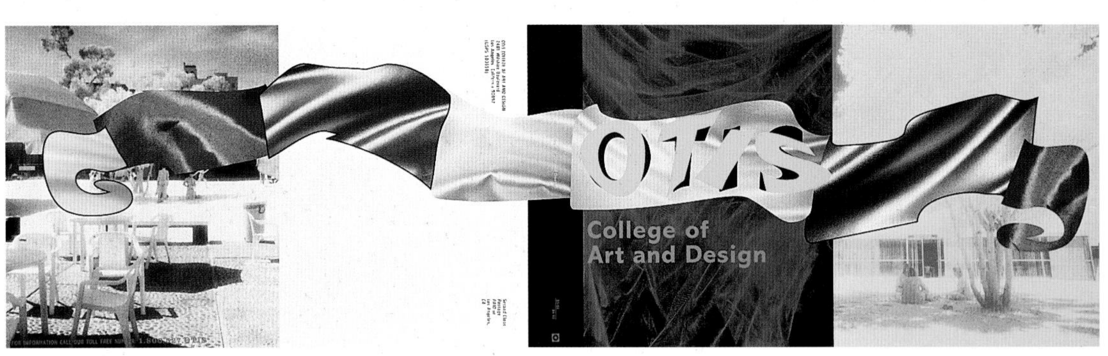

Otis College of Art and Design 93-94/94-95

Fold-out cover and catalogue spreads

DESIGNERS Lisa Nugent, Whitney Lowe, Somi Kim

DESIGN COMPANY ReVerb

PHOTOGRAPHER Dennis Keeley

PRINCIPAL TYPEFACES Clarendon, Steile Futura, Script

CLIENT Otis College of Art and Design

USA, 1993

The catalogue's theme, "set things in motion", is expressed through the use of shifting type and flowing, banner-inspired shapes. The density of type and image is intended to reflect the energy of campus activity.

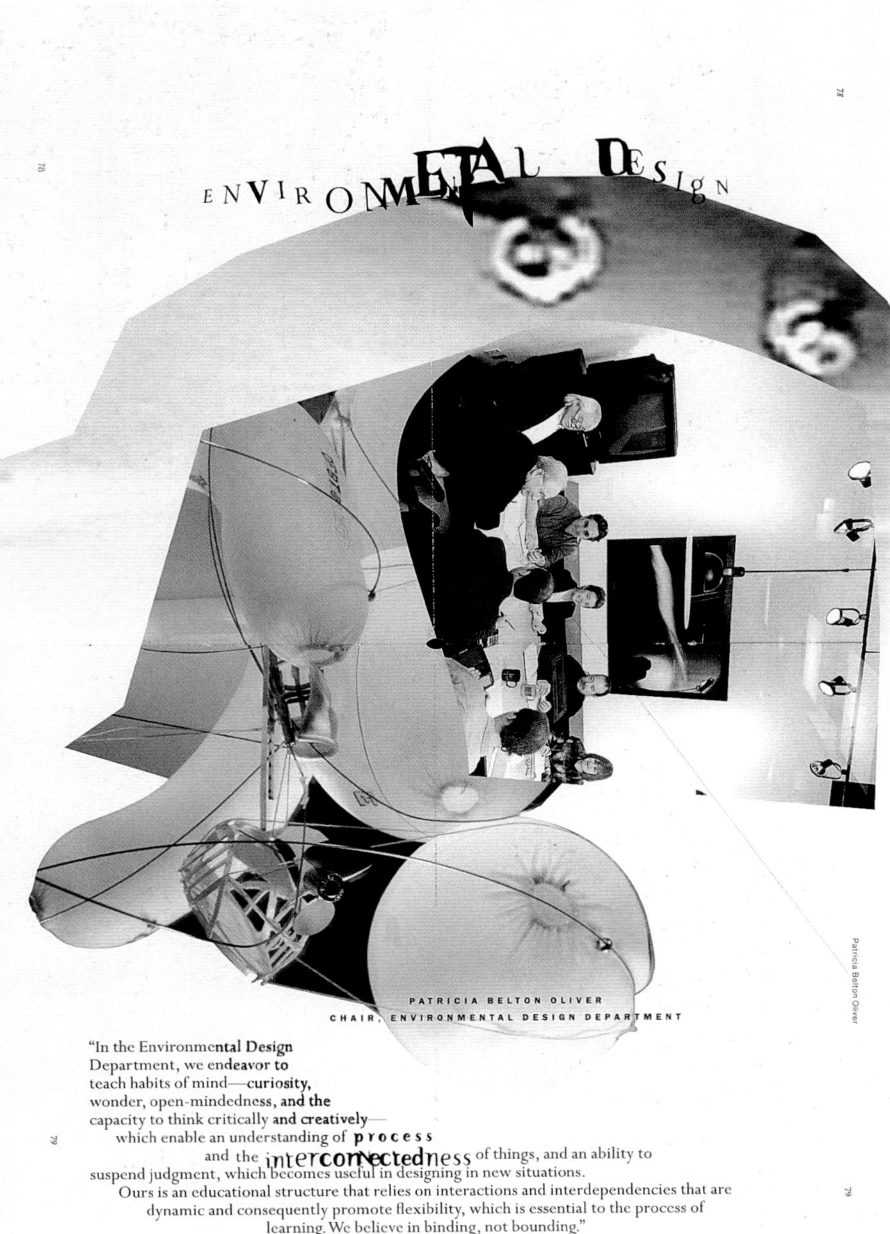

PATRICIA BELTON OLIVER
CHAIR, ENVIRONMENTAL DESIGN DEPARTMENT

"In the Environmental Design Department, we endeavor to teach habits of mind—**curiosity**, wonder, open-mindedness, **and the** capacity to think critically **and creatively**— which enable an understanding of **process** and the **interconnectedness** of things, and an ability to suspend judgment, which becomes useful in designing in new situations. Ours is an educational structure that relies on interactions and interdependencies that are dynamic and consequently promote flexibility, which is essential to the process of learning. We believe in binding, not bounding."

ENVIRONMENTAL DESIGN

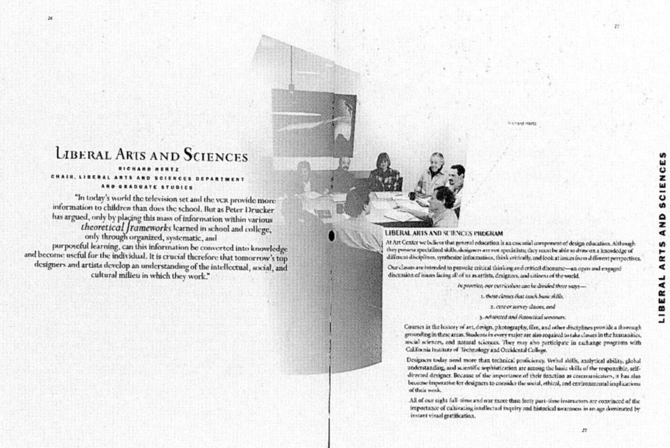

Art Center College of Design Catalog 1995-96

Catalogue spreads

DESIGN DIRECTOR Rebeca Méndez
DESIGNER Darin Beaman
ASSOCIATE DESIGNER Chris Haaga
PHOTOGRAPHER Steven A. Heller
PRINCIPAL TYPEFACES Perpetua, Minion, Franklin Gothic, Helvetica, Tema Cantante, Lip
CLIENT Art Center College of Design

USA, 1994

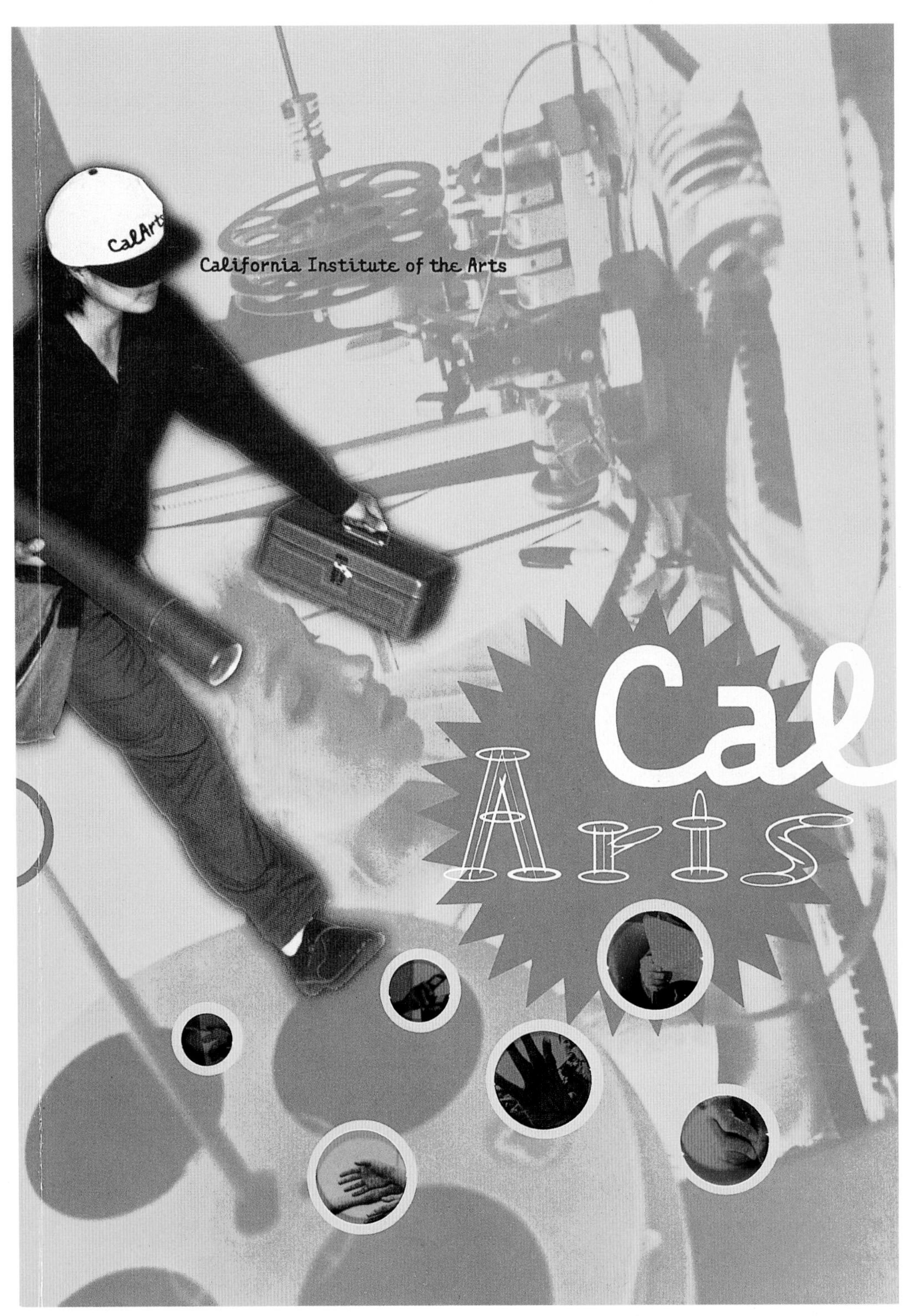

CalArts

Cover and spreads from California Institute of the Arts catalogue, 1995-97

DESIGNERS Somi Kim, Barbara Glauber
DESIGN COMPANIES ReVerb, Heavy Meta
PHOTOGRAPHERS Steven A. Gunther, Paula Riff, Raymond Hahn, Stephen Callis
PRINCIPAL TYPEFACES Arbitrary, Jot, One Iota, OutWest, Platelet, Tribulation, Wormwood
CLIENT California Institute of the Arts

USA, 1994

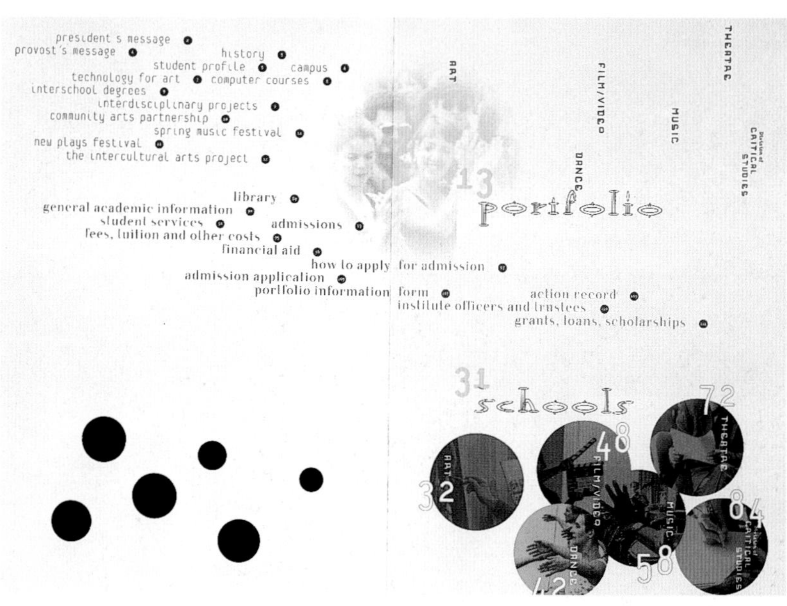
president's message
provost's message
history
student profile
campus
technology for art
computer courses
interschool degrees
interdisciplinary projects
community arts partnership
spring music festival
new plays festival
the intercultural arts project
library
general academic information
student services
admissions
fees, tuition and other costs
financial aid
how to apply for admission
admission application
portfolio information form
action record
institute officers and trustees
grants, loans, scholarships
ART
FILM/VIDEO
MUSIC
THEATRE
DANCE
13 portfolio
31 schools
32 ART
48 FILM/VIDEO
72 THEATRE
58 MUSIC
42 DANCE
84

This is a school of film and video makers—
the tool may be a camera, an optical printer or computer.
Any path the moving image has taken in the past
or might take in the future is kept open for exploration and use.
Since enthusiasm underlies all creative and imaginative
production, we welcome highly motivated students
with an independent and daring approach towards their discipline.
● We offer an education based on comprehensively designed and tested curricula
with a strong emphasis on artistic and intellectual boldness.
The courses, classes and workshops combine practical training in skills and craftsmanship with theoretical inquiry. Working and production progress in constant dialogue with aesthetic reflection and critical thinking. ● The Live Action program establishes a laboratory for innovative, unconventional forms of experimental, narrative and documentary film and video making. Experimental Animation and Character Animation, both internationally renowned programs, nourish individual development as well as the technical facility of their students. Joint computer labs provide facilities in these areas that keep pace with advancing technologies. ● The interschool program Directing for Theatre, Video and Cinema (offered in partnership with the School of Theatre) furnishes young directors and actors with fundamentals upon which they can rely in their future profession. ● To produce vivid and vigorous works of art, student film and video makers need an inspiring exchange with their colleagues, teachers and mentors. To shape, deepen and enrich their visions, the School relies on three interdependent assets: a body of curious, courageous, and challenging students with a critical power of judgment and ingenuity; an outstanding faculty with exemplary workmanship freely sharing their experience and knowledge; and an inventory of equipment, facilities and machinery which is continually renewed and upgraded. ● One factor which makes CalArts special is the presence of different arts in one setting. Students can benefit from this prolific contiguity, and for this reason we urge them to take courses in the disciplines of other Schools and to participate in all the activities and potentials the Institute provides. As the saying goes: someone who knows nothing but chemistry, doesn't know it well at all.
school of film/video

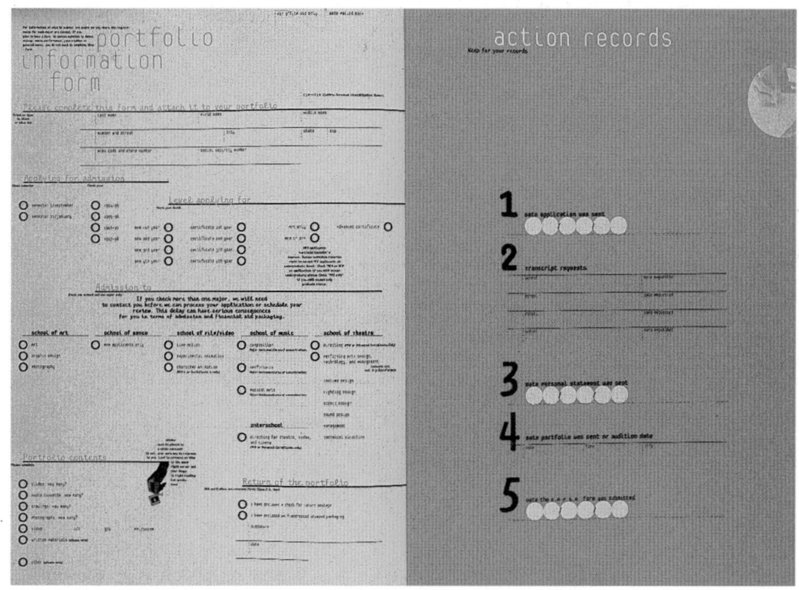
portfolio information form
action records
1
2
3
4
5

Flyer for a lecture by Edward Fella
DESIGNER Edward Fella
PRINCIPAL TYPEFACES By Fella's CalArts students
CLIENT Art Center College of Design

USA, 1995

Flyer for a lecture by Mike Fink
DESIGNER Edward Fella
PRINCIPAL TYPEFACE OutWest
CLIENT Graphic Design Program, California Institute of the Arts

USA, 1993

Edward Fella's lecture "announcements" are made, with some perversity, long after the event itself is over. As with his earlier Detroit Focus Gallery series, their defiantly non-digital, hand-lettered inventions refer not to the visiting artists and designers (except in the case of his own lectures) but to Fella's pet themes and predilections. The poster for graphic designer Mike Fink featuring Fella's typeface OutWest takes its cue from another historical "Miche Phinck", who in the early 1800s earned a wild west reputation as a brawler, braggart and marksman.

Flyer for a lecture by Edward Fella
DESIGNER Edward Fella
PRINCIPAL TYPEFACES Custom-made for the project, Cooper Black
CLIENT Central Michigan University Department of Art

USA, 1995

Flyer for a lecture by Nick Bell
DESIGNER Edward Fella
PRINCIPAL TYPEFACES Custom-made for the project
CLIENT Graphic Design Program, California Institute of the Arts

USA, 1994

Flyer for a lecture by Rebeca Méndez

DESIGNER Edward Fella

PRINCIPAL TYPEFACES Custom-made for the project

CLIENT Graphic Design Program, California Institute of the Arts

USA, 1993

Flyer for a lecture by Neville Brody

DESIGNER Edward Fella

PRINCIPAL TYPEFACES Peter Regular, Marsha Demi, Greg Bold, Jan Ultra, Cindy Light, Bobby Italic

CLIENT Graphic Design Program, California Institute of the Arts

USA, 1994

Errant Bodies

Cultural journal cover
DESIGNER Louise Sandhaus
PRINCIPAL TYPEFACES OutWest, Walbaum
CLIENT Brandon LaBelle

USA, 1994

Errant Bodies

Cultural journal cover
DESIGNER Louise Sandhaus
PRINCIPAL TYPEFACES Suburban, Monoline Script, Grotesque
CLIENT Brandon LaBelle, Louise Sandhaus

USA, 1994

Poster for a literary reading

DESIGNER Brian Schorn

DESIGN COMPANY ReVerb

PRINCIPAL TYPEFACES Letraset Sourcebook, Gill Sans

Self-published

USA, 1993

Surreal vol. 2 no. 3

Arts magazine cover
DESIGNER Brian Schorn
PRINCIPAL TYPEFACES Harting, Madrid, Onyx, Blackoak, Kaufmann
CLIENT *Surreal*

USA, 1994

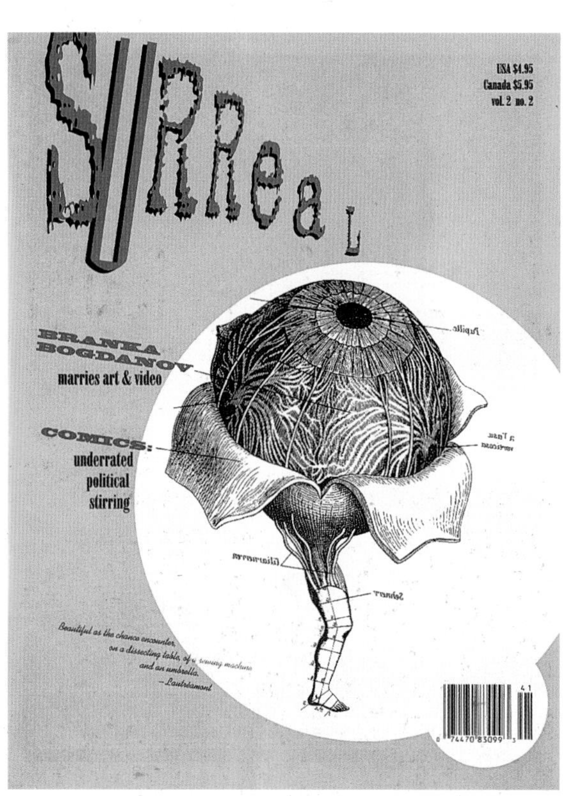

Surreal vol. 2 no. 2

Arts magazine cover
DESIGNER Brian Schorn
PRINCIPAL TYPEFACES Harting, Madrid, Technocrat, Shelley
CLIENT *Surreal*

USA, 1994

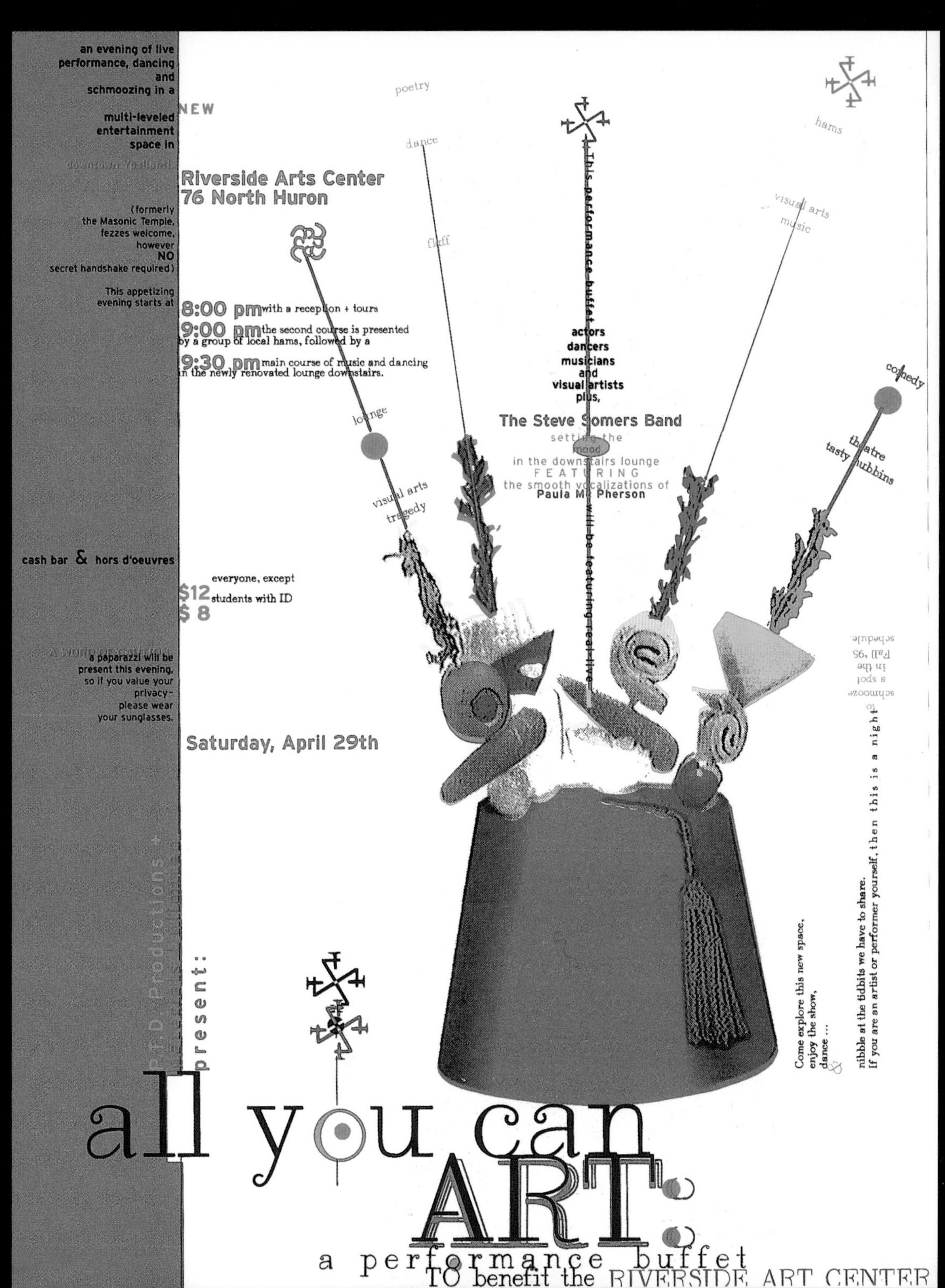

All You Can Art

Poster for a performance buffet

DESIGNERS/PHOTOGRAPHERS Susan LaPorte, George LaRou
DESIGN COMPANY Exquisite Corps
PRINCIPAL TYPEFACES Fancy Single, Interstate
CLIENT P.T.D. Productions

USA, 1995

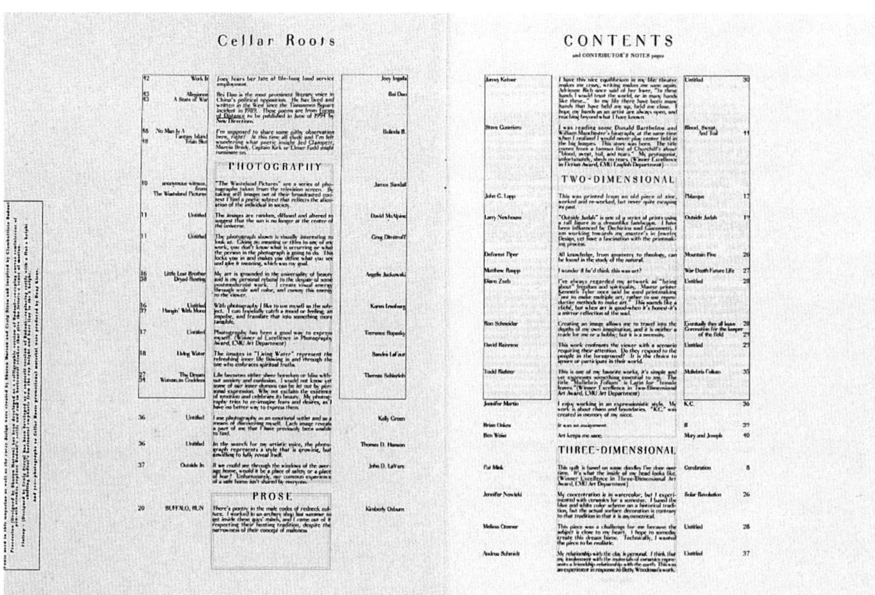

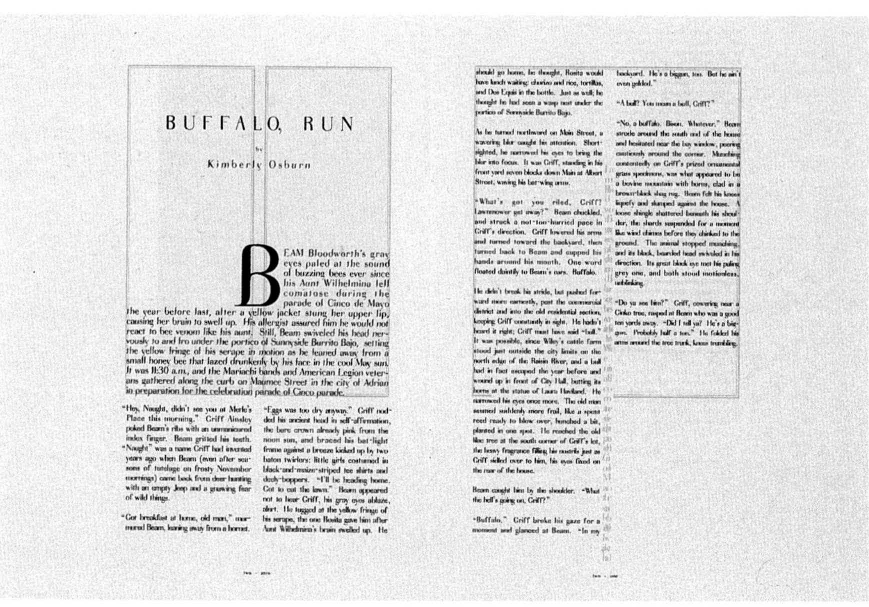

The 1994 *Cellar Roots* was designed as a response to conservative criticism of the design of previous issues. The golden mean, the Arts and Crafts movement and nuances found in letterpress were used as references and the typefaces Flattop and Procession also contain a historical reference to the structure and proportions of Bodoni. The satirical aim was to produce a "beautiful magazine" to showcase the art and literature department's work.

Cellar Roots

Cover and spreads from a magazine of literary and visual arts

FACULTY ADVISER	George LaRou
DESIGNERS	Craig Steen, Sharon Marson
DESIGN COMPANY	Eastern Michigan University Design Department
PRINCIPAL TYPEFACES	Flattop, Procession
CLIENT	Eastern Michigan University Student Media

USA, 1994

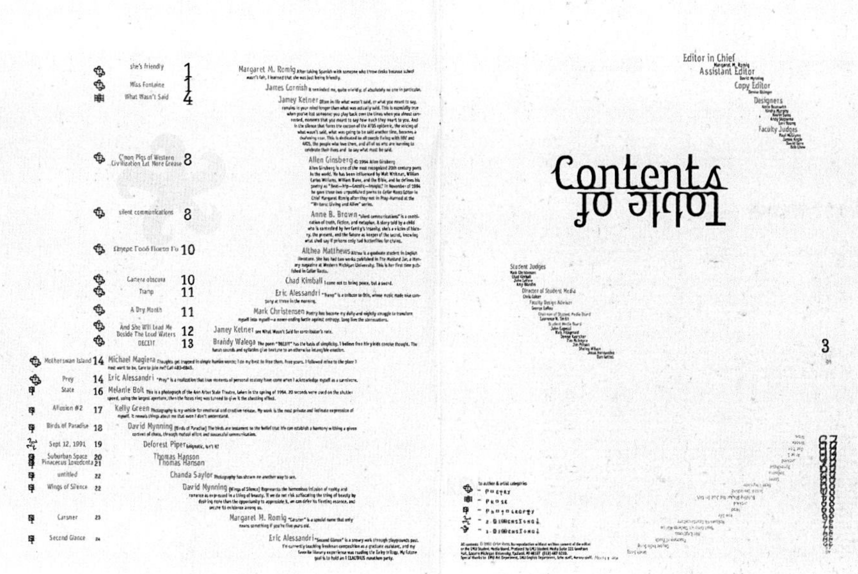

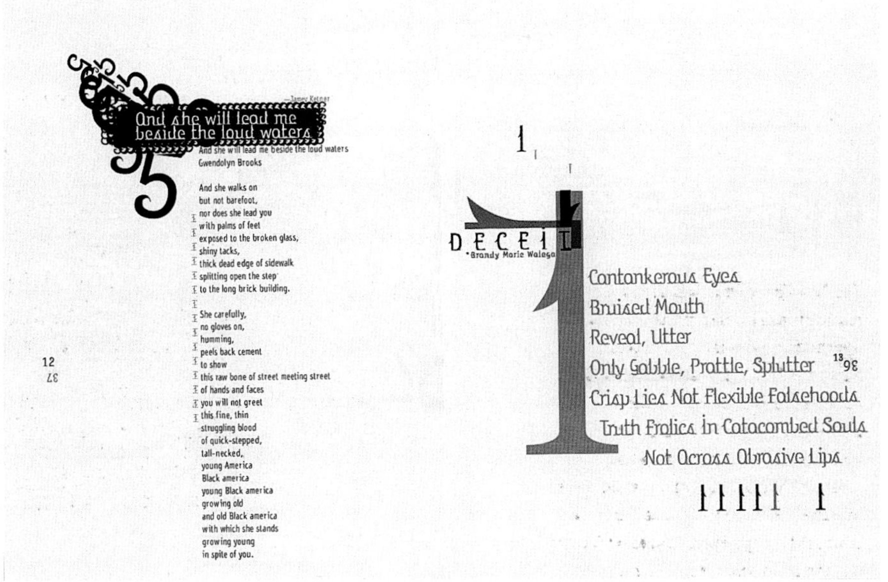

Cellar Roots

Cover and spreads from a magazine
of literary and visual arts

FACULTY ADVISER George LaRou

DESIGNERS Anne Bourselth, Kindra Murphy, Kevin Sams, Andy Slopsema, Lori Young

DESIGN COMPANY Eastern Michigan University Design Department

PRINCIPAL TYPEFACES Celly, Starlight

CLIENT Eastern Michigan University Student Media

USA, 1995

Dress Like the Boss

Poster

DESIGNER Elliott Peter Earls
DESIGN COMPANY The Apollo Program
PRINCIPAL TYPEFACE Helvetica

Self-published
USA, 1993

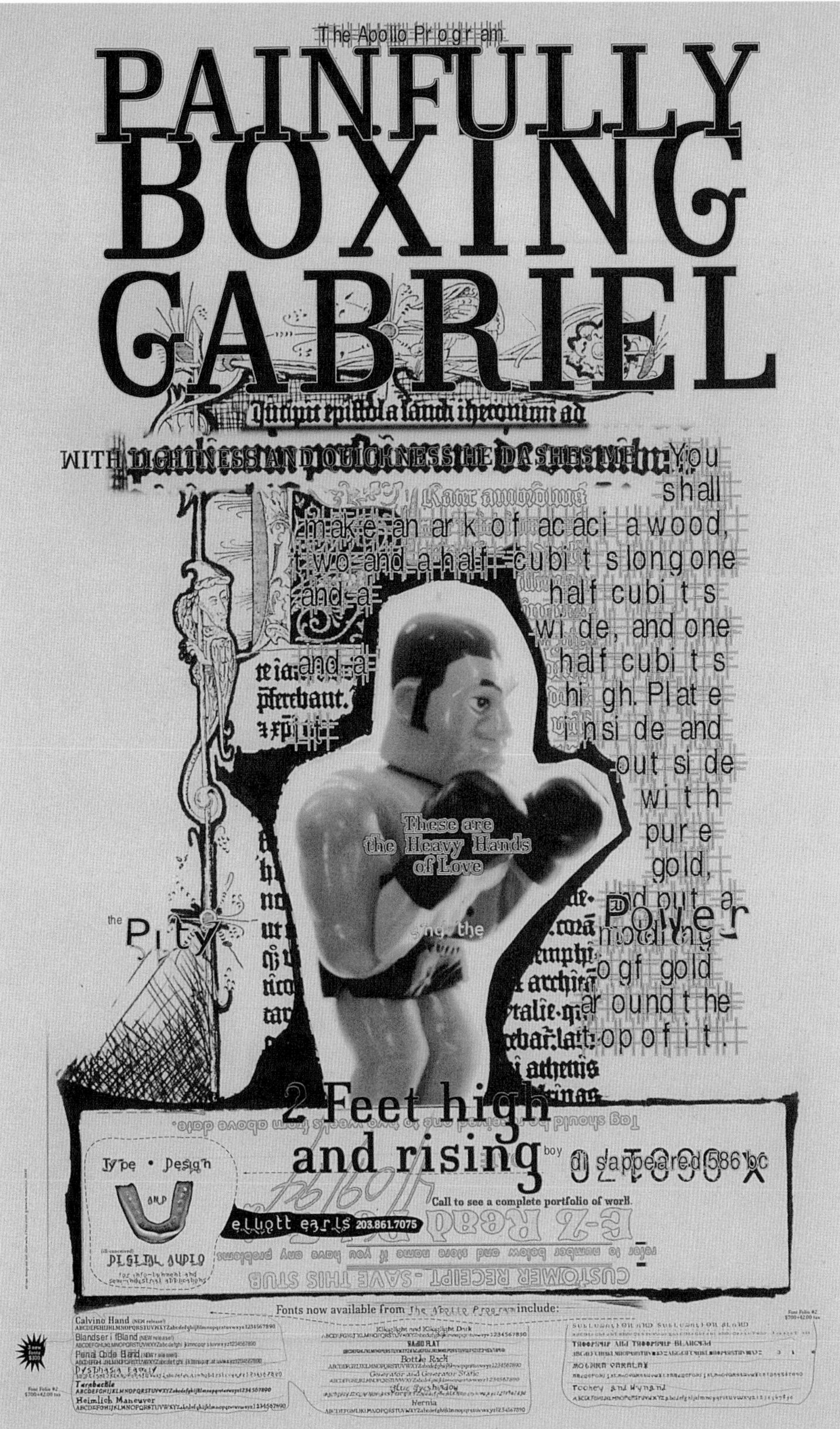

In his self-published posters, often designed to promote his own typefaces, Elliott Peter Earls poses fundamental questions about experimental design. "How do we restore radicality to the creative process when pluralism renders all work valid and no work taboo?" he asks. "How can we deal with the pervasive 'legitimation of the subversive'?" Earls's personal answer is the literary concept of defamiliarisation. With his bizarre typography he makes the familiar strange and the strange familiar and in the process questions the viewer's assumptions about "form" itself.

Painfully Boxing Gabriel

Poster

DESIGNER Elliott Peter Earls
DESIGN COMPANY The Apollo Program
PHOTOGRAPHER The Apollo Program
PRINCIPAL TYPEFACES Calvino Hand, Bland Serif Bland

Self-published
USA, 1995

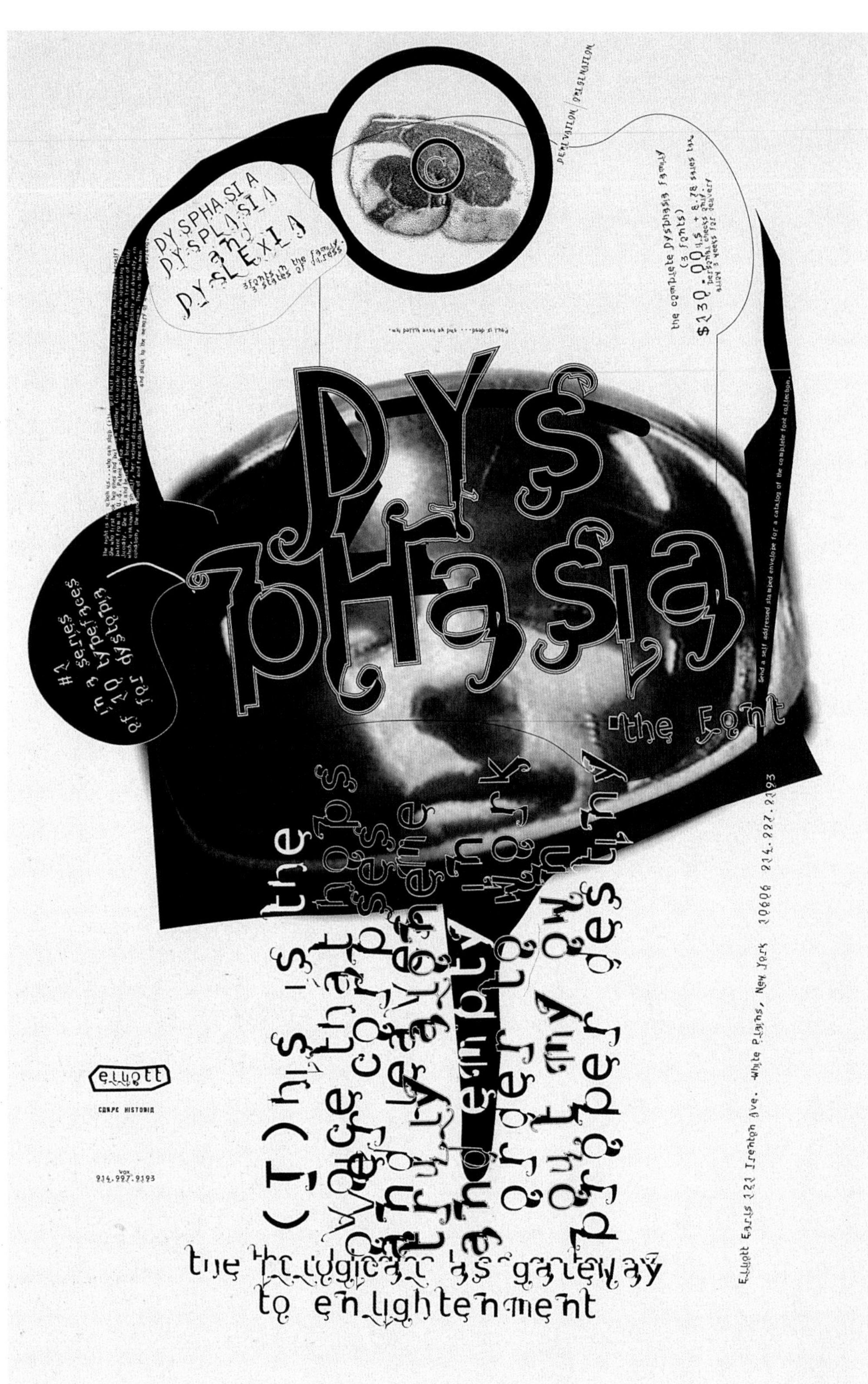

Dysphasia, Dysplasia, Dyslexia

Poster advertising three typefaces

DESIGNER Elliott Peter Earls

DESIGN COMPANY The Apollo Program

PHOTOGRAPHER The Apollo Program

PRINCIPAL TYPEFACES Dysphasia, Dysplasia, Dyslexia

Self-published

USA, 1995

The Conversion of Saint Paul

Poster
DESIGNER Elliott Peter Earls
DESIGN COMPANY The Apollo Program
PHOTOGRAPHER The Apollo Program
PRINCIPAL TYPEFACES Mothra Paralax, Toohey, Wynand

Self-published
USA, 1995

Now Time no. 3

Cover and contents spread from a magazine of social and cultural criticism

DESIGNERS Somi Kim, Whitney Lowe, Susan Parr, Lorraine Wild, Caryn Aono, Andrea Fella
DESIGN COMPANY ReVerb
ILLUSTRATOR Michael Greco
PRINCIPAL TYPEFACES Antique Olive, Souvenir
CLIENT A.R.T. Press

USA, 1993

Now Time is sponsored, in part, by the generosity of individuals who are interested in supporting art and culture in Los Angeles through a forum which allows for a wide diversity of voices from people working to free the Human Spirit!

All contributions to Now Time are tax deductible to the full extent of the law
Friends of Now Time will join our masthead and will be invited to our special events
Please make out your check to Art Resources Transfer, Inc., earmarked "Now Time."

$24	Subscriber
$100	Friend
$250	Friend
$500	Friend
$1000	Friend

Friends:
Neil Denari
Kwang-Sub and Sura Kim
Sinan and Graeme Revell

Tina Lhotsky a Light Teacher from the Andromeda Galaxy, landing on Venice Beach.

Contents:

NOW TIME is published by A.R.T. Press.

Spring Summer 1993

NOW TIME no. 3

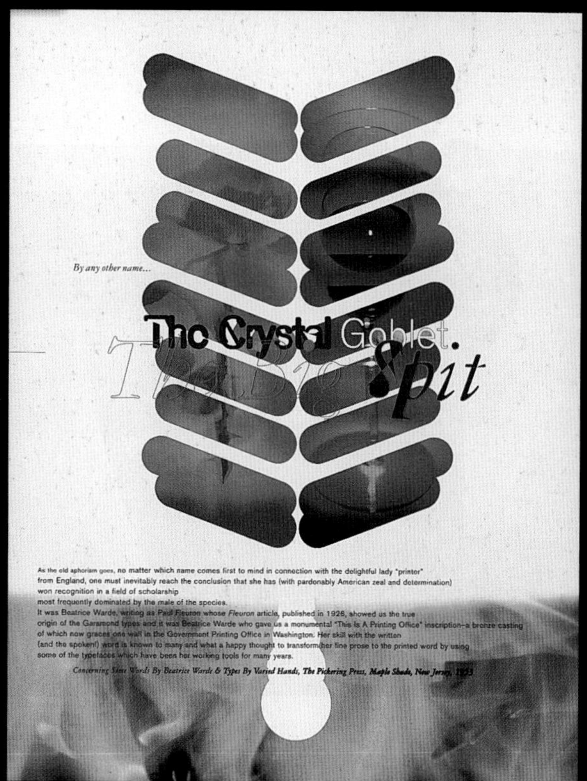

The Crystal Goblet.The Big Spit

Pages from a visual essay published in the promotion *Rethinking Design II: The Future of Print*

DESIGNER Allen Hori
EDITORS Michael Bierut, Emily Hayes
DESIGN COMPANY Bates Hori
PHOTOGRAPHERS Christopher Weil, Allen Hori
PRINCIPAL TYPEFACES Akzidenz Grotesk, Melior, Garamond
CLIENT Mohawk Paper Mills

USA, 1995

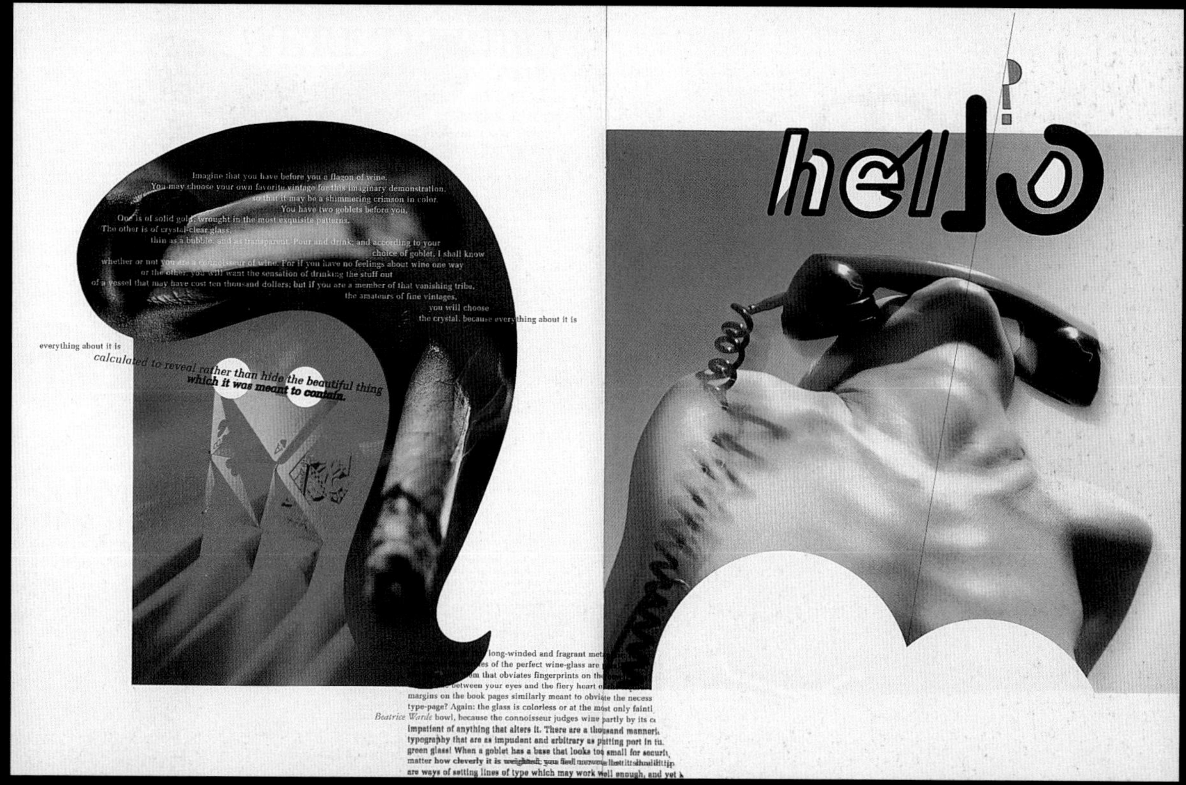

Fluxus Vivus

Poster for a month-long Fluxus festival

DESIGNERS/DIGITAL IMAGING	Rick Valicenti, Mark Rattlin
DESIGN COMPANY	Thirst
PRINCIPAL TYPEFACES	News Gothic, random video grabs
CLIENT	Arts Club of Chicago

USA, 1993

A House Swarming!

Pages from a poem/foreword for a journal of literature and art

DESIGNER/PHOTOGRAPHER	Stephen Farrell
WRITER	D. R. Heiniger
PRINCIPAL TYPEFACES	Beach Savage, Werkman Round, Evangelic, typewriter
CLIENT	*Private Arts*

USA, 1994

Fire at J. D. Salinger's House

Unpublished poetry promotion/font specimen poster

DESIGNER Stephen Farrell

WRITER Daniel X. O'Neil

PRINCIPAL TYPEFACE Tetsuo Organic

USA, 1993

Stephen Farrell's pieces with the poet Daniel X. O'Neil are rare but highly suggestive examples of close creative collaboration between designer and writer. In *Injured Child*, text and typeface illustrate each other. Both are commentaries on brokenness: the poem on the broken social and political structures of Europe, the typefaces – Farrell's own designs – on the fractured nature of communication in English.

Injured Child Flown to London

Limited edition print

DESIGNER/ILLUSTRATOR Stephen Farrell

WRITER Daniel X. O'Neil

PRINCIPAL TYPEFACES Entropy, Commonworld, Stamp Gothic

Self-published

USA, 1994

ALTHOUGH THE COMPUTER AIDS IN CERTAIN DESIGN TASKS, MUCH AS THE TECHNOLOGY OF LASERS AIDS THE SURGEON, ULTIMATELY THE HAND AND EYE ARE THE PRIMARY TOOLS.

TYPE BECOMES A SPECIMEN, NOT ON THE SHEET, BUT ON THE OPERATING TABLE. LETTERS CAN NOW BE EXPLORED AS LIVING, ORGANIC WONDERS BY REMOVING OLD TISSUES, TRANSPLANTING NEW ORGANS, OR GRAFTING NEW LIMBS

THE RESULTANT FORMS, SOMETIMES CURIOUS ANOMALIES, SOMETIMES FLORAL BEAUTIES, INEVITABLY CHALLENGE THE CONCEPTION OF TYPOGRAPHY TODAY.

BRIAN SCHORN

TYPOGRAPHY

IN THE INTERACTIVE WORLD IS FLUID,
AND BOTH THE

TEXT AND THE DESIGN

CAN BE OPEN TO

RE-INTERPRETATION & RE-CONFIGURATION

BY THE

READER/USER.

THE OPTIONS MAY EXIST AS VARIABLES CREATED BY THE

AUTHOR/DESIGNER,

OR DESIGN MAY BE ALLOWED TO ROAM FREE, OPEN TO

CROSS-FERTILIZATION.

MICHAEL WORTHINGTON

THE DOMINANT AND REPRESSIVE ROLE OF THE TEXT OVER THE IMAGE IS BREAKING DOWN. AS THE DESIRE TO FIX IMAGE CONNOTATION IS REPLACED BY A MORE INCLUSIVE AND OPEN UNDERSTANDING, THE BOUNDARIES BETWEEN WORDS, SOUNDS AND IMAGES DISSOLVE INTO THE ELECTRONIC FLOW.

JEFFERY KEEDY

student

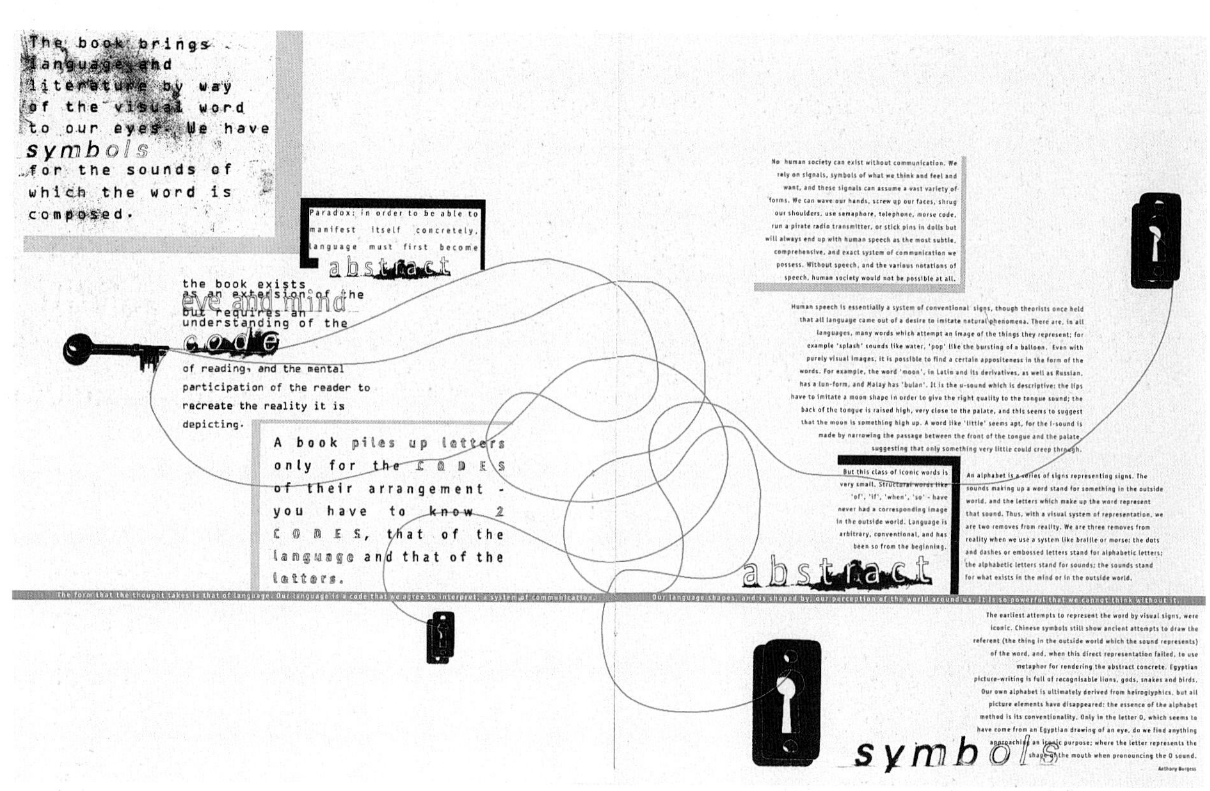

The book brings language and literature by way of the visual word to our eyes. We have symbols for the sounds of which the word is composed.

Paradox: in order to be able to manifest itself concretely, language must first become abstract

the book exists as an extension of the eye and mind but requires an understanding of the code of reading, and the mental participation of the reader to recreate the reality it is depicting.

A book piles up letters only for the CODES of their arrangement - you have to know 2 CODES, that of the language and that of the letters.

The form that the thought takes is that of language. Our language is a code that we agree to interpret, a system of communication.

No human society can exist without communication. We rely on signals, symbols of what we think and feel and want, and these signals can assume a vast variety of forms. We can wave our hands, screw up our faces, shrug our shoulders, use semaphore, telephone, morse code, run a pirate radio transmitter, or stick pins in dolls but will always end up with human speech as the most subtle, comprehensive, and exact system of communication we possess. Without speech, and the various notations of speech, human society would not be possible at all.

Human speech is essentially a system of conventional signs, though theorists once held that all language came out of a desire to imitate natural phenomena. There are, in all languages, many words which attempt an image of the things they represent; for example 'splash' sounds like water, 'pop' like the bursting of a balloon. Even with purely visual images, it is possible to find a certain appositeness in the form of the words. For example, the word 'moon', in Latin and its derivatives, as well as Russian, has a lun-form, and Malay has 'bulan'. It is the u-sound which is descriptive: the lips have to imitate a moon shape in order to give the right quality to the tongue sound; the back of the tongue is raised high, very close to the palate, and this seems to suggest that the moon is something high up. A word like 'little' seems apt, for the i-sound is made by narrowing the passage between the front of the tongue and the palate, suggesting that only something very little could creep through.

But this class of iconic words is very small. Structural words like 'of', 'if', 'when', 'so' - have never had a corresponding image in the outside world. Language is arbitrary, conventional, and has been so from the beginning.

An alphabet is a series of signs representing signs. The sounds making up a word stand for something in the outside world, and the letters which make up the word represent that sound. Thus, with a visual system of representation, we are two removes from reality. We are three removes from reality when we use a system like braille or morse: the dots and dashes or embossed letters stand for alphabetic letters; the alphabetic letters stand for sounds; the sounds stand for what exists in the mind or in the outside world.

abstract

Our language shapes, and is shaped by, our perception of the world around us. It is so powerful that we cannot think without it.

The earliest attempts to represent the word by visual signs, were iconic. Chinese symbols still show ancient attempts to draw the referent (the thing in the outside world which the sound represents) of the word, and, when this direct representation failed, to use metaphor for rendering the abstract concrete. Egyptian picture-writing is full of recognisable lions, gods, snakes and birds. Our own alphabet is ultimately derived from heiroglyphics, but all picture elements have disappeared: the essence of the alphabet method is its conventionality. Only in the letter O, which seems to have come from an Egyptian drawing of an eye, do we find anything approaching an iconic purpose; where the letter represents the shape of the mouth when pronouncing the O sound.

Anthony Burgess

symbols

The Magazine of the Book

Magazine spreads presenting research from the project "When is a book not a book?"

DESIGNERS Vivienne Cherry, Seònaid MacKay

PRINCIPAL TYPEFACES Custom-made for the project

Royal College of Art
Great Britain, 1995

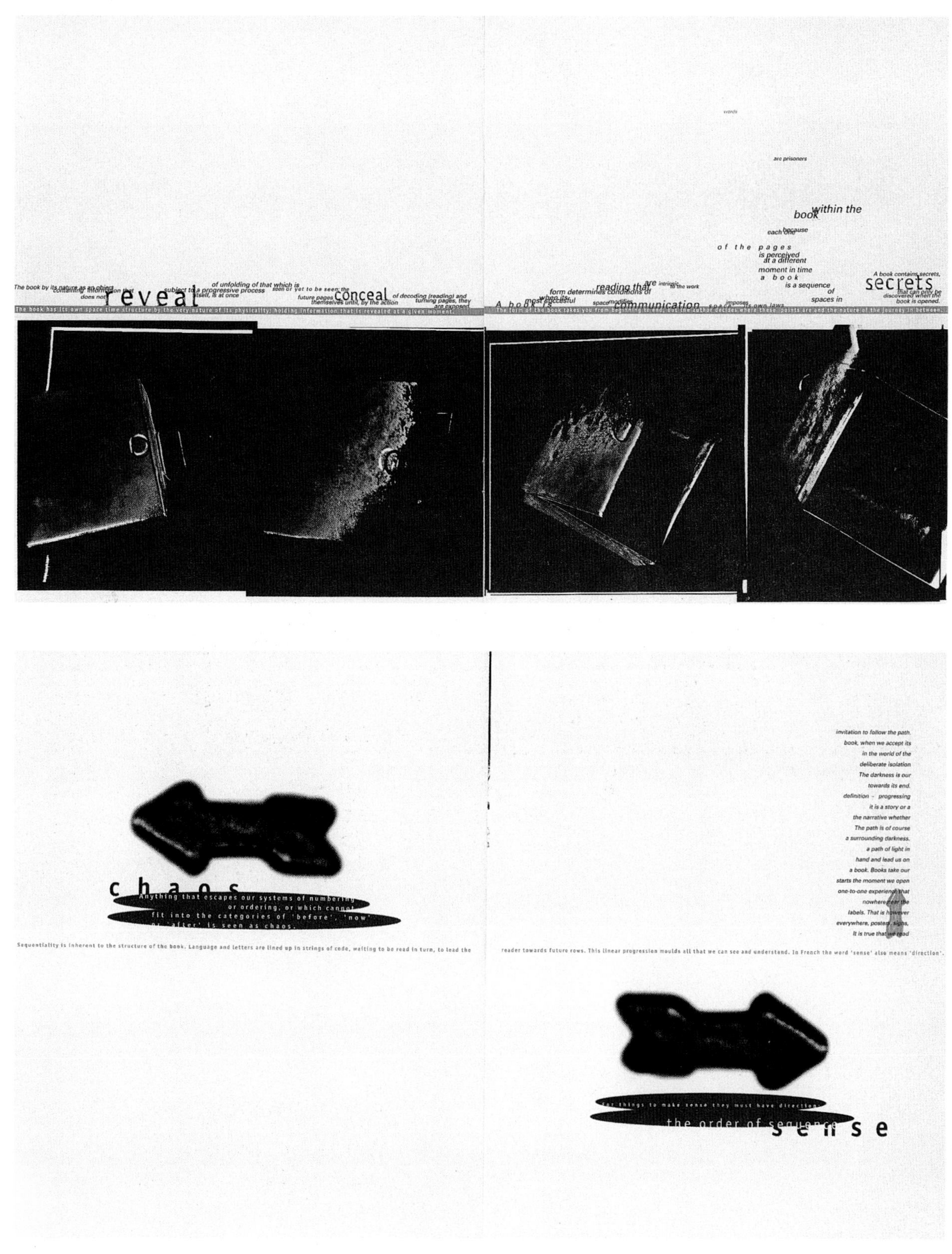
The book by its nature as an object containing information that does not
reveal
subject to a progressive process itself, is at once
of unfolding of that which is
seen or yet to be seen; the future pages themselves until, by the action
conceal
of decoding (reading) and turning pages, they are exposed.
The book has its own space time structure by the very nature of its physicality; holding information that is revealed at a given moment.
book within the
each one because
of the pages
is perceived
at a different
moment in time
a book
is a sequence
of
spaces in
A book contains secrets,
secrets
that can only be
discovered when the
book is opened.
form determines conditions of
reading that
are intrinsic to the work
communication
imposes its own laws
The form of the book takes you from beginning to end, but the author decides where these points are and the nature of the journey in between.
chaos
Anything that escapes our systems of numbering or ordering, or which cannot fit into the categories of 'before', 'now' or 'after' is seen as chaos.
Sequentiality is inherent to the structure of the book. Language and letters are lined up in strings of code, waiting to be read in turn, to lead the
reader towards future rows. This linear progression moulds all that we can see and understand. In French the word 'sense' also means 'direction'.
invitation to follow the path.
book, when we accept its
in the world of the
deliberate isolation
The darkness is our
towards its end.
definition - progressing
it is a story or a
the narrative whether
The path is of course
a surrounding darkness.
a path of light in
hand and lead us on
a book. Books take our
starts the moment we open
one-to-one experience that
nowhere near the
labels. That is however
everywhere, posters, signs,
It is true that we read
the order of sequence
sense

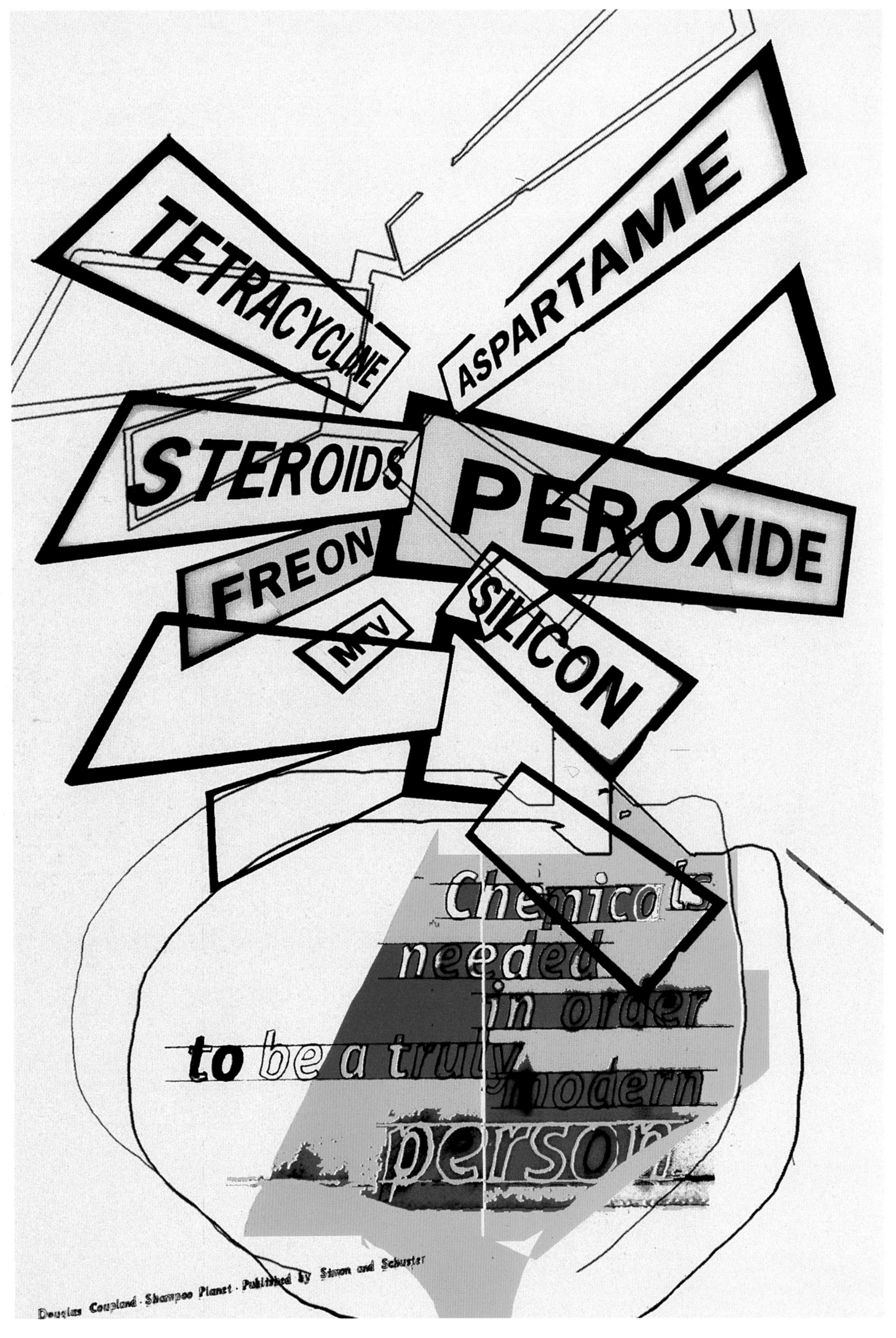
TETRACYCLINE
ASPARTAME
STEROIDS
PEROXIDE
FREON
SILICON
MTV
Chemicals
needed
in order
to be a truly
modern
person
Douglas Coupland · Shampoo Planet · Published by Simon and Schuster

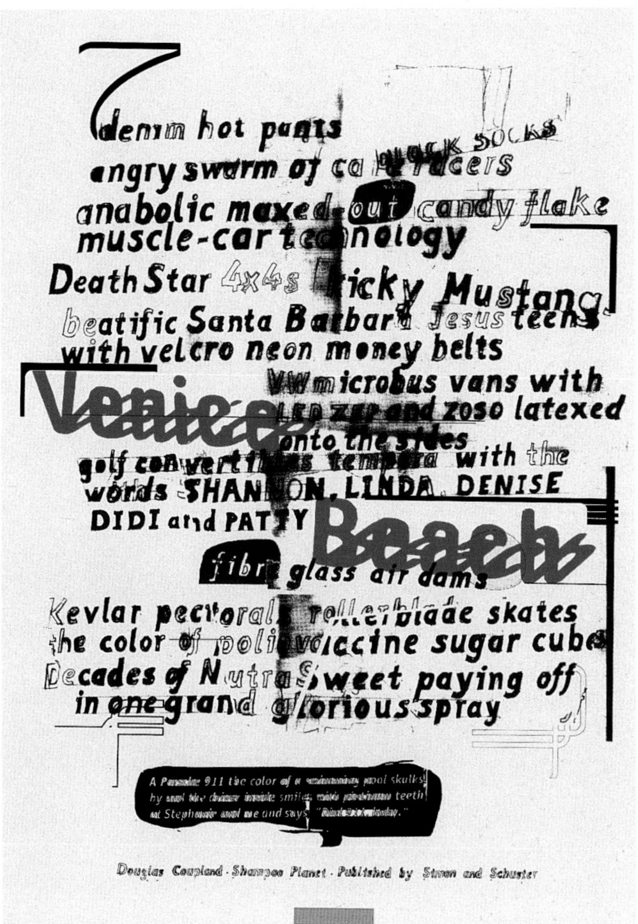

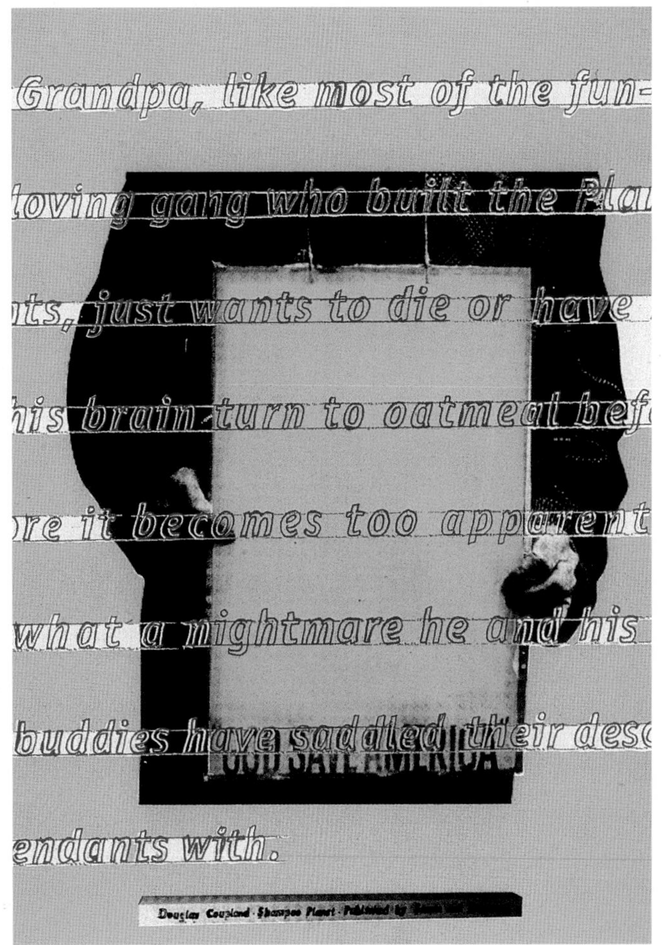

Chemicals
Venice Beach
Grandpa

Poster project based on Douglas Coupland's novel *Shampoo Planet*

DESIGNER Martin Carty

PRINCIPAL TYPEFACES Custom-made for the project

Royal College of Art
Great Britain, 1995

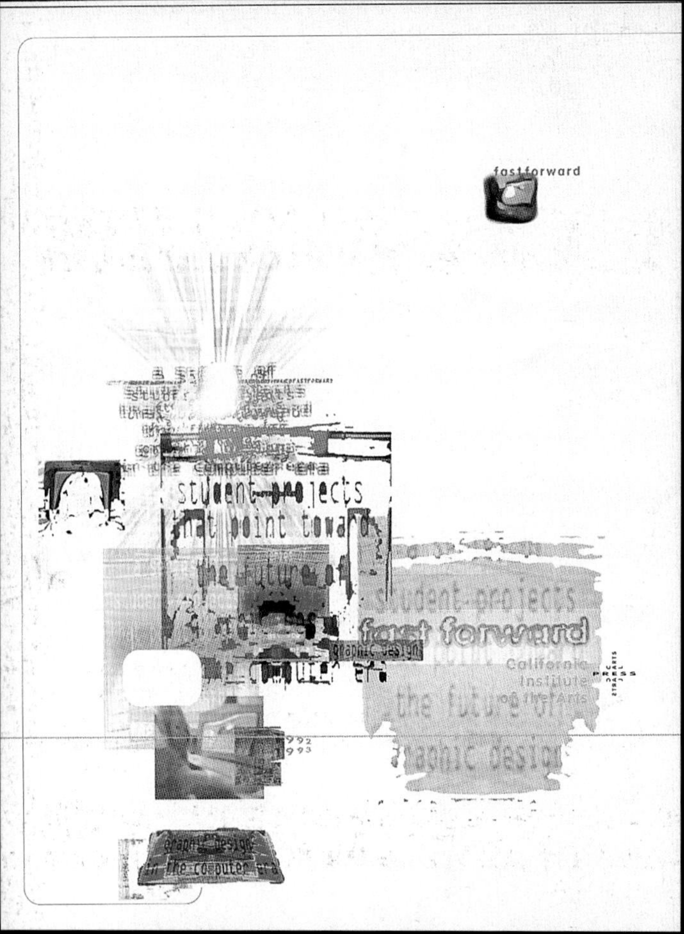

Fast Forward

Book documenting a series of lectures and projects about graphic design in the computer era

ART DIRECTOR Jeffery Keedy
DESIGNERS James Stoecker (front), Margo Johnson (back)
PRINCIPAL TYPEFACES Keedy Sans, VAG Rounded

California Institute of the Arts
USA, 1993

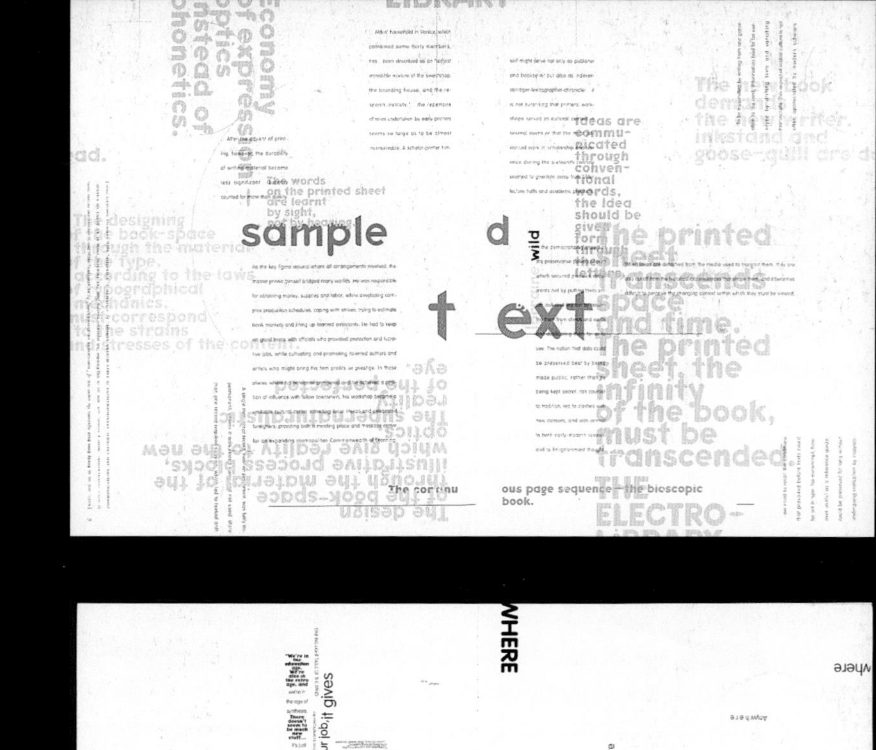

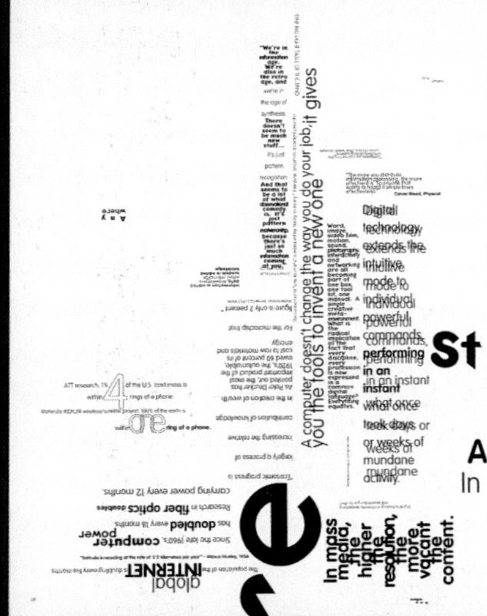

The dominant and repressive role of the text over the image is breaking down.

As the desire to fix image connotation is replaced by a more inclusive and open understanding, the boundaries between words, sounds and images dissolve

Hyper-typography

From Whitespace to Cyberspace

Mr. Keedy

In preparation for the "new media" and the the cutting edge of...

graphic design is moving forward by imagining possible futures. These futures are as idiosyncratic as they are complex, a logical response to our current cultural context.

Fast Forward

Essay spreads

T DIRECTOR Jeffery Keedy

WRITERS Lorraine Wild, Eric Martin, Jeffery Keedy

DESIGNERS Shawn Mckinney, Shelley Stepp, Scott Saltsman

TYPEFACES Keedy Sans, VAG Rounded

California Institute of the Arts

USA, 1993

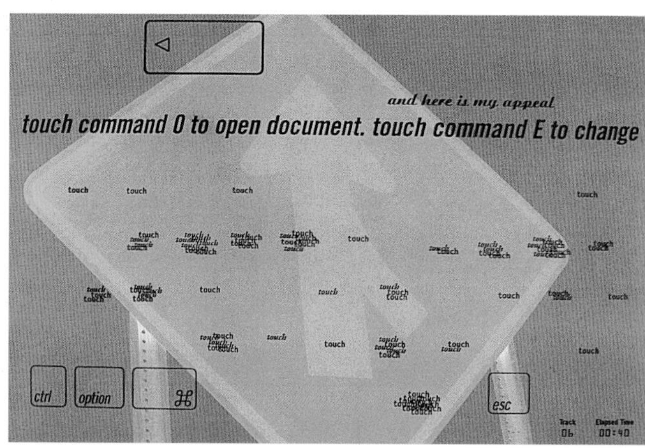

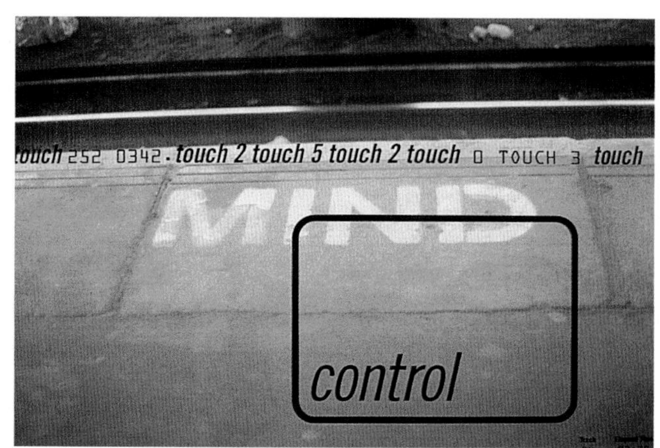

In this short self-published book, the vernacular type of the computer keyboard is juxtaposed with banal imagery to question the nature of binary touch and our relationship with digital technology. Is escape from this seductive environment possible? asks the designer. Who controls whom?

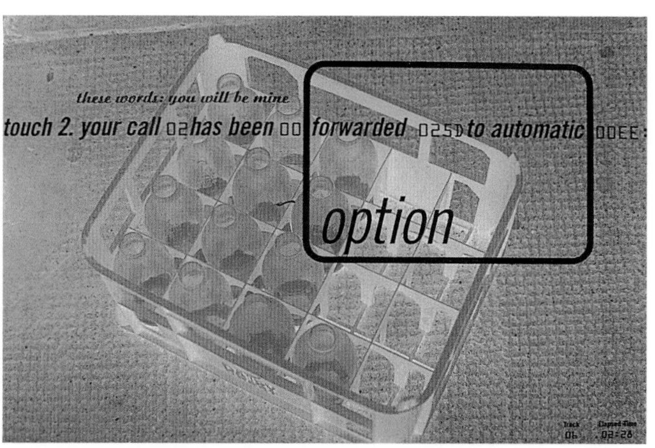

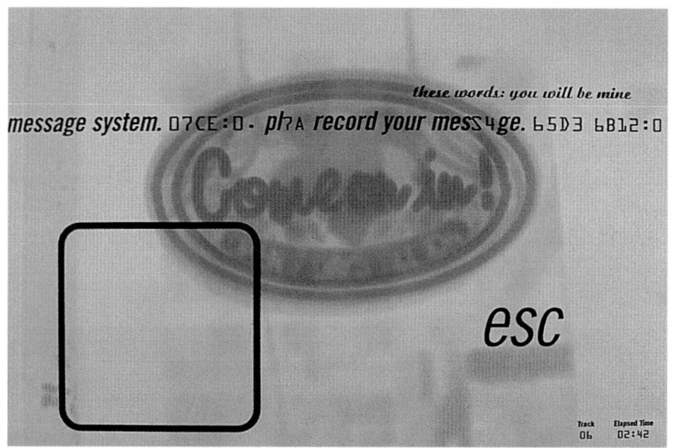

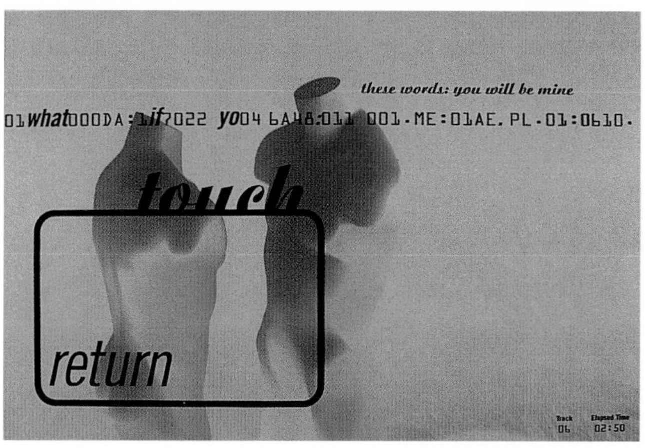

MIN/MAX

Book pages

WRITER/DESIGNER Liisa Salonen

PRINCIPAL TYPEFACES OCRA, Ariston, Trade Gothic, Peignot

Cranbrook Academy of Art

USA, 1995

Systems

Poster/mailer
NER/PHOTOGRAPHER Jeremy Francis Mende
PRINCIPAL TYPEFACE Univers

Cranbrook Academy of Art
USA, 1994

The self-published poster discusses cultural and individual fragmentation and the contemporary schizophrenia of identity and memory. The piece invites viewer response via a mail-back card so that both emotional and analytical information can be re-entered into the creative process, thereby evolving it.

And the body-vehicle,
moving across the landscape,
interpreting, re-interpreting,
feeds its conclusions
back into intself: Evolving.
Each cycle spins a thread,
stringing displaced fragme
into a subjective sequence.
Each of us, with our questions,
ties the past and the future
to our present.
re-input
questions
become milestones,
pathways:
nodes in a mental landscape
Superhighways re-introducing a continuity of language, object, image, and place
A mapwork of common states of mind.
staccato moments
//instances//
occupying the whole
field of vision
nonlinear
image of
place
and flickering between moments
phasing in and out of time-incremental, I
ask a question
ideal
vs.
real
how
much
time
is
left
sharp
fragment of time
amplified and intense
because it is
//now//
Bridges
among
water.
Folks straggling along vast stretches of concrete,
heading into the plane.
Even the words floating in air make blue shadows.
Aorta
Central vein
APPROVED BY:
DRAWN BY
REVISED
DRAWING NUMBER
Hey guess what? What? I've learned how to talk. Great.
The person whose head
was incomplete burst into tears.
//two systems// text + design: jeremy francis mende subtext: excerpts from China by bob perelman thanks: carolyn steinbeck
ience itself. Please re-input the perceived product.

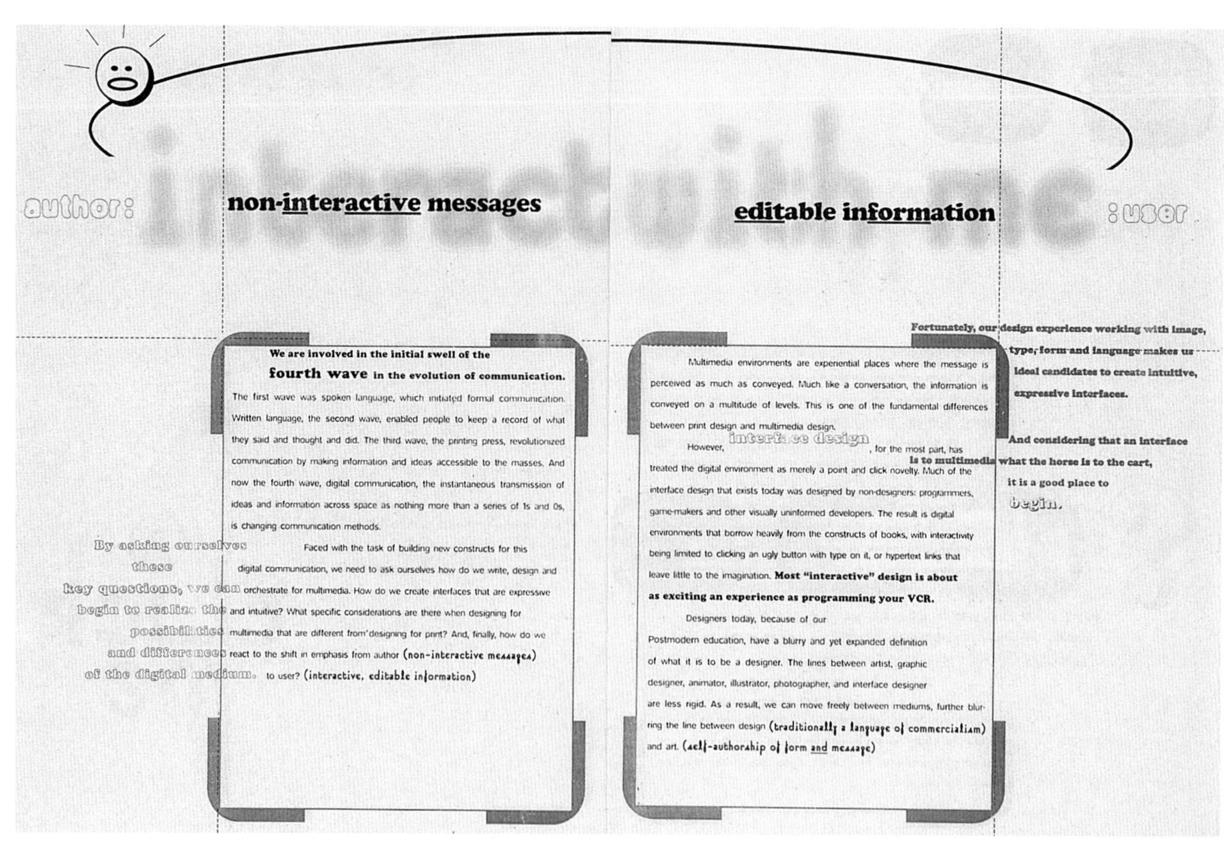

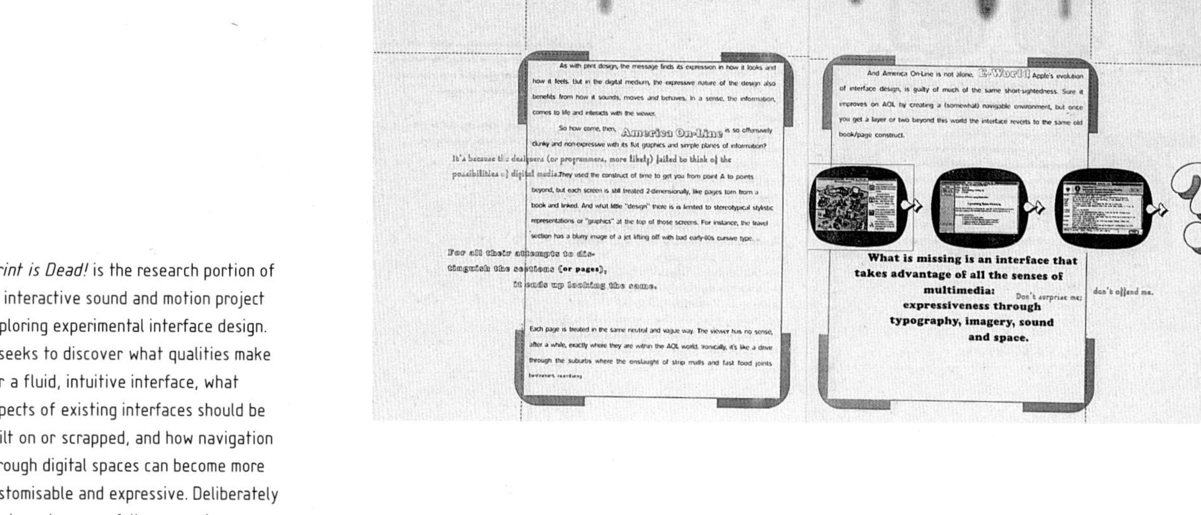

Print is Dead! is the research portion of an interactive sound and motion project exploring experimental interface design. It seeks to discover what qualities make for a fluid, intuitive interface, what aspects of existing interfaces should be built on or scrapped, and how navigation through digital spaces can become more customisable and expressive. Deliberately crude and purposefully arcane in appearance, the hand-printed book is intended to have a charm and tactility that most multimedia experiences presently lack.

Print is Dead! Or so it seems

Spreads from a thesis project

WRITER/DESIGNER Richard Shanks

PRINCIPAL TYPEFACES Cooper Black, Suburban

California Institute of the Arts
USA, 1995

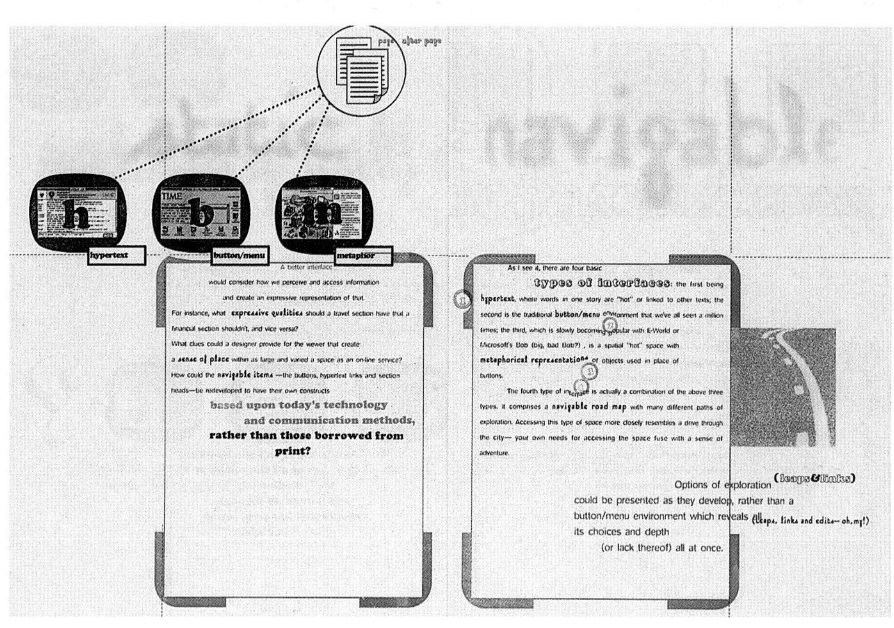

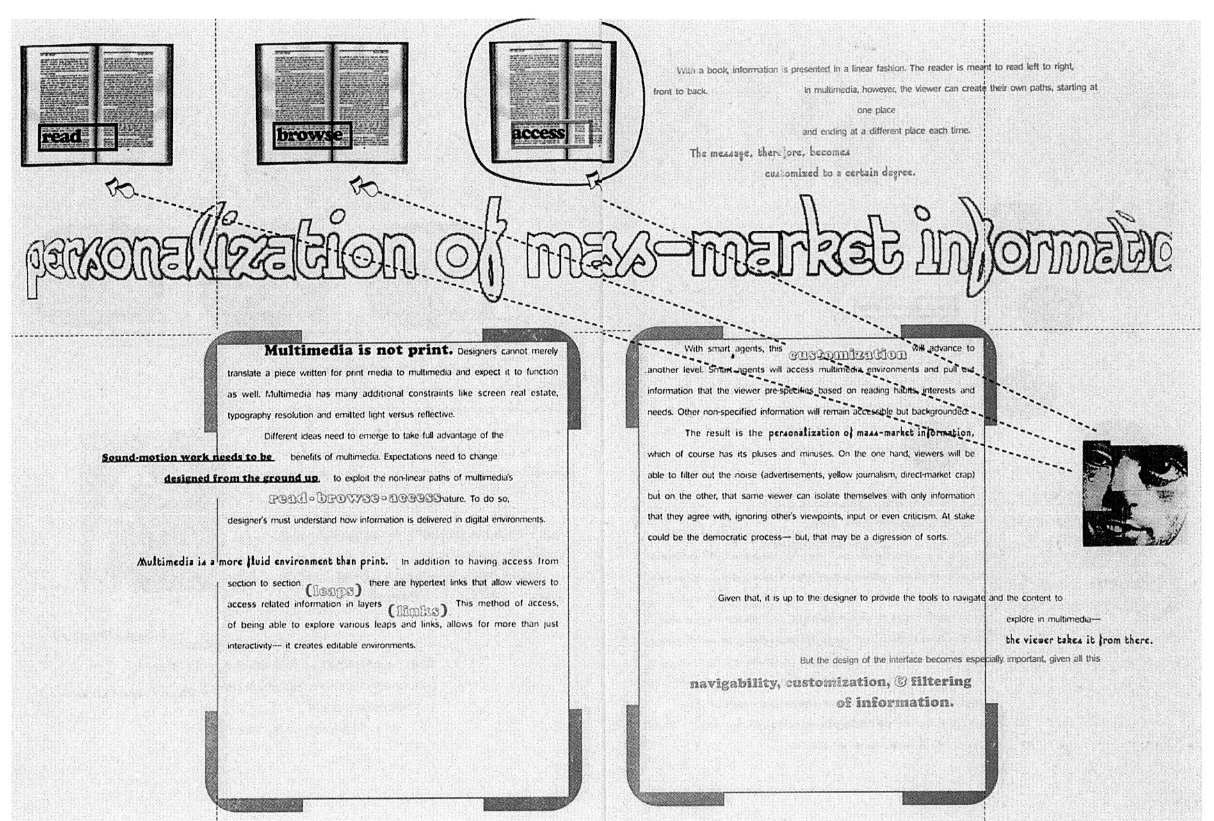

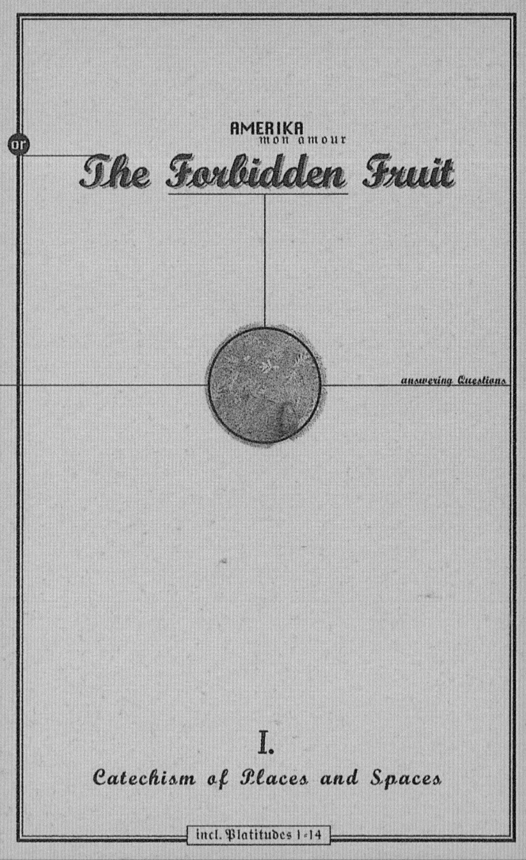

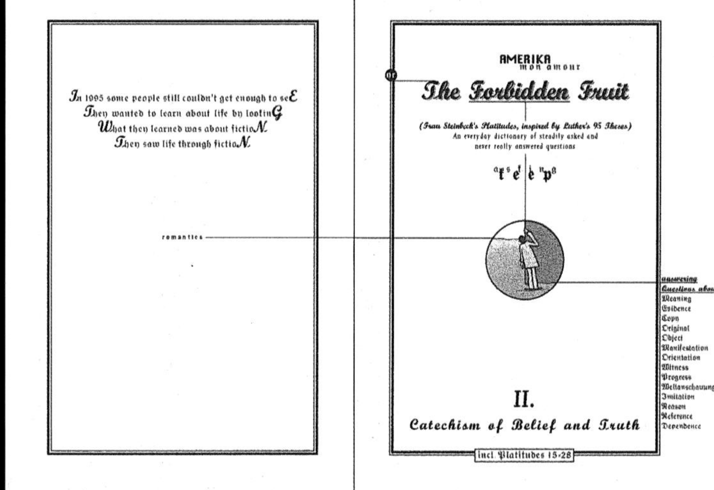

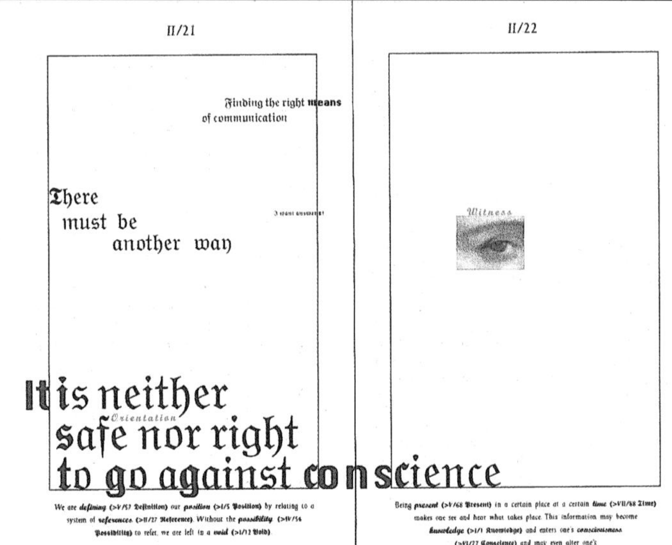

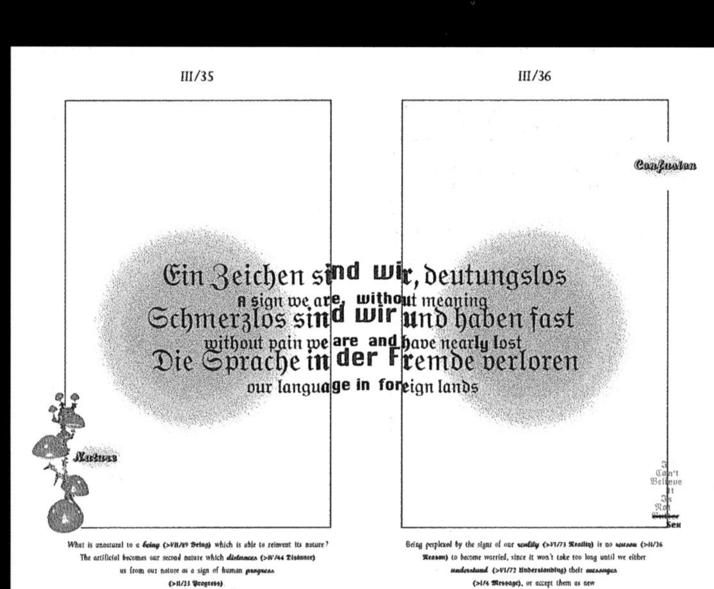

Amerika Mon Amour or the Forbidden Fruit

Cover and spreads from a thesis project

WRITER/DESIGNER Carolyn Steinbeck

PRINCIPAL TYPEFACES Wittenberg, Fraktur, Script Bold, Chicago

Cranbrook Academy of Art

USA, 1995

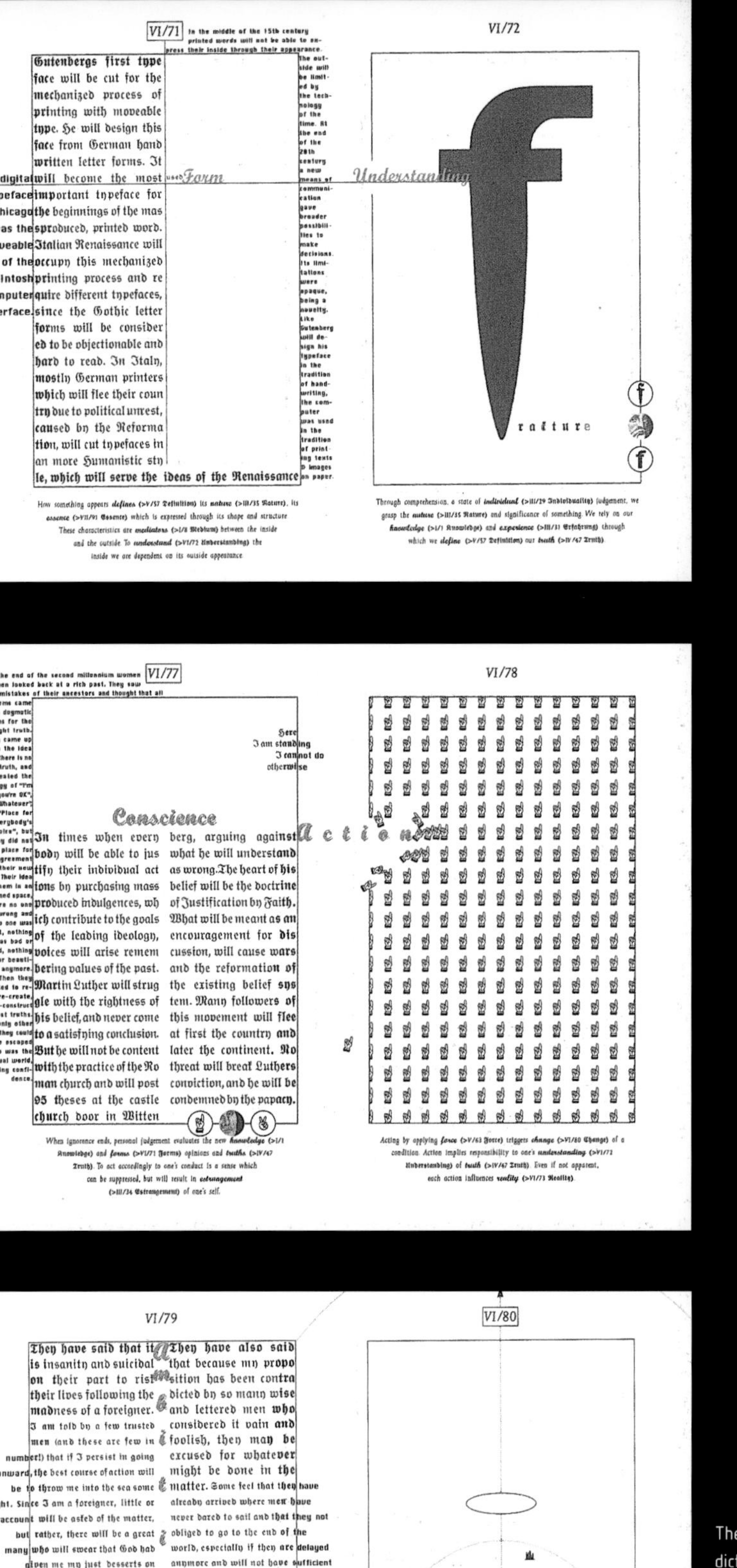

The thesis, subtitled "An everyday dictionary of steadily asked and never really answered questions", takes the form of seven self-published booklets – "chatechisms" of places and spaces, of belief and truth, of experiences, of driving forces, of women and men, of influences, and of conclusions. The booklets frame 95 cross-referenced platitudes – one per page – inspired by the 95 theses arguing against the sale of indulgences nailed to the church door in sixteenth-century Wittenberg by Martin Luther.

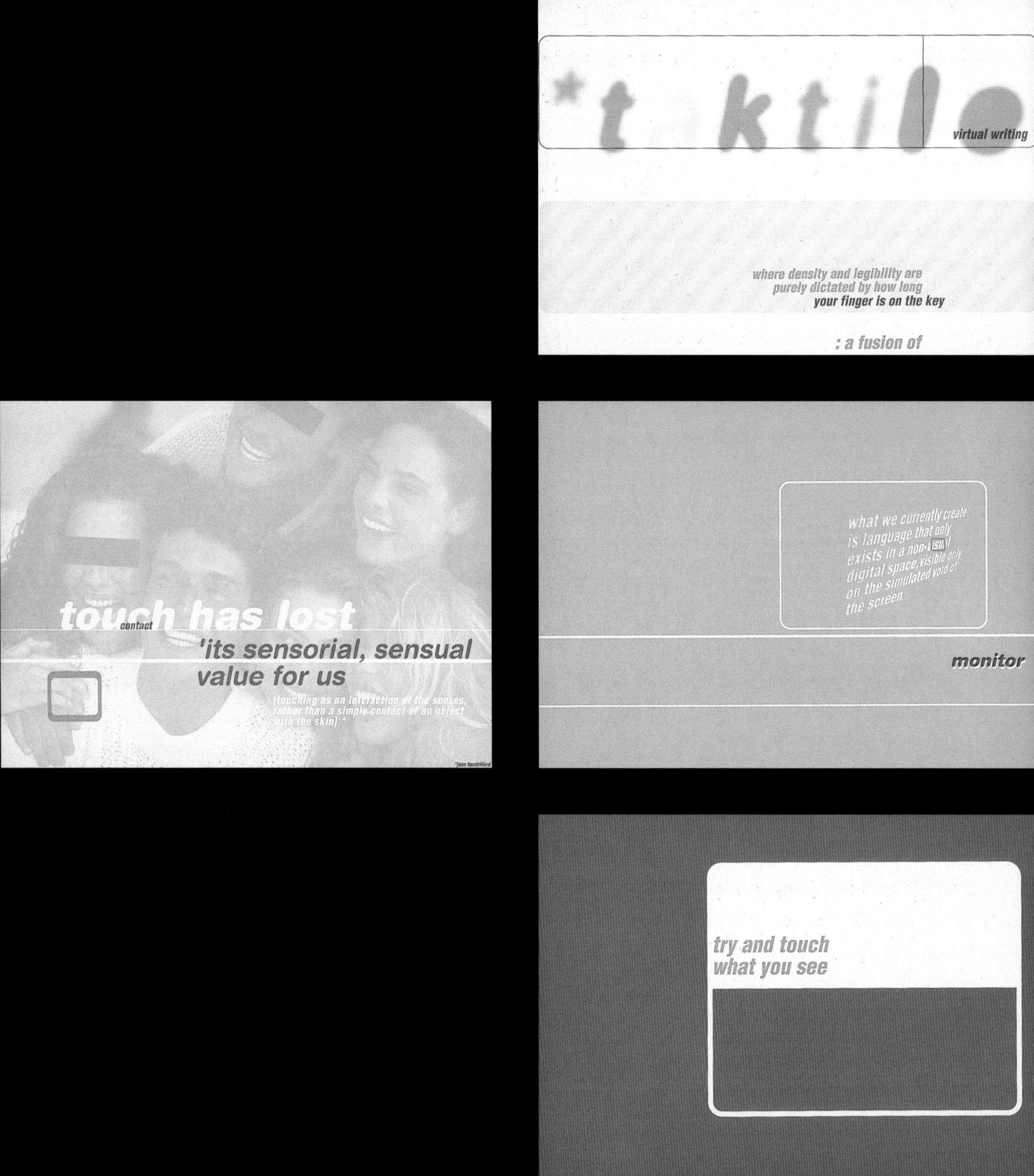
*t ktil
virtual writing
where density and legibility are
purely dictated by how long
your finger is on the key
: a fusion of
touch has lost
contact
'its sensorial, sensual
value for us
(touching as an interaction of the senses,
rather than a simple contact of an object
with the skin)'*
*jean baudrillard
what we currently create
is language that only
exists in a non-visual
digital space, visible only
on the simulated void of
the screen
monitor
try and touch
what you see

Taktile

Wall panels for a typeface project

WRITER/DESIGNER Ben Tibbs
PROGRAMMING ASSISTANCE Tony Side
PRINCIPAL TYPEFACES Taktile, Helvetica

Royal College of Art
Great Britain, 1995

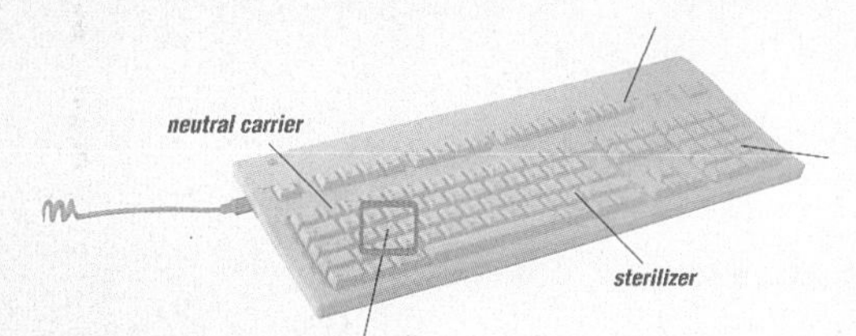

literacy will become learning to type on a keyboard

Digital technology and the keyboard have had a profound effect on the physical nature of writing. The emotional directness of mark-making on a surface has been reduced to the uniform pressing of a key. Taktile is an attempt to restore the physicality of writing by combining the tangible and the digital: the longer your finger rests on a key, the more impact it will make on the character's density and legibility.

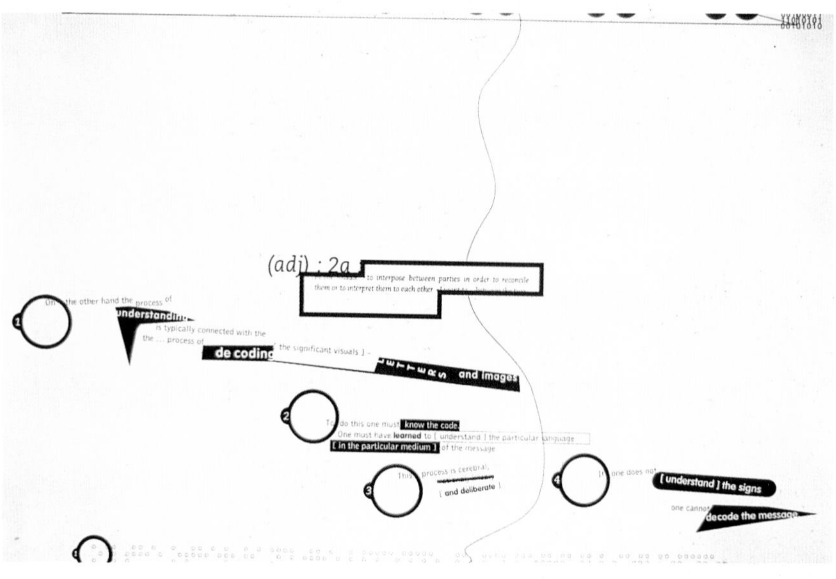

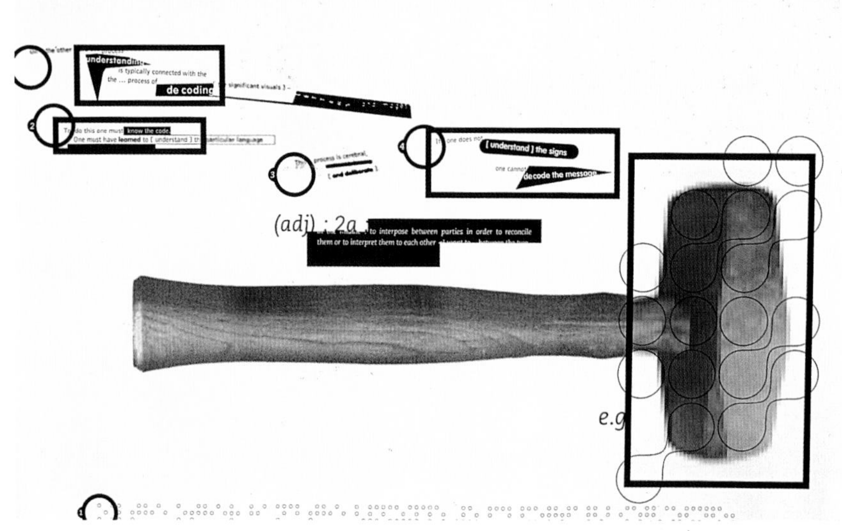

Irony
Mediate

Broadsheets from "Lexicon" project
DESIGNER Weston Bingham
PRINCIPAL TYPEFACES Caecilia, VAG Rounded, Rotis Sans, State, Dr No

California Institute of the Arts
USA, 1994

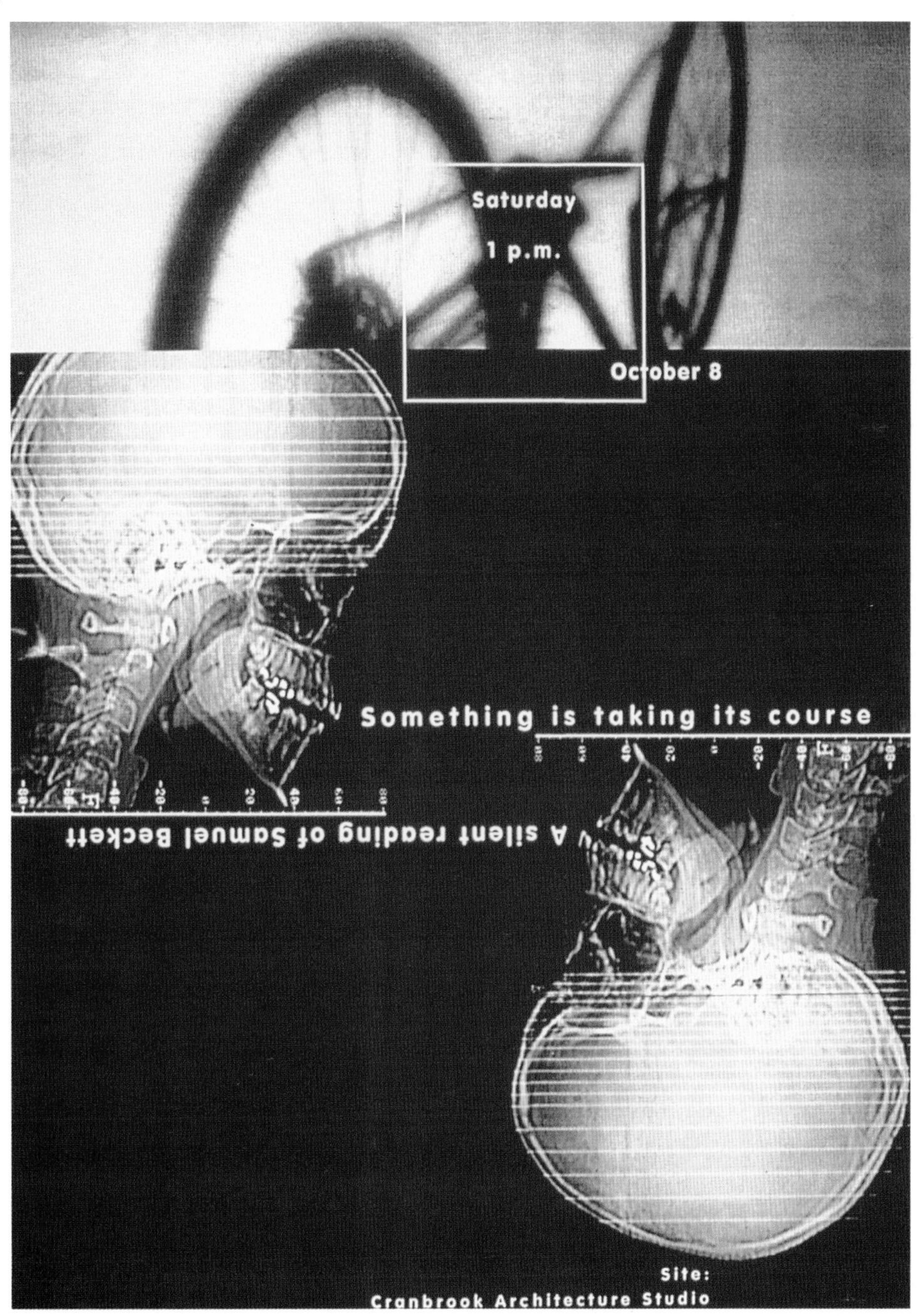

Beckett #1

Poster for a performance based
on Samuel Beckett's *Endgame*

DESIGNERS Jeremy Francis Mende, Jeff Talbot
PRINCIPAL TYPEFACE VAG Rounded
CLIENT Jeff Talbot

Cranbrook Academy of Art
USA, 1995

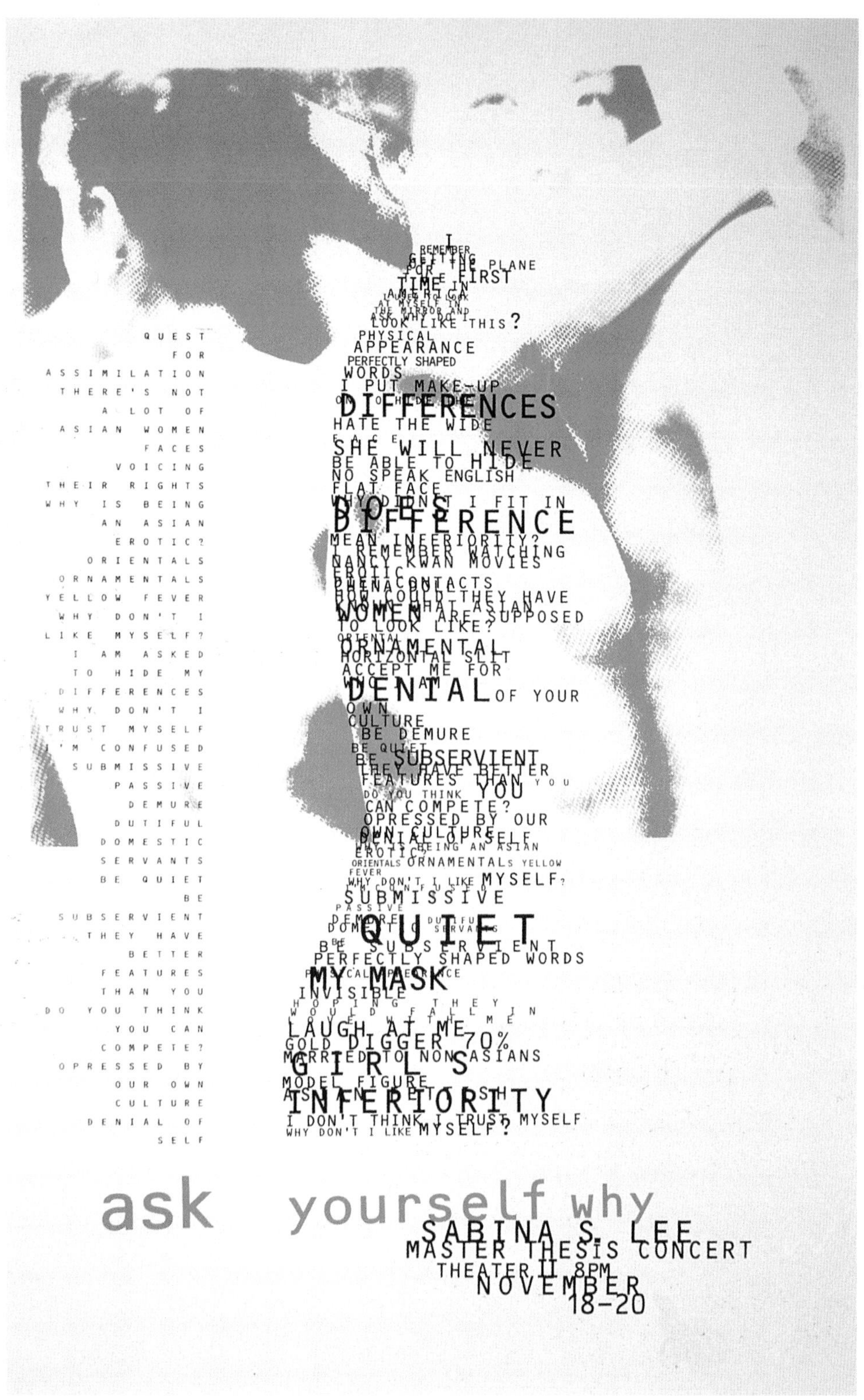

Ask Yourself Why

Concert poster

DESIGNER Michael Worthington

PRINCIPAL TYPEFACE Letter Gothic

CLIENT Dance School

California Institute of the Arts

USA, 1993

Suture

Poster project
DESIGNER Vivienne Cherry
PHOTOGRAPHER Annelise Howard Phillips
PRINCIPAL TYPEFACES Custom-made for the project

Royal College of Art
Great Britain, 1995

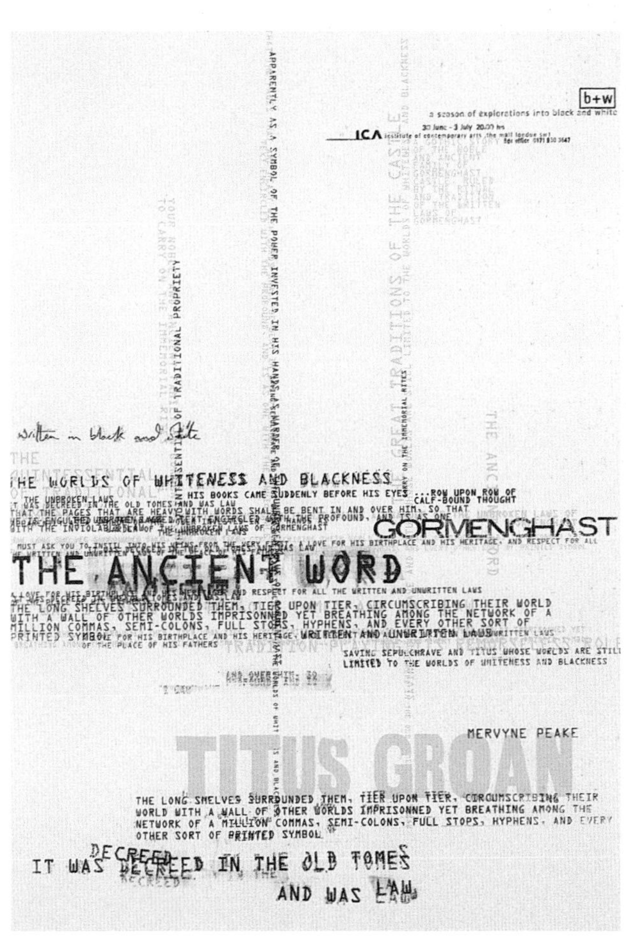

Titus Groan

Poster project
DESIGNER Vivienne Cherry
PRINCIPAL TYPEFACES Custom-made for the project

Royal College of Art
Great Britain, 1995

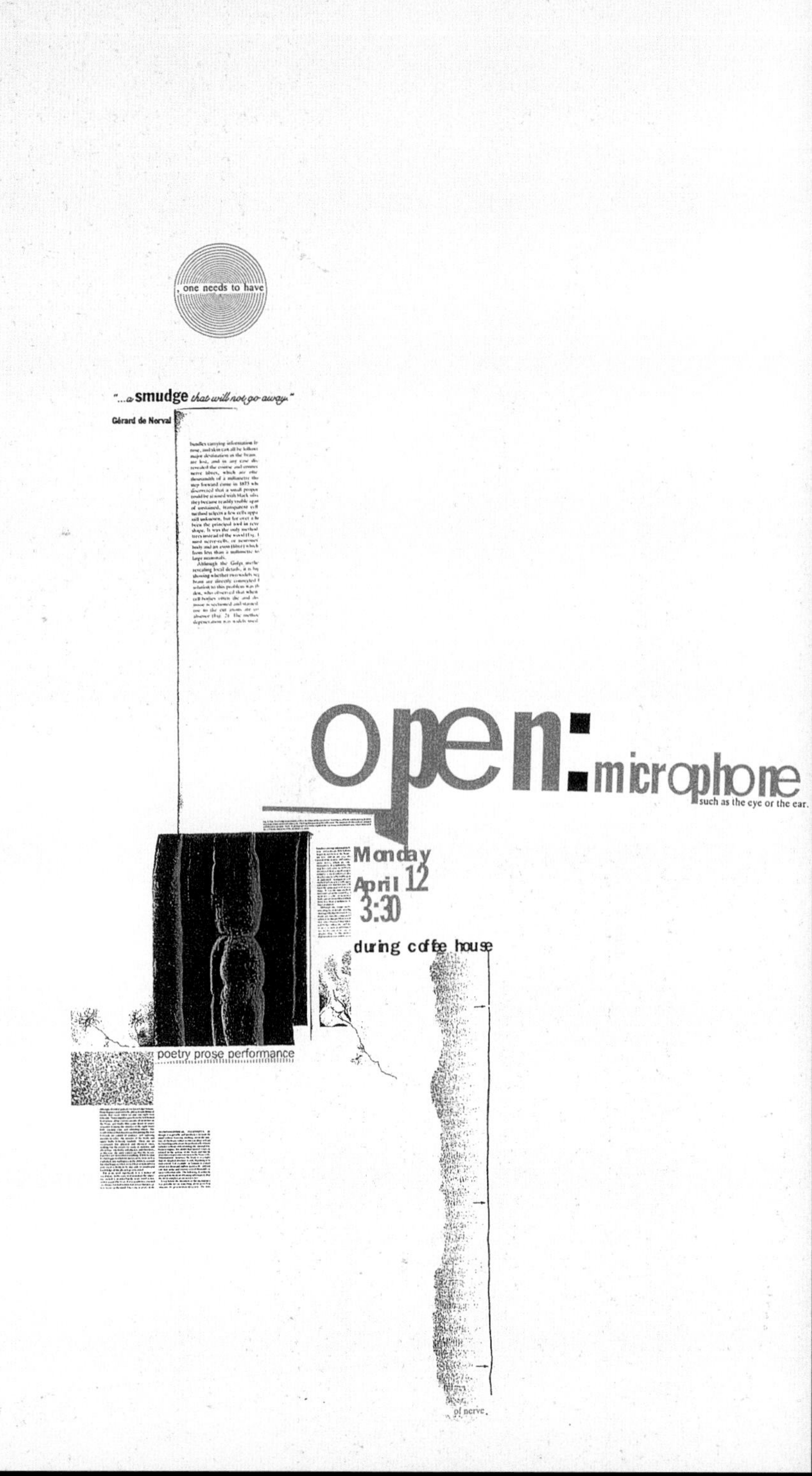

Open Microphone: A Smudge

Poster announcing an open reading on campus

DESIGNER Brian Schorn

PRINCIPAL TYPEFACES Trade Gothic, Snell Roundhand

CLIENT Open Microphone Series

Cranbrook Academy of Art

USA, 1993

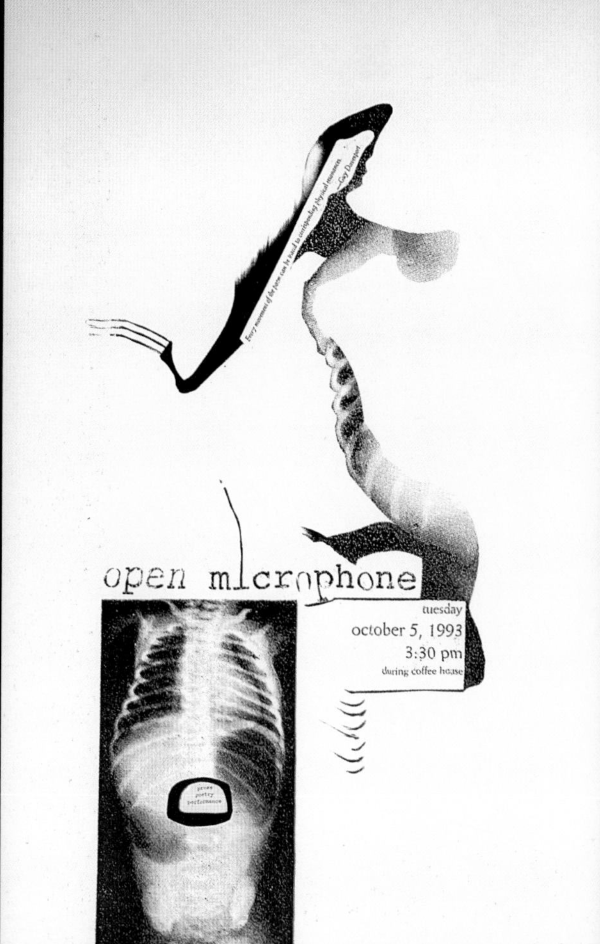

Open Microphone: Resonances

Poster announcing an open reading on campus

DESIGNER Brian Schorn
PRINCIPAL TYPEFACES Courier, Weiss
CLIENT Open Microphone Series

Cranbrook Academy of Art
USA, 1993

Open Microphone: Gates of Hell

Poster announcing an open reading on campus

DESIGNER Brian Schorn
PRINCIPAL TYPEFACES Cochin, Ocraelliot Black, Century Schoolbook
CLIENT Open Microphone Series

Cranbrook Academy of Art
USA, 1993

Kathy Acker: Postmodern Novelist

Poster announcing a reading

DESIGNER / Brian Schorn

PRINCIPAL TYPEFACE / Serifa

CLIENT / Department of English, Wayne State University

Cranbrook Academy of Art

USA 1994

Trust (105 Minutes)

Film poster

DESIGNER Brian Schorn

PRINCIPAL TYPEFACES Charlemagne, Avenir

Faculty Show

Poster
DESIGNER Michael Worthington
PRINCIPAL TYPEFACES Wood Type, Dead History, Compacta

California Institute of the Arts
USA, 1995

70s Party

Poster
DESIGNER Michael Worthington
PRINCIPAL TYPEFACES Fellaparts, Wedgie
CLIENT Student Council

California Institute of the Arts
USA, 1994

Patty Dance

Dance Poster

DESIGNER Deborah Littlejohn

PRINCIPAL TYPEFACES Matrix, Hubba Bubba, Suburban, Koo Koo

California Institute of the Arts

USA, 1995

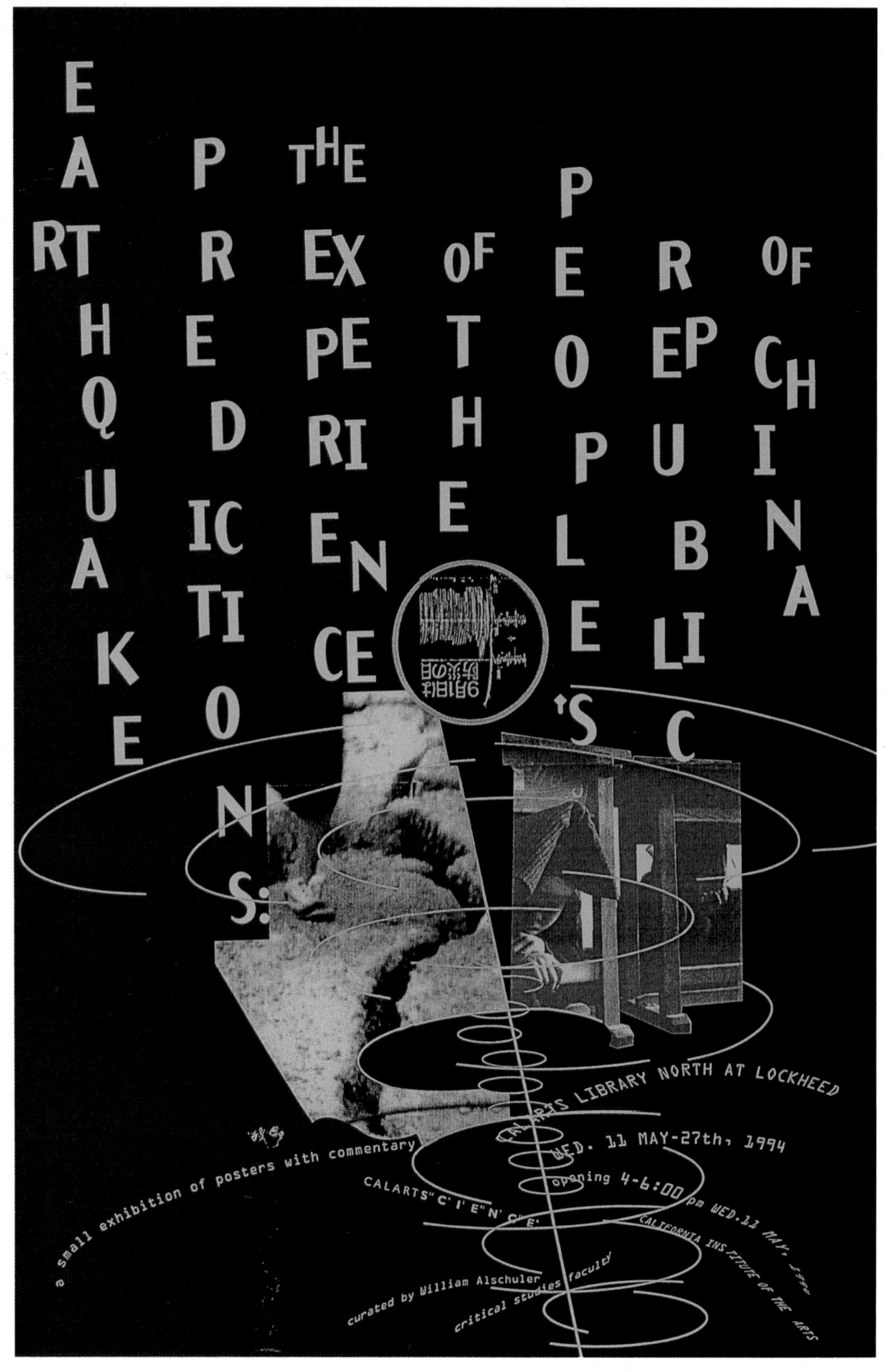

Earthquake Predictions

Exhibition poster
DESIGNER Deborah Littlejohn
PRINCIPAL TYPEFACES Barry Sans, OCRA
CLIENT Critical Studies Department

California Institute of the Arts
USA, 1994

Mike Kelley

Poster announcing a lecture
DESIGNERS Deborah Littlejohn, Shawn McKinney
PRINCIPAL TYPEFACE Arbitrary Sans
CLIENT Visiting Artist Program

California Institute of the Arts
USA, 1993

The designers scanned in many elements and dragged them together to create a succession of alternative designs. Believing the poster to be finished, they pulled back to discover that the scattered typographic matter on the pasteboard more closely reflected the artist's attitude than their careful composition.

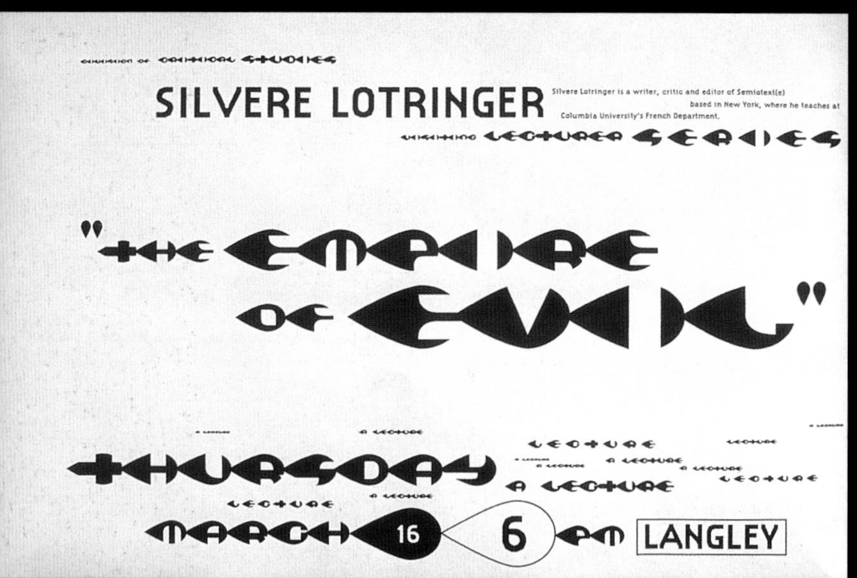

Silvere Lotringer

Poster announcing a lecture
DESIGNER Geoff McFetridge
PRINCIPAL TYPEFACES Tear, Citizen
CLIENT Visiting Artist Program

California Institute of the Arts
USA, 1995

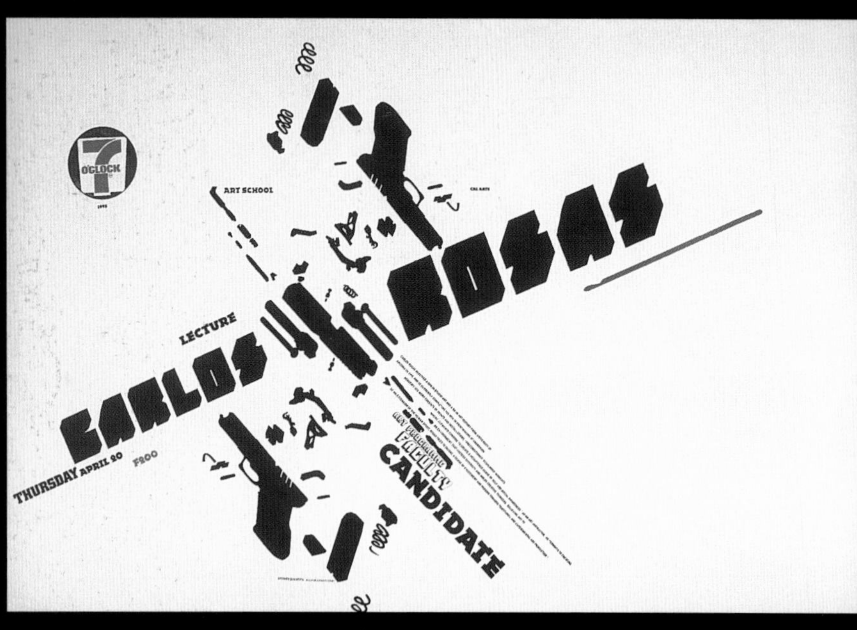

Carlos Rosas

Poster announcing a lecture
DESIGNERS Geoff McFetridge, Kevin Lyons
PRINCIPAL TYPEFACES Shaft, Dynamo, Bell Gothic
CLIENT Visiting Artist Program

California Institute of the Arts
USA, 1994-95

Sissy Space

Poster for an evening of gay cabaret

DESIGNER Michael Worthington

PRINCIPAL TYPEFACES Sissy, Killer Klown, Dominatrix, Koo Koo Fatboy, Suburban

California Institute of the Arts

USA, 1994

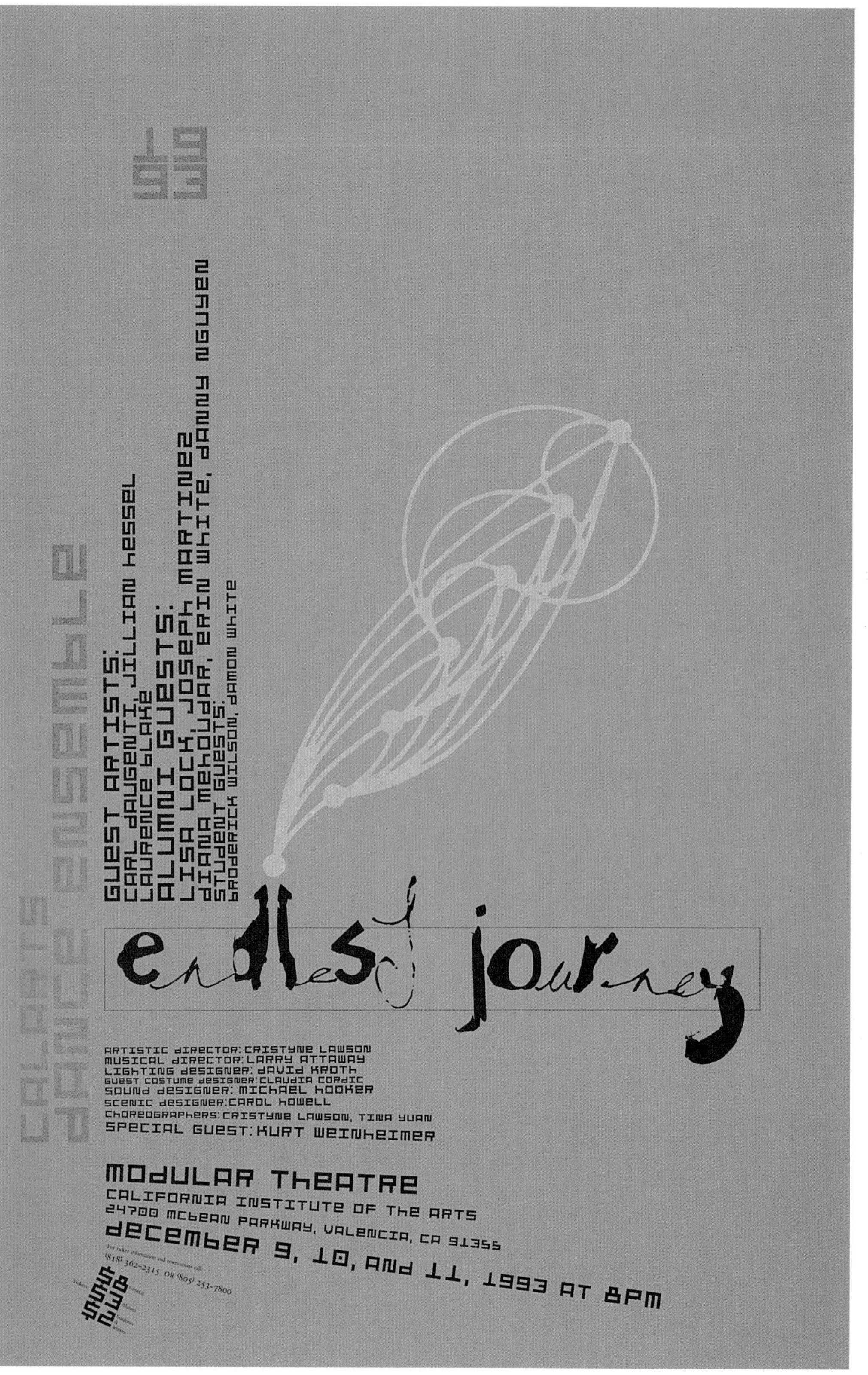

Endless Journey

Dance poster
DESIGNER Michael Worthington
PRINCIPAL TYPEFACES Gridlock, Eugenius
CLIENT Dance School
California Institute of the Arts
USA, 1993

The structure of the design is related to the general nature of dance and to the specific choreography of *Endless Journey* (further referenced by the diagram of infinity) in which dancers flowed in and out of a trench in the stage. The Gridlock type designed by Austin Putman masses together to form the "audience" for the more animated Eugenius "dancers" designed by Worthington himself.

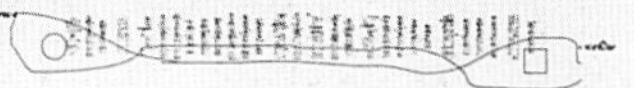

humanachine

The Cyborg or the Cyborg or cybernetic organism cybernetic organism implies that the implies that the conscious conscious mind steers the mind steers the meaning of the Greek meaning of the Greek kybernetes our organic kybernetes our organic life. Organic life life. Organic life energy ceases to energy ceases to initiate our mental initiate our mental gestures. Can we ever gestures. Can we ever be fully present when be fully present when we live through a we live through a surrogate body surrogate body standing in for us? The standing in for us? The stand-in self stand-in self lacks the vulnerability lacks the vulnerability and fragility of our and fragility of our primary identity primary identity. The stand-in self can The stand-in self can never fully represent never fully represent us. The more we us. The more we mistake the mistake the cyberbodies cyberbodies for ourselves, the for ourselves, the more the machine more the machine twists ourselves into twists ourselves into the protheses the protheses we are wearing we are wearing.

Melding: Humanachine

Poster project on the theme of cyberspace

DESIGNER Margo Johnson

PRINCIPAL TYPEFACES Hybrid digital typefaces

California Institute of the Arts
USA, 1993

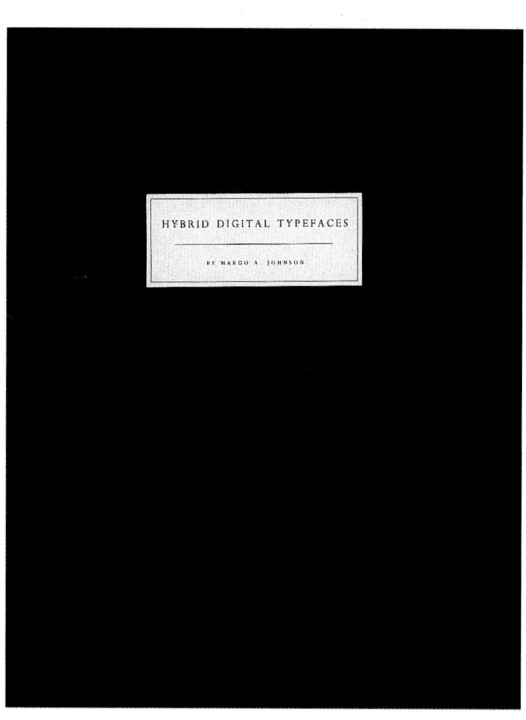

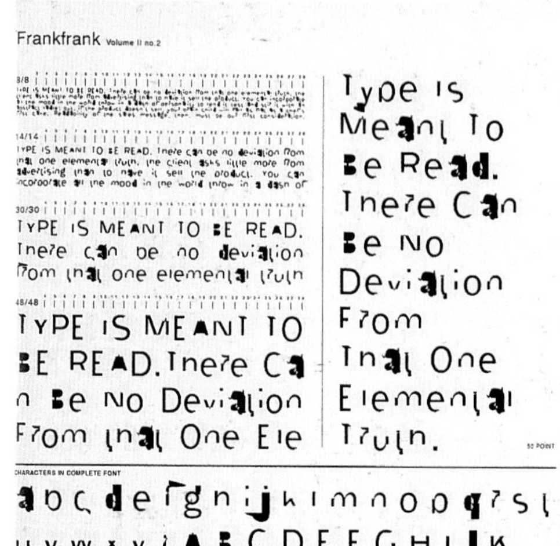

Hybrid Digital Typefaces

Cover and pages from a thesis project book

DESIGNER Margo Johnson

PRINCIPAL TYPEFACES Hybrid digital typefaces

California Institute of the Arts

USA, 1993

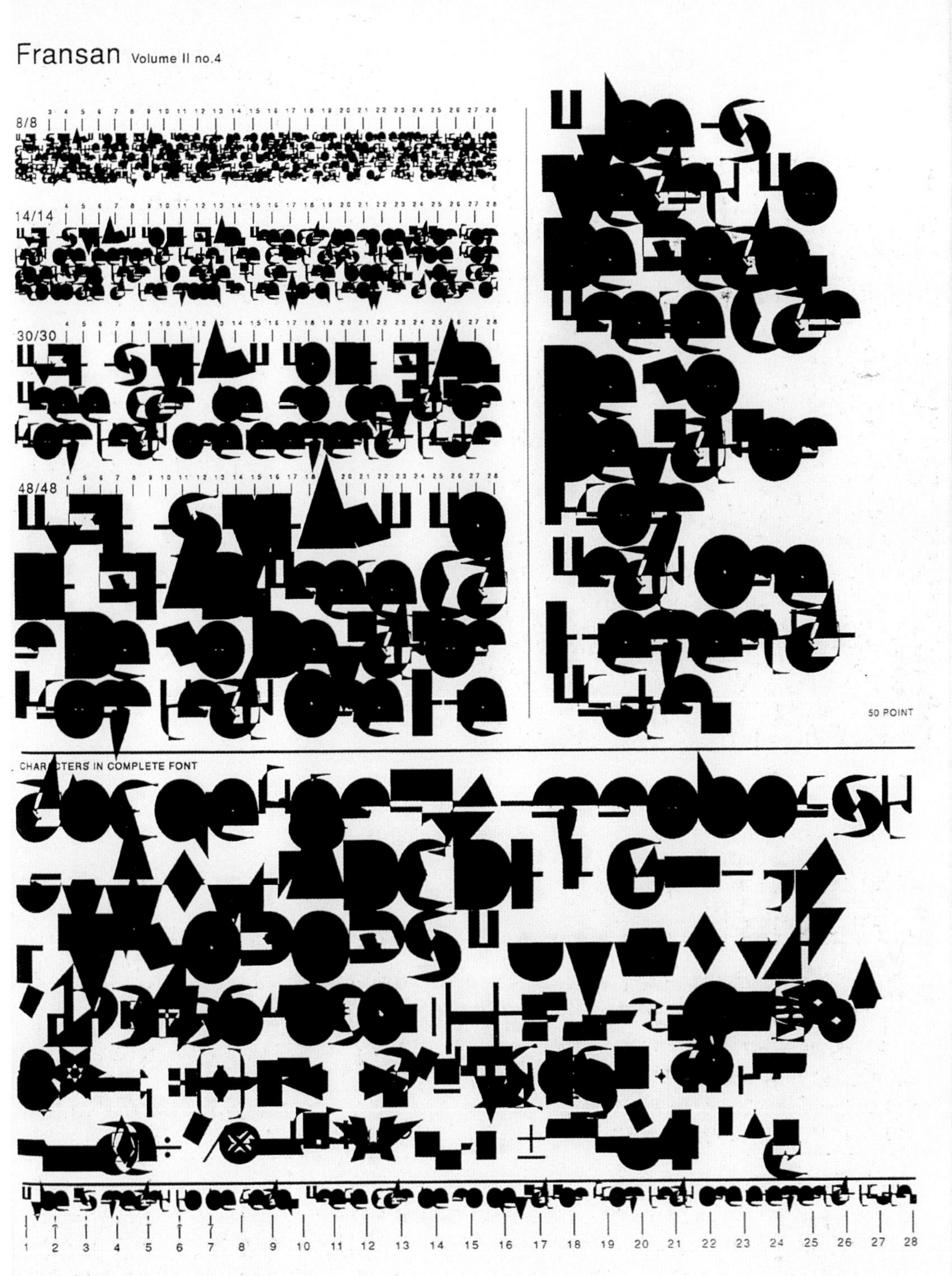

By applying a numerical matrix to three existing typefaces – Cooper Black, Franklin Gothic, Kuenstler Script – Johnson discovered she could produce random and unexpected letterforms. Three series of 20 new fonts were generated, each named and ordered according to the matrix. A traditional type specimen book, with an introduction and diagrams, showcases the 60 hybrid typefaces and gives the project an air of technological parody.

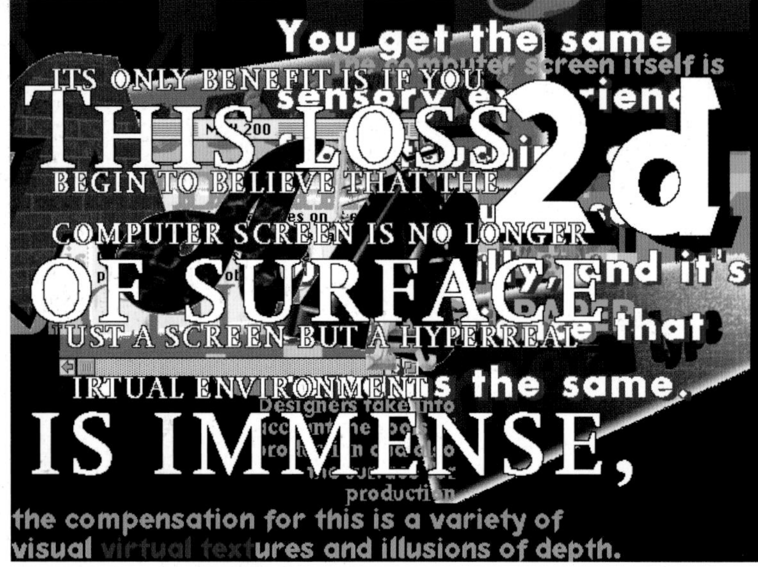

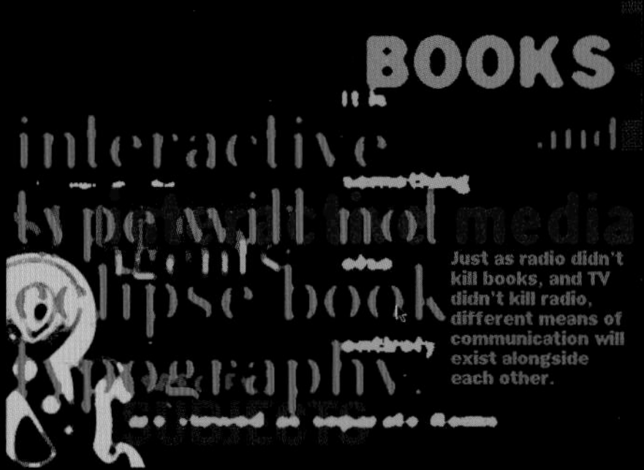

Michael Worthington's thesis, included on California Institute of the Arts' 25th Anniversary CD-ROM, explores the possibilities for type in the interactive medium and asks why it is so often neglected in design for the screen. Mostly typographic in content, the piece offers a fluid illustration of its own arguments that takes the viewer on a sound-and-motion journey into typography's near future.

BOOKS

interactive

Digital Luddites

Just as radio didn't kill books, and TV didn't kill radio, different means of communication will exist alongside each other.

fear the book will be replaced by the "push button literacy of givens"

Race, gender and other physical attributes are irrelevent on the net, the interface becomes the only-face and also the only-body.

where information is accepted rather than challenged.

Contrary to this is the fact that users on the internet are readier to enter into dialogue and debate, perhaps due to "techno anonymity."

"push button literacy of givens"

Hypertype

Screen-based thesis project

WRITER/DESIGNER Michael Worthington

California Institute of the Arts
USA, 1995

Andy Altmann *23, 24, 25, 28, 29, 40, 102, 104, 105*
Born in 1962, Andy Altmann graduated with a BA from St. Martin's School of Art, London in 1985 and received an MA from the Royal College of Art in 1987. He formed Why Not Associates with David Ellis and Howard Greenhalgh immediately after college. The company has worked with a variety of clients from both the private and public sectors, including Next Directory, the Royal Mail, Hull City Council and the Royal Academy.

Caryn Aono *176*
Born in Chicago in 1959, Caryn Aono took a Bachelor of Science in graphic design from Illinois State University in 1981. She received an MFA in graphic design from Cranbrook Academy of Art in 1985. Since 1988, she has been art director of California Institute of the Arts' Public Affairs Office and she is also on the faculty of the graphic design programme. Her work has been included in the American Center for Design's 100 Show.

Chris Ashworth *64, 65, 76, 77, 138, 139*
Born in Leeds in 1969, Chris Ashworth studied for an HND in graphic design at York College of Arts and Technology, graduating in 1990. In the same year, he set up Orange, which concentrated on youth-related projects. In 1995, he joined Neil Fletcher and Amanda Sissons to form the design team Substance. Clients include MTV and Ray Gun Publishing.

Phil Baines *134, 135*
Born in Kendal, Westmorland in 1958, Phil Baines graduated with a BA from St Martin's School of Art, London in 1985 and an MA from the Royal College of Art in 1987. In 1990, he took up a residency at the Crafts Council and, since 1991, he has taught graphic design at Central Saint Martins. His letterpress typography has appeared in several exhibitions, including "British Design: New Traditions" at the Boymans van Beuningen Museum, Rotterdam in 1989.

Jonathan Barnbrook *72, 73, 74, 75, 78, 94, 95*
Born in 1966, Jonathan Barnbrook graduated with a BA from Central Saint Martins College of Art & Design, London in 1988 and an MA from the Royal College of Art in 1990. After art school he began working in London as a freelance. He directs typography and live-action commercials through Tony Kaye Films. His typefaces Mason and Exocet are released by Emigre Fonts. In 1996, he launched his own type foundry, Virus.

Richard Bates *84*
With partner Allen Hori, Richard Bates is co-principal of the design group Bates Hori. His work has been exhibited internationally in the 1990 touring exhibition "Cranbrook Design: The New Discourse" and at the Design Museum, London and the GGG Gallery, Tokyo. He has received recognition in the *I.D. Annual Design Review* and the American Center for Design's 100 Show.

Weston Bingham *200*
Born in 1968, Weston Bingham completed a BFA at the Pratt Institute in Brooklyn. After professional experience with Chermayeff & Geismar in New York, he began graduate studies at California Institute of the Arts.

Andrew Blauvelt *150, 151*
Born in 1964, Andrew Blauvelt received a BFA from Herron School of Art and an MFA from Cranbrook Academy of Art. He teaches at North Carolina State University and in 1995 occupied the interim chair of graphic design at Cranbrook. As a designer, he works for cultural and educational clients. In 1990, his work was exhibited in the touring exhibition "Cranbrook Design: the New Discourse" and he has received recognition in the *I.D. Annual Design Review*. He edited the *Visible Language* series "New Perspectives: Critical Histories of Graphic Design" and writes for *Emigre* and *Eye*.

Frédéric Bortolotti *120, 121*
Born in 1965, Frédéric Bortolotti studied at the Ecole Nationale des Arts Appliques and the Ecole Nationale des Beaux-Art in Paris. With his design studio vertmiroir, he has worked on projects for the Centre Pompidou, the Institut du Monde Arabe and has created corporate identities for private clients including Cofinoga. Bortolotti is founder of the Bulldozer project and publishes his own work under the name The Red Dozer.

Anne Burdick *109, 112, 113, 151*
Born in 1962, Anne Burdick graduated with an MFA from California Institute of the Arts. From 1995-96, she was assistant professor of graphic design at North Carolina State University. As well as teaching and maintaining her own practice, she has written widely about design. In 1995, she guest edited and produced *Emigre* nos. 35 and 36, "Mouthpiece: Clamor over Writing and Design".

Raul Cabra *80*
Born in Bogota, Columbia in 1964, Raul Cabra attended the School of Architecture in Caracas, Venezuela. He went on to study graphic design at California College of Arts and Crafts in San Francisco, graduating with a BFA in 1988. Cabra has worked as a senior designer at Tenazas Design in San Francisco on corporate and non-profit communication projects. In 1992, he became co-principal, with Martin Venezky, of the design group Diseño. In 1995, his work was included in the American Center for Design's 100 Show.

David Carson *12, 52, 53, 54, 55, 56, 57, 137*
Born in Corpus Christi, Texas, David Carson began his career as an art director/designer at *Transworld Skateboarding* magazine in 1983. He was art director of *Beach Culture* magazine from 1989-91 and art director of *Raygun* from 1992-95. He now divides his time between studios in New York and California. He has worked on commercials for Coca-Cola, Sega and other clients. *The End of Print: The Graphic Design of David Carson* was published in 1995. He is art director of *Speak* magazine.

Martin Carty *186, 187*
Born in 1968, Martin Carty completed a BA in graphic design at Central Saint Martins College of Art & Design, London in 1992 and an MA at the Royal College of Art in 1995. He has freelanced for Theatre de Complicite, *i-D* magazine and other clients. He is a partner with Ben Tibbs in the design team Automatic.

Vivienne Cherry *184, 185, 203*
Born in Derby in 1970, Vivienne Cherry graduated with a BA in graphic design from Brighton Polytechnic in 1992. A year later, after working as a designer at Mitchell Beazley publishers, she began an MA in graphic design at the Royal College of Art. Since 1995, she has worked as a freelance.

Scott Clum *9, 58, 59*
Born in 1964, Scott Clum studied at the Munson Williams Proctor Institute of Fine Art. He has been principal of Ride Design, based in Silverton, Oregon, since 1989. He is design director of *Bikini* magazine and, in 1991, launched his own magazine, *Blur*. His work has been recognised by the American Center for Design's 100 Show and by the Type Directors Club of New York.

Denise Gonzales Crisp *112*
Born in 1955, Denise Gonzales Crisp worked professionally for seven years before entering the graduate programme in graphic design at California Institute of the Arts. She has taught typography at Art Center College of Design and Otis College of Art and Design.

Richard Curren *20, 21*
Born in San Francisco in 1969, Richard Curren received a BFA from the University of Houston, Texas in 1993. He worked for the Houston Museum of Natural Science, designing computer-animated interactive kiosks. In 1994, he joined Jager Di Paola Kemp Design.

Zsolt Czakó *8, 142*
Born in Pécs, Hungary in 1965, Zsolt Czakó studied photography and graphic design at the Hungarian Academy of Applied Arts, Budapest from 1989-93, and undertook postgraduate studies in typography from 1993-94. In 1993, he was a co-founder of the creative workshop ART 'i csók, which undertakes projects for national and international clients. He exhibits regularly and, in 1994, was an organiser and participant in "New Typography", held in Pécs.

Michael Davies *62, 63*
Born in 1970, Michael Davies graduated from Kingston University with a BA in graphic design in 1993. Since then, he has worked at Lippa Pearce and as a designer at The Body Shop.

Barry Deck *136, 137, 144*
Born in Mount Peasant, Iowa in 1962, Barry Deck graduated with a BFA from Northern Illinois University in 1986 and an MFA from California Institute of the Arts in 1989. He has designed a number of well-known and widely distributed typefaces, including Template Gothic. He has worked for Viacom and Atlantic Records, designing for both print and screen.

Barbara De Wilde *46*
Working at Alfred A. Knopf in New York, Barbara De Wilde concentrates on the design of books and literature.

Mark Diaper *62, 63*
Born in 1967, Mark Diaper studied at Middlesex Polytechnic, graduating with a BA in graphic design. He has worked at Newell & Sorrell and Lippa Pearce for IBM, Decca, Waterstones and The Terence Higgins Trust.

Joan Dobkin *153*
After graduating with a BFA from Rhode Island School of Design and an MFA from the School of the Art Institute of Chicago, Joan Dobkin's main interest lay in painting and drawing. She later began a freelance career in design and completed an MFA at Cranbrook Academy of Art. She is assistant professor of graphic design at Ohio University and also maintains a freelance practice.

Elliott Peter Earls *60, 61, 172, 173, 174, 175*
Born in 1965, Elliott Peter Earls studied for an MFA at Cranbrook Academy of Art before gaining professional experience at De Harak and Poulin Associates and Elektra Records in New York. Through his company the Apollo Program, based in Greenwich, Connecticut, he releases typefaces and CD-ROMs. He has worked for Master Card International, Sony Records, the Voyager Company and *Plazm*.

Birgit Eggers *63*
Born in 1968, Birgit Eggers was educated at the F. H. Hamburg, graduating in 1993. Since then, she has worked as a freelance, first in London and from 1995 in Amsterdam. Her clients include the publishers Hamlyn.

David Ellis *23, 24, 25, 28, 29, 40, 102, 104, 105*
Born in 1962, David Ellis graduated with a BA from St. Martin's School of Art, London in 1985 and received an MA from the Royal College of Art in 1987. He formed Why Not Associates with Andy Altmann and Howard Greenhalgh immediately after college. The company has worked with a variety of clients from both the private and public sectors, including Next Directory, the Royal Mail, Hull City Council and the Royal Academy.

Stephen Farrell *96, 179, 180, 181*
Born in 1968, Stephen Farrell gained a Bachelor of Science degree in industrial design from Ohio State University. He is a proponent of visual/verbal integration, which he explores in contributions to the literary and arts journal *Private Arts*. He is a full-time faculty member in the graphic design/digital imaging department of Ray College of Design in Chicago. His fonts are distributed by [T-26].

Andrea Fella *176*
Born in 1969, Andrea Fella studied design and twentieth-century culture at the University of Michigan. She worked for the Los Angeles-based firm ReVerb for four years. In 1995, she became associate art director of *I.D.* magazine.

Edward Fella *15, 106, 162, 163, 164, 165*
Born in Detroit, Michigan in 1938, Edward Fella practised commercial art and design for many years before entering Cranbrook Academy of Art in 1985. Since graduating with an MFA, he has worked for a number of cultural clients and currently teaches on the graphic design programme at California Institute of the Arts.

Detlef Fiedler *101, 114, 115, 116, 117*
Born in 1955, Detlef Fiedler is a member of the Berlin design group Cyan. The group view themselves as avant-garde in the traditional sense. Designing books, posters and magazines, they have so far worked exclusively for clients in the cultural sector.

Neil Fletcher *64, 65, 139*
Born in 1969, Neil Fletcher studied graphic design at Hook College of Art and Technology from 1987-89. In 1991, he established Pd-p, working for Sheffield University Union of Students and other clients. In 1995, he joined Chris Ashworth and Amanda Sissons to form the design team Substance. Clients include MTV and Ray Gun Publishing.

Barbara Glauber *122, 123, 160, 161*
Born in Buffalo, New York in 1962, Barbara Glauber received an MFA from California Institute of the Arts. She teaches at the Cooper Union, New York and is a critic on the graphic design programme at Yale University. She has a New York-based design studio and concentrates on publication design and information graphics for educational and cultural clients. In 1993, she curated the exhibition "Lift and Separate: Graphic Design and the Quote Unquote Vernacular" at the Cooper Union.

Heike Grebin *100*
Born in Rostock in 1959, Heike Grebin studied architecture at the Hochschule für Architektur und Bauwesen in Weimar and went on to work as an architect for four years. In the late 1980s, she worked as a typographer for a children's book publisher and in 1990 she joined Grappa, the Berlin design group. Grappa are committed to working on low budgets for cultural institutions and many of their clients are based in East Berlin's historic centre.

April Greiman *18, 19*
Born in 1948, April Greiman graduated with a BFA from Kansas City Art Institute in 1970 and pursued graduate studies at the Design School in Basel from 1970-71. Her Los Angeles-based practice, known for its pioneering use of technology, is involved with interactive and multimedia projects, as well as graphic, motion and environmental design. A former director of the visual communications programme at California Institute of the Arts, she serves as graduate adviser for Art Center College of Design, Pasadena and is an instructor at the Southern California Institute of Architecture. A one-woman exhibition was staged at the Arc en Rêve Centre d'Architecture, Bordeaux, France in 1994 and subsequently toured.

Julian Harriman-Dickinson *86*
Born in 1972, Julian Harriman-Dickinson studied graphic design, graduating with a BA. He has worked for Lowe Howard-Spink as a designer/typographer. He won a D&AD gold award while still a student.

Daniela Haufe *101, 114, 115, 116, 117*
Born in 1966, Daniela Haufe is a member of the Berlin design group Cyan. The group view themselves as avant-garde in the traditional sense. Designing books, posters and magazines, they have so far worked exclusively for clients in the cultural sector.

Andrew Henderson *26, 27*
Born in New York in 1967, Andrew Henderson graduated from Minneapolis College of Art and Design in 1995. He assisted Jan Jancourt on the redesign of the *Utne Reader* and is the magazine's associate art director.

Allen Hori *33, 177*
With partner Richard Bates, Allen Hori is co-principal of the design group Bates Hori. His work has been exhibited internationally in the 1990 touring exhibition "Cranbrook Design: The New Discourse" and at the Design Museum, London and the GGG Gallery, Tokyo. He has received recognition in the *I.D. Annual Design Review* and the American Center for Design's 100 Show.

Karl Hyde *140, 141*
Born in England in 1957, Karl Hyde graduated from art school with a BA in sculpture, installation and video. In 1980, he formed the rock group Freur with John Warwicker and Richard Smith. With Smith and Darren Emerson, he launched Underworld. He is a member of the design collective Tomato.

Jan Jancourt *26, 27, 150*
Born in Minnesota in 1957, Jan Jancourt studied for a Bachelor of Science in design at Bemidji State Univerisity from 1977-81. He completed an MFA at Cranbrook Academy of Art in 1985. He was an intern at Studio Dumbar and, since 1986, has been associate professor at Minneapolis College of Art and Design, while pursuing a freelance career with projects for the Walker Art Center and other clients. His work was exhibited in "Holland in Form: Dutch Design 1945-87" at the Stedelijk Museum and in the 1990 touring exhibition, "Cranbrook Design: The New Discourse".

Damian Jaques *124, 125*
Born in 1965, Damian Jaques completed a BA in fine art at Portsmouth Polytechnic in 1988, and an MA in print-making at Wimbledon School of Art in 1991.

Alicia Johnson *53*
Born in 1960, Alicia Johnson studied at Hutchins School, a liberal arts programme at the UC Sonoma. She is president and co-director of Johnson & Wolverton, based in Portland, Oregon. The company's clients include Amnesty International, The Democratic National Committee, the AVIA Group International and Ray Gun Publishing.

Andrew Johnson *89, 103*
Born in Essex in 1968, Andrew Johnson was educated at Brighton Polytechnic, graduating with a BA in 1990, and at the Royal College of Art, graduating with an MA in 1992. As a freelance, his clients have included the Institute of Contemporary Arts, the London Ecology Centre and RTZ Corporation. He has collaborated with Nick Oates on theatre publicity material. In 1995, he became art director of *Blueprint* magazine.

Margo Johnson *108, 188, 215, 216, 217*
Born in Toledo, Ohio in 1964, Margo Johnson followed a BFA from the University of Michigan with an MFA at California Institute of the Arts. Since graduating in 1993, she has worked in Los Angeles in a variety of media for clients in the music industry and television. She teaches design and typography at Otis College of Art and Design. Her *Hybrid Digital Typefaces* project was included in the American Center for Design's 100 Show.

Jason Kedgley *49*
Born in 1969, Jason Kedgley gained a BA in graphic design from the London College of Printing and an MA from Central Saint Martins College of Art & Design. He is a member of the design collective Tomato.

Jeffery Keedy *108, 122, 183, 188, 189*
Born in Battle Creek, Michigan in 1957, Jeffery Keedy gained a BFA in graphic design and photography at Western Michigan University in 1981. After a period of professional experience in Boston and Honolulu, he studied for an MFA at Cranbrook Academy of Art, graduating in 1985. He moved to Los Angeles to teach at California Institute of the Arts and was director of its graphic design programme from 1991-95. A polemical post-modernist in his writings, he is a regular contributor to design publications such as *Emigre* and *Eye*. In 1991, his typeface Keedy Sans was released by Emigre Fonts. In 1996, he launched a number of new faces through his type foundry, Cipher.

Chip Kidd *47*
Born in 1964, Chip Kidd was educated at Pennsylvania State University, graduating with a BA in graphic design in 1986. Since then, he has worked as a book jacket designer at Alfred A. Knopf in New York. His designs have been included in the American Center for Design's 100 Show for five years running. In addition to coverage in the design press, his work has been featured in *Time* magazine and *The New York Times*.

Somi Kim *66, 67, 156, 157, 160, 161, 176*
Born in 1962, Somi Kim gained a BA from Harvard University in 1984 and an MFA from California Institute of the Arts in 1989. In 1990, she was a founding partner of ReVerb, a Los Angeles-based design firm whose clients range from grass-roots community centres to corporations, museums and foundations. She is a graduate adviser for Art Center College of Design, Pasadena and a visiting lecturer at Cranbrook Academy of Art and other schools.

Doug Kisor *154, 155*
Born in Mason, Michigan in 1949, Doug Kisor has been working in design education since he completed an MFA in graphic design at Michigan University in 1984. He is director of the graphic design studies programme at Eastern Michigan University. His work has been included in the *AIGA Annual* and the American Center for Design's 100 Show. He is working with the Graphic Design Education Association to develop international exchange programmes and has co-developed the Rotterdam-based de Program, which hosts a group of international participants, who work with leading practitioners, theorists and educators.

Jacques Koeweiden *128, 129*
Born in 1957, Jacques Koeweiden studied at the Royal Academy of Art and Design in Den Bosch from 1978-83. In 1985, he became art director of *Vinyl* magazine and in 1986 he formed Koeweiden Postma with Paul Postma. The company works for international corporate and cultural clients, including Chiat/Day, Glaxo, the Hogeschule of Amsterdam, the Royal Dutch PTT, UNICEF and Nike. They received a gold award in the 1993 Typography International Awards and were featured in the "Dutch Design" exhibition at the Design Museum, London in 1991.

Susan Lally *126*
After completing a BFA in painting at the University of Illinois in 1983, Susan Lally went on to graduate studies in graphic design at Cranbrook Academy of Art. She has worked as a freelance designer with various design groups in Chicago and designs for a variety of media with Zun Design. Her work was included in the 1990 touring exhibition "Cranbrook Design: the New Discourse" and she has received recognition in the American Center for Design's 100 Show and *How* magazine's *International Annual of Design*.

Susan LaPorte *92, 169*
Born in 1965, Susan LaPorte received a BFA from the University of Illinois, Chicago and an MFA from California Institute of the Arts. In the early 1990s, she worked as an intern at CalArts and the Walker Art Center. Since 1993, she has been assistant professor of graphic design at Eastern Michigan University. Her typefaces were used in the first five issues of *Raygun* and have also appeared in *Emigre*. She was included in the American Center for Design's 100 Show in 1993 and 1995.

George LaRou *123, 169, 170, 171*
Born in Maine, George LaRou received an MFA from California Institute of the Arts in 1990. He taught for four years at Eastern Michigan University and is an associate professor at Maine College of Art. His work has been featured in the American Center for Design's 100 Show in 1994 and 1995, and in the exhibition "Lift and Separate" at the Cooper Union, New York in 1993.

Dominic Lippa *62*

Born in 1962, Dominic Lippa studied graphic design at London College of Printing from 1981-84. He worked at Smith & Milton, Michael Thierens and Newell & Sorrell, before setting up Lippa Pearce Design with Harry Pearce and Giles Calver in 1990. He was art director of *Baseline* for five years. Clients include the Royal Mail, Boots the Chemist and Waitrose. He is on the executive committee of London's Typographic Circle and has judged the RSA Student Awards for three years.

Deborah Littlejohn *209, 210, 211*

Born in Raleigh, North Carolina in 1966, Deborah Littlejohn graduated with a BFA in design from Western Carolina University in 1992. She completed an MFA at California Institute of the Arts in 1994. She has worked for ReVerb in Los Angeles and led an Internet workshop at CalArts. She is a designer in the Walker Art Center's design department.

Whitney Lowe *66, 67, 156, 157, 176*

Born in 1958, Whitney Lowe was educated at California Polytechnic State University and Art Center College of Design, Pasadena, graduating in 1982. He worked for Knoll International and Anthon Beeke's studio in Amsterdam before, in 1990, becoming a founding partner of ReVerb, a Los Angeles-based design firm whose clients range from grass-roots community centres to corporations, museums and foundations.

Kevin Lyons *212*

Born in 1969, Kevin Lyons graduated from Rhode Island School of Design with a BFA in film in 1988. He recently completed an MFA at California Institute of the Arts.

Seònaid MacKay *184, 185*

Born in 1970, Seònaid MacKay studied graphic design at Glasgow School of Art, graduating with a BA in 1993, and at the Royal College of Art, graduating with an MA in 1995. She is a designer/film-maker and has exhibited at the Edinburgh Film Festival and Cherbourgh Film Festival. She works for Simple Productions, a graphic and moving-image production company.

P. Scott Makela *30, 31, 32, 78, 79, 97, 145*

Born in St. Paul, Minnesota in 1960, P. Scott Makela took a degree in political science before completing a BFA in visual communication at Minneapolis College of Art and Design in 1984. From 1989-91, he studied for an MFA in graphic design at Cranbrook Academy of Art. His first business venture was Makela + Knickelbine Design in Los Angeles. Words and Pictures for Business and Culture, his current venture, is a "multi-aspect" company dealing with advanced design technologies. Clients include Warner Brothers Records, Nike and PBS. He worked as a consultant on the 1990 touring exhibition "Cranbrook Design: The New Discourse". In 1996, he was appointed joint chair (with Laurie Haycock Makela) of the graphic design programme at Cranbrook Academy of Art.

Geoff McFetridge *7, 212*

Born in 1971, Geoff McFetridge worked as a freelance designer for snowboard and skateboard companies between studies at Alberta College of Art in Calgary, Canada and California Institute of the Arts. He completed his MFA in 1995.

Shawn McKinney *189, 211*

Born in 1960, Shawn McKinney majored in liberal arts/English at Tulane University, graduating with a BA in 1982. He started at the Texan design firm of Fuller, Dyal and Stamper as a copywriter, leaving four years later as a senior level graphic designer. He completed an MFA in graphic design at California Institute of the Arts in 1992. In 1995, he became a lecturer in computer graphic design at Wanganui Regional Community Polytechnic in New Zealand.

Jeremy Francis Mende *192, 193, 201*

After gaining a first degree in psychology at UCLA in 1991, Jeremy Francis Mende worked as an art director on various magazines. In 1995, he completed an MFA in graphic design at Cranbrook Academy of Art. He was an intern at Studio Dumbar in 1994.

Rebeca Méndez *152, 158, 159*

Born in 1962, Rebeca Méndez graduated from Art Center College of Design, Pasadena in 1984. She worked for several design firms in Los Angeles before rejoining the college as its designer in 1989. She is now its design director, a post that involves both teaching and practice. She was awarded designer of the year in both 1991 and 1992 by The Council for the Advancement and Support of Education and her work has appeared in the American Center for Design's 100 Show and the *I.D.*'s *Annual Design Review*. Her designs are included in the permanent collections of the Library of Congress, the Cooper-Hewitt, National Design Museum and the Getty Center.

Jennifer Moody *98*

Born in 1965, Jennifer Moody graduated from Western Michigan University with a BFA and went on to complete an MFA at California Institute of the Arts in 1993. She worked in Chicago as a designer at Cagney & McDowell and ABC-TV. In 1993, she took a position in CalArts' Office of Public Affairs. Her work has been selected for the American Center for Design's 100 Show. She is a partner with Gail Swanlund in the Los Angeles design firm Nice.

James Moore *66, 67*

Born in 1971, James Moore graduated from California Institute of the Arts with a BFA in 1993. He works as a designer at the Los Angeles-based design firm ReVerb.

Patrick Morrissey *24, 25, 28, 29, 104, 105*

Born in 1972, Patrick Morrissey studied graphic design at the London College of Printing, graduating with a BA in 1994. He freelances for Why Not Associates in London.

Roelof Mulder *132, 133*

After studying fine art at the Arnhem Institute for the Arts, Roelof Mulder founded a gallery, released an artist's book, *Speed is what we need*, and exhibited paintings and sculptures internationally. He became involved in interior and fashion design in the early 1990s and began to work full time as a graphic designer in 1992. His clients include the Dutch Red Cross and the Stedelijk Museum, Amsterdam. He won the Rotterdam Design Prize in 1993. Since 1994, he has taught graphic design at the Arnhem Institute and, in 1995, he became an editor and designer of the Dutch architectural quarterly *Forum*.

Robert Nakata *10, 41, 42, 43, 44, 45*

Born in Toronto in 1960, Robert Nakata attended the Ontario College of Art from 1979-83. After working as a designer in Canada for two years, he completed an MFA at Cranbrook Academy of Art in 1985. He has worked for design firms in the United States and the Netherlands, including McCoy & McCoy in Michigan and Studio Dumbar in the Hague. He is now with Wieden & Kennedy in Amsterdam. His work was included in the 1990 touring show "Cranbrook Design: The New Discourse" and more recently in "Displaced Voices", a two-person show with Allen Hori at DDD Gallery, Osaka, Japan.

Lisa Nugent *66, 67, 143, 156, 157*

Born in 1955, Lisa Nugent was educated at California State University, Long Beach and California Institute of the Arts, graduating with an MFA in 1988. In 1990, she was a founding partner of ReVerb, a Los Angeles-based design firm whose clients range from grass-roots community centres to corporations, museums and foundations. From 1990-94, she taught experimental design and computer typography at Otis College of Art and Design. In 1993, she was a juror for the Type Directors Club of New York awards.

Nick Oates *89*

Born in 1968, Nick Oates was educated at Central Saint Martins College of Art & Design, London, graduating with a BA in 1990, and at the Royal College of Art, graduating with an MA in 1992. As a student, he was an intern at Hard Werken Design in the Netherlands. He has worked as a freelance designer in London for Diesel Jeans, Paul Smith and other clients and has collaborated with Andrew Johnson on theatre publicity material.

Susan Parr *176*

Born in 1959, Susan Parr was educated at Pacific NW College of Art and Parsons School of Design, graduating with a BFA in 1986. For four years she had her own graphic design studio. In 1990, she was a founding partner of ReVerb, a Los Angeles-based design firm whose clients range from grass-roots community centres to corporations, museums and foundations.

John Plunkett *15, 16, 34, 35, 36, 37*

After graduating with a degree in communication design from California Institute of the Arts in 1977, John Plunkett worked with Colin Forbes and Dan Friedman at Pentagram in New York. With partner Barbara Kuhr, he is responsible for the look and feel of both *Wired* magazine and *HotWired*, the first Web-based publication on the Internet. Plunkett + Kuhr's design office is based in Park City, Utah and clients include Carnegie Hall Museum and the Sundance Film Festival. In 1995, *Wired* won the National Magazine Award for design from the American Society of Magazine Editors.

Paul Postma *128, 129*

Born in 1958, Paul Postma studied at the Royal Academy of Art and Design in Den Bosch from 1979-84. He worked at Samenwerkende Ontwerpers in Amsterdam and went on to become art director of *Vinyl* magazine from 1985-86. In 1986, he formed Koeweiden Postma with Jacques Koeweiden. The company works for international corporate and cultural clients, including Chiat/Day, Glaxo, the Hogeschule of Amsterdam, the Royal Dutch PTT, UNICEF and Nike. They received a gold award in the 1993 Typography International Awards and were featured in the "Dutch Design" exhibition at the Design Museum, London in 1991.

Chris Priest *40*

Born in 1967, Chris Priest graduated from Central Saint Martins College of Art & Design, London with a BA in graphic design in 1989. He worked for Why Not Associates for several years and, in 1995, teamed up with Jo Wright to form the London-based Studio Barbara.

Pam Racs *82*

Born in 1964, Pam Racs was educated in graphic design at Art Center College of Design, Pasadena. Since 1994, she has been a designer at Johnson & Wolverton.

Paul Sahre *88, 93*

Born in 1964, Paul Sahre was educated at Kent State University, where he completed a BFA in 1987 and an MFA in 1990. From 1992-93, he worked as senior designer at Rutka Weadock, and he is now creative director of GKV Design. He maintains a freelance practice, offering his services free to the non-profit Fells Point Corner Theatre. His work was been recognised by the American Center for Design's 100 Show.

Katie Salen *118, 119*

Born in 1967, Katie Salen was educated at the University of Texas at Austin, graduating with a BFA, and at Rhode Island School of Design, graduating with an MFA in graphic design. She was assistant professor of design at the Virginia Commonwealth University and, from 1995, assistant professor in the department of art and art history at the University of Texas. She maintains a freelance practice, designing mainly for non-profit clients. Since 1993, she has been editor and designer of the design journal *Zed*. Her work has been recognised by the American Center for Design's 100 Show.

Liisa Salonen *190, 191*
An expatriate American, living in Canada, Liisa Salonen completed a Bachelor of Science in design at the University of Michigan in 1971 and undertook graduate studies at Cranbrook Academy of Art. She has worked as a designer and art director for institutional publications.

Louise Sandhaus *106, 113, 166*
After studying graphic design at California Institute of the Arts and graduating with a BFA in 1993 and an MFA in 1994, Louise Sandhaus was designer-in-residence at the Jan van Eyck Akademie, Maastricht in 1995. She has been a commercial designer since 1980, and has worked on projects with ReVerb in Los Angeles and Total Design in the Netherlands. Her work was included in the American Center for Design's 100 Show in 1995. She is designer, writer and co-publisher of the journal *Errant Bodies*.

Brian Schorn *167, 168, 182, 204, 205, 206, 207*
Born in 1961, Brian Schorn undertook two years of pre-med at Oakland University, a BFA in photography at the Center for Creative Studies, an MFA in photography at the University of Michigan, an MFA in creative writing at Brown University, and an MFA in graphic design at Cranbrook Academy of Art. While at Cranbrook, he worked as an intern for ReVerb in Los Angeles. His writing and design have been published in *Emigre* and he has been recognised by the Type Directors Club of New York.

Richard Shanks *194, 195*
After completing a bachelor's degree in graphic design and English at the University of Michigan in 1988, Richard Shanks worked in advertising. In 1990, he set up his own design practice, Visual Thinking. In 1995, he completed an MFA at California Institute of the Arts.

Laura Lacy-Sholly & James Sholly *130*
Both born in 1965, Laura Lacy-Sholly and James Sholly are partners in the design group Antenna. Clients include the Indiana Civil Liberties Union, Indianapolis Museum of Art, Stonycreek farms and Indianapolis Zoo. They were visiting artists at Cranbrook Academy of Art in 1993 and at the School of the Art Institute of Chicago in 1994. Their work was included in the American Center for the Design's 100 Show in 1992, 1993 and 1994.

Amanda Sissons *64, 65, 139*
After graduating from the London College of Printing with a BA in graphic and media design, in 1995, Amanda Sissons worked for the design group Area. In 1995, she joined Chris Ashworth and Neil Fletcher to form the design team Substance.

Carolyn Steinbeck *196, 197*
Born in 1967 in Berlin, Carolyn Steinbeck studied graphic design at Fachochschule in Darmstadt, Germany before winning a Fulbright scholarship to attend Cranbrook Academy of Art. She gained her MFA in 1995.

Shelley Stepp *189*
Born in 1950, Shelley Stepp graduated with an MFA from California Institute of the Arts in 1994. She subsequently became director of CalArts' Mac Lab for graphic design. She also works as a freelance designer for CalArts' Office of Public Affairs and other clients.

James Stoecker *188*
Born in 1963, James Stoecker completed a BFA in graphic design at Western Carolina University in 1987. He worked as an assistant art director at Whittle Communications in Tennessee for four years and, in 1993, completed an MFA at California Institute of the Arts. He works as art director at Electric Image Incorporated, Pasadena and is a part-time faculty member of the graphic design department of San Jose State University.

Gail Swanlund *108, 110*
Born in St. Paul, Minnesota in 1957, Gail Swanlund gained a BFA from the University of Minnesota in 1981. After working as a designer for several years, she completed an MFA at California Institute of the Arts in 1992. She worked for two years as a graphic designer at *Emigre* magazine and, since 1995, has taught at CalArts. She is a partner with Jennifer Moody in the Los Angeles design firm Nice.

Carlo Tartaglia *7, 22, 127*
Born in 1971, Carlo Tartaglia studied graphic design at Ravensbourne College of Design and Communication. In 1995, he completed an MA in graphic design at the Royal College of Art.

Simon Taylor *70, 71, 76, 77*
Born in 1965, Simon Taylor gained a BA in graphic design. He is a member of the design collective Tomato.

Anusch Thielbeer *99*
Born in Hamburg in 1963, Anusch Thielbeer studied industrial design at Kiel College from 1985-89. She began collaborating with the Berlin design group Grappa in 1993. Grappa are committed to working on low budgets for cultural institutions and many of their clients are based in East Berlin's historic centre.

Joseph Thomas *81, 85*
Born in Swansea, Wales in 1968, Joseph Thomas studied graphic design at Bristol Polytechnic and went on to Central Saint Martins College of Art & Design, London, graduating with an MA in 1991. He co-founded the design company Push. Clients include cultural organisations such as South West Arts and the British Film Institute.

Ben Tibbs *198, 199*
Born in 1970, Ben Tibbs studied graphic design at Glasgow School of Art, graduating with a BA in 1993, and at the Royal College of Art, graduating with an MA in 1995. In 1992, his work was including in the touring exhibition "Autogeddon" and he won the Scottish Art Director's Student Award. He has lectured in graphic design at Glasgow School of Art and Kingston University. He is a partner with Martin Carty in the design team Automatic.

Andreas Trogisch *100*
Born in Riesa in 1959, Andreas Trogisch studied exhibition design at the Fachschule für Werbung and Gestaltung from 1983-88. In 1989, he became a founder member of the design collective Grappa. The group are committed to working on low budgets for cultural institutions and many of their clients are based in East Berlin's historic centre. He has taught at the Merz-Akademie in Stuttgart and the Hdk in Berlin.

Alexei Tylevich *50, 51, 68, 69, 146, 147, 148, 149*
Born in Minsk, Belarus in 1972, Alexei Tylevich completed a BA in painting at Minsk School of Art. He went on graduate from Minneapolis College of Art and Design with a BFA in graphic design. He now lives and works in the United States. He has designed for print and screen for Sega, Airwalk Shoes and other clients. His work was selected for the American Center for Design's 100 Show in 1993.

Rick Valicenti *38, 39, 178*
Born in 1951, Rick Valicenti was educated at Bowling Green State University, graduating in with a BFA in 1973, and the University of Iowa, graduating with an MFA in photography in 1976. In 1982, he established R. Valicenti Design in Chicago and, in 1988, he set up the design group Thirst, which now operates from Barrington, Illinois. Thirstype was initiated in 1992 to release new typeface designs. He has been on the board of directors of the American Institute of Graphic Arts, chairman of the American Center for Design's 100 Show and a juror of the President's Design Awards.

Rudy VanderLans *17, 109, 110, 111*
Born in 1955, Rudy VanderLans studied graphic design at the Royal Academy of Fine Art in the Hague, graduating in 1979. After working for several years as a designer in the Netherlands, he moved to California and studied photography in the masters programme at the University of California, Berkeley. In 1984, he co-founded *Emigre*, a general arts and culture magazine. Early issues featured the digital typefaces of his partner, Zuzana Licko, and this led to the setting up of Emigre Fonts, which releases typefaces by Licko and other designers. *Emigre* itself went on to become an international forum for the new typography. Clients include Apple Computer and San Francisco's Artspace. A ten-year retrospective book, *Emigre: Graphic Design into the Digital Realm*, was published in 1994.

Martin Venezky *56, 60, 61, 80, 90*
Born in 1957, Martin Venezky attended the Hopkins Center Design Studio at Dartmouth College, New Hampshire, graduating with a BA in 1980. He worked as a designer for several years before completing an MFA at Cranbrook Academy of Art in 1993. After an internship at Studio Dumbar, he returned on graduation to work at the company. He now works in San Francisco, both independently and in partnership with Raul Cabra as Diseño. His work was included in the American Center for Design's 100 Show in 1993, 1994 and 1995.

John Warwicker *48, 76, 77, 140, 141*
Born in London in 1955, John Warwicker completed a BA in graphic design at Camberwell School of Art in 1977. In 1980, he completed an MA in visual communication at Birmingham Polytechnic, where he became involved in research into electronic interactive media. In the early 1980s, he worked with Karl Hyde and Richard Smith as a member of the rock group Freur and as a creative director at Da Gama. He became head of art and video at A&M Records and from 1987-91 he was creative director at Vivid I.D. He is a member of the design collective Tomato.

Lorraine Wild *106, 189, 176*
After studying at Yale University and Cranbrook Academy of Art, Lorraine Wild began a career as a designer of books on art, architecture and design for Rizzoli, MIT Press, the Museum of Contemporary Art in Los Angeles and other clients. She was director of the graphic design programme at California Institute of the Arts and writes about design history, theory and criticism for *Emigre*, *I.D.* and other publications. In 1990, she was a founding partner of ReVerb, a Los Angeles-based design firm whose clients range from grass-roots community centres to corporations, museums and foundations. In 1995, she left ReVerb to work as a freelance.

Cornel Windlin *11, 87, 91, 131*
Born in 1964, Cornel Windlin studied at the Schule für Gestaltung in Lucerne. He spent the late 1980s and early 1990s in London, working, among others, for Neville Brody. He now runs his own studio in Zurich. His work has been published in *Graphic Agitation* (1993) and *Wear Me* (1995).

Hal Wolverton *53, 82, 83*
Born in 1960, Hal Wolverton studied on scholarship at the University of Washington's Pratt Institute. He is president and co-director of Johnson & Wolverton, based in Portland, Oregon. The company's clients include Amnesty International, The Democratic National Committee, the AVIA Group International and Ray Gun Publishing.

Graham Wood *10, 49*
Born in Beckenham, Kent in 1965, Graham Wood completed a BA and an MA in graphic design at Central Saint Martins College of Art & Design, London. He is a member of the design collective Tomato and works in a variety of media, including print and video.

Michael Worthington *183, 202, 208, 213, 214, 218, 219*
Born in 1966, Michael Worthington graduated from Central Saint Martins College of Art & Design, London with a BA in 1991. He worked as a partner in the London-based design group Studio Dm and taught design at Central Saint Martins and Oxford Brookes University. In 1995, he completed an MFA at California Institute of the Arts. He has worked on projects for ReVerb and teaches at CalArts.